James Surowiecki is a staff writer at the *New Yorker*, where he writes the popular business column, 'The Financial Page'. His work has appeared in a wide range of publications, including the *New York Times*, the *Wall Street Journal*, *Artforum*, *Wired* and *Slate*. He lives in Brooklyn, New York.

Praise for *The Wisdom of Crowds*

'A bright and lucid columnist for the *New Yorker* . . . [Surowiecki] knows how to make a convincing, sometimes entertaining case' *Sunday Times*

'Surowiecki's intelligent book . . . is a valuable argument to the contempt for the crowd . . . an antidote to the notion that a camel is a horse designed by committee' *Guardian*

'*The Wisdom of Crowds* is a handsome addition to the books that combine the verve of smart magazine writing with a whiff of academia . . . a fantastically stylish counter to the expert-knows-best line . . . an offbeat argument for democracy. In the future, "crowd pleaser" might no longer be such a half-hearted compliment' *GQ*

'Dazzling . . . It will turn your world upside down . . . the most brilliant book on business, society and everyday life that I've read in years' Malcolm Gladwell, author of *The Tipping Point*

'Clear and intelligent . . . A rich and interesting book that sends the mind wandering in many directions' Bryan Appleyard, *New Statesman*

'Thanks to Surowiecki's use of experiments and examples little known outside academia, it's convincingly put' *Evening Standard*

'Simple, elegant and counterintuitive' *Daily Telegraph*

'A hymn of praise to the judgement of the many' *The Economist*

'Striking' *Independent*

'Erudite and entertaining . . . he has a rare gift for combining rigorous thought with entertaining examples' *Financial Times*

'[Surowiecki] makes a persuasive case' *The Times*

'Lightly written, well-argued and deftly assembled . . . intelligent, engaging and provocative' *Herald*

'Striking . . . the group approves of Surowiecki's book – and in a big way' *Scotland on Sunday*

'Consistently fascinating' *Director*

D0315546

THE WISDOM OF CROWDS

WHY THE MANY ARE SMARTER THAN THE FEW

JAMES SUROWIECKI

An *Abacus* Book

First published in the United States of America in 2004 by
Doubleday, a division of Random House, Inc.
First published in Great Britain by Little, Brown in 2004
This edition published by Abacus in 2005

A CIP catalogue record for this book is available from the British Library.

ISBN 0 349 11605 9

Printed and bound in Great Britain by Clays Ltd, St Ives plc

Abacus
An imprint of
Time Warner Book Group UK
Brettenham House
Lancaster Place
London WC2E 7EN

www.twbg.co.uk

To Mom and Dad

CONTENTS

PART II

THE WISDOM
OF CROWDS

I

One day in the fall of 1906, the British scientist Francis Galton left his home in the town of Plymouth and headed for a country fair. Galton was eighty-five years old and beginning to feel his age, but he was still brimming with the curiosity that had won him renown—and notoriety—for his work on statistics and the science of heredity. And on that particular day, what Galton was curious about was livestock.

Galton's destination was the annual West of England Fat Stock and Poultry Exhibition, a regional fair where the local farmers and townspeople gathered to appraise the quality of each other's cattle, sheep, chicken, horses, and pigs. Wandering through rows of stalls examining workhorses and prize hogs may seem to have been a strange way for a scientist (especially an elderly one) to spend an afternoon, but there was a certain logic to it. Galton was a man obsessed with two things: the measurement of physical and mental qualities, and breeding. And what, after all, is a livestock show but a big showcase for the effects of good and bad breeding?

Breeding mattered to Galton because he believed that only a very few people had the characteristics necessary to keep societies healthy. He had devoted much of his career to measuring those characteristics, in fact, in order to prove that the vast majority of people did not have them. At the International Exhibition of 1884 in London, for instance, he set up an "Anthropometric Laboratory," where he used devices of his own making to test exhibition-goers on, among other things, their "Keenness of Sight and of Hearing, Colour Sense, Judgment of Eye, [and] Reaction Time." His experiments left him with little faith in the intelligence of the average person, "the stupidity and wrong-headedness of many men and women being so great as to be scarcely credible." Only if power and control stayed in the hands of the select, well-bred few, Galton believed, could a society remain healthy and strong.

As he walked through the exhibition that day, Galton came across a weight-judging competition. A fat ox had been selected and placed on display, and members of a gathering crowd were lining up to place wagers on the weight of the ox. (Or rather, they were placing wagers on what the weight of the ox would be *after* it had been "slaughtered and dressed.") For sixpence, you could buy a stamped and numbered ticket, where you filled in your name, your address, and your estimate. The best guesses would receive prizes.

Eight hundred people tried their luck. They were a diverse lot. Many of them were butchers and farmers, who were presumably expert at judging the weight of livestock, but there were also quite a few people who had, as it were, no insider knowledge of cattle. "Many non-experts competed," Galton wrote later in the scientific journal *Nature*, "like those clerks and others who have no expert knowledge of horses, but who bet on races, guided by newspapers, friends, and their own fancies." The analogy to a democracy, in which people of radically different abilities and interests each get one vote, had suggested itself to Galton immediately. "The average competitor was probably as well fitted for making a just estimate of the dressed weight of the ox, as an average voter is of judging the merits of most political issues on which he votes," he wrote.

Galton was interested in figuring out what the "average voter" was capable of because he wanted to prove that the average voter was capable of very little. So he turned the competition into an im-

promptu experiment. When the contest was over and the prizes
had been awarded, Galton borrowed the tickets from the organiz-
ers and ran a series of statistical tests on them. Galton arranged the
guesses (which totaled 787 in all, after he had to discard thirteen
because they were illegible) in order from highest to lowest and
graphed them to see if they would form a bell curve. Then, among
other things, he added all the contestants' estimates, and calculated the mean of the group's guesses. That number represented,
you could say, the collective wisdom of the Plymouth crowd. If the
crowd were a single person, that was how much it would have
guessed the ox weighed.

Galton undoubtedly thought that the average guess of the
group would be way off the mark. After all, mix a few very smart
people with some mediocre people and a lot of dumb people, and
it seems likely you'd end up with a dumb answer. But Galton was
wrong. The crowd had guessed that the ox, after it had been
slaughtered and dressed, would weigh 1,197 pounds. After it had
been slaughtered and dressed, the ox weighed 1,198 pounds. In
other words, the crowd's judgment was essentially perfect. Perhaps
breeding did not mean so much after all. Galton wrote later: "The
result seems more creditable to the trustworthiness of a democratic
judgment than might have been expected." That was, to say the
least, an understatement.

II

What Francis Galton stumbled on that day in Plymouth was the
simple, but powerful, truth that is at the heart of this book: under
the right circumstances, groups are remarkably intelligent, and are
often smarter than the smartest people in them. Groups do not
need to be dominated by exceptionally intelligent people in order to
be smart. Even if most of the people within a group are not especially well-informed or rational, it can still reach a collectively wise

decision. This is a good thing, since human beings are not perfectly designed decision makers. Instead, we are what the economist Herbert Simon called "boundedly rational." We generally have less information than we'd like. We have limited foresight into the future. Most of us lack the ability—and the desire—to make sophisticated cost-benefit calculations. Instead of insisting on finding the best possible decision, we will often accept one that seems good enough. And we often let emotion affect our judgment. Yet despite all these limitations, when our imperfect judgments are aggregated in the right way, our collective intelligence is often excellent.

This intelligence, or what I'll call "the wisdom of crowds," is at work in the world in many different guises. It's the reason the Internet search engine Google can scan a billion Web pages and find the one page that has the exact piece of information you were looking for. It's the reason it's so hard to make money betting on NFL games, and it helps explain why, for the past fifteen years, a few hundred amateur traders in the middle of Iowa have done a better job of predicting election results than Gallup polls have. The wisdom of crowds has something to tell us about why the stock market works (and about why, every so often, it stops working). The idea of collective intelligence helps explain why, when you go to the convenience store in search of milk at two in the morning, there is a carton of milk waiting there for you, and it even tells us something important about why people pay their taxes and help coach Little League. It's essential to good science. And it has the potential to make a profound difference in the way companies do business.

In one sense, this book tries to describe the world as it is, looking at things that at first glance may not seem similar but that are ultimately very much alike. But this book is also about the world as it might be. One of the striking things about the wisdom of crowds is that even though its effects are all around us, it's easy to miss, and, even when it's seen, it can be hard to accept. Most of us, whether as voters or investors or consumers or managers, believe that valuable knowledge is concentrated in a very few hands (or, rather, in a very few heads). We assume that the key to solving problems or making good decisions is finding that one right person who will have the answer. Even when we see a large crowd of people, many of them not especially well-informed, do something amazing like, say, predict the outcomes of horse races, we are more likely to attribute that success to a few smart people in the crowd than to the crowd itself. As sociologists Jack B. Soll and Richard Larrick put it, we feel the need to "chase the expert." The argument of this book is that chasing the expert is a mistake, and a costly one at that. We should stop hunting and ask the crowd (which, of course, includes the geniuses as well as everyone else) instead. Chances are, it knows.

III

Charles Mackay would have scoffed at the idea that a crowd of people could know anything at all. Mackay was the Scottish journalist who, in 1841, published *Extraordinary Popular Delusions and the Madness of Crowds,* an endlessly entertaining chronicle of mass manias and collective follies, to which the title of my book pays homage. For Mackay, crowds were never wise. They were never even reasonable. Collective judgments were doomed to be extreme. "Men, it has been well said, think in herds," he wrote. "It will be seen that they go mad in herds, while they only recover their senses slowly, and one by one." Mackay's take on collective madness is not an unusual one. In the popular imagination, groups tend to make people either dumb or crazy, or both. The speculator Bernard Baruch, for instance, famously said: "Anyone taken as an individual is tolerably sensible and reasonable—as a member of a crowd, he at once becomes a blockhead." Henry David Thoreau lamented: "The mass never comes up to the standard of its best member, but on the contrary degrades itself to a level with the lowest." Friedrich Nietzsche wrote, "Madness is the exception in individuals but the rule in groups," while the English historian Thomas Carlyle put it succinctly: "I do not believe in the collective wisdom of individual ignorance."

Perhaps the most severe critic of the stupidity of groups was the French writer Gustave Le Bon, who in 1895 published the polemical classic *The Crowd: A Study of the Popular Mind*. Le Bon was appalled by the rise of democracy in the West in the nineteenth century, and dismayed by the idea that ordinary people had come to wield political and cultural power. But his disdain for groups went deeper than that. A crowd, Le Bon argued, was more than just the sum of its members. Instead, it was a kind of independent organism. It had an identity and a will of its own, and it often acted in ways that no one within the crowd intended. When the crowd did act, Le Bon argued, it invariably acted foolishly. A crowd might be brave or cowardly or cruel, but it could never be smart. As he wrote, "In crowds it is stupidity and not mother wit that is accumulated." Crowds "can never accomplish acts demanding a high degree of intelligence," and they are "always intellectually inferior to the isolated individual." Strikingly, for Le Bon, the idea of "the crowd" included not just obvious examples of collective wildness, like lynch mobs or rioters. It also included just about any kind of group that could make decisions.

So Le Bon lambasted juries, which "deliver verdicts of which each individual juror would disapprove." Parliaments, he argued, adopt laws that each of their members would normally reject. In fact, if you assembled smart people who were specialists in a host of different fields and asked them to "make decisions affecting matters of general interest," the decisions they would reach would be no better, on the whole, than those "adopted by a gathering of imbeciles."

Over the course of this book, I follow Le Bon's lead in giving the words "group" and "crowd" broad definitions, using the words to refer to everything from game-show audiences to multibillion-dollar corporations to a crowd of sports gamblers. Some of the groups in this book, like the management teams in Chapter 9, are tightly organized and very much aware of their identities as groups. Other crowds, like the herds of cars caught in traffic that I write about in Chapter 7, have no formal organization at all. And still others, like the stock market, exist mainly as an ever-changing collection of numbers and dollars. These groups are all very different, but they have in common the ability to act collectively to make decisions and solve problems—even if the people in the groups aren't always aware that's what they're doing. And what is demonstrably true of some of these groups—namely, that they are smart and good at problem solving—is potentially true of most, if not all, of them. In that sense, Gustave Le Bon had things exactly backward. If you put together a big enough and diverse enough group of people and ask them to "make decisions affecting matters of general interest," that group's decisions will, over time, be "intellectually [superior] to the isolated individual," no matter how smart or well-informed he is.

I V

Judging the weight of an ox is hardly a complex task. But, as I suggested above, collective intelligence can be brought to bear on a wide variety of problems, and complexity is no bar. In this book, I concentrate on three kinds of problems. The first are what I'll call *cognition* problems. These are problems that have or will have definitive solutions. For example, "Who will win the Super Bowl this year?" and "How many copies of this new ink-jet printer will we sell in the next three months?" are cognition problems. So, too, is, "How likely is it that this drug will be approved by the FDA?" Questions to which there may not be a single right answer, but to which some answers are certainly better than others—such as, "What would be the best place to build this new public swimming pool?"—are cognition problems, too.

The second kind of problem is what's usually called a *coordi-*

nation problem. Coordination problems require members of a group (market, subway riders, college students looking for a party) to figure out how to coordinate their behavior with each other, knowing that everyone else is trying to do the same. How do buyers and sellers find each other and trade at a fair price? How do companies organize their operations? How can you drive safely in heavy traffic? These are all problems of coordination.

The final kind of problem is a *cooperation* problem. As their name suggests, cooperation problems involve the challenge of getting self-interested, distrustful people to work together, even when narrow self-interest would seem to dictate that no individual should take part. Paying taxes, dealing with pollution, and agreeing on definitions of what counts as reasonable pay are all examples of cooperation problems.

A word about structure. The first half of this book is, you might say, theory, although leavened by practical examples. There's a chapter for each of the three problems (cognition, coordination, and cooperation), and there are chapters covering the conditions that are necessary for the crowd to be wise: diversity, independence, and a particular kind of decentralization. The first half begins with the wisdom of crowds, and then explores the three conditions that make it possible, before moving on to deal with coordination and cooperation.

The second part of the book consists of what are essentially case studies. Each of the chapters is devoted to a different way of organizing people toward a common (or at least loosely common) goal, and each chapter is about the way collective intelligence either flourishes or flounders. In the chapter about corporations, for instance, the tension is between a system in which only a few people exercise power and a system in which many have a voice. The chapter about markets starts with the question of whether markets can be collectively intelligent, and ends with a look at the dynamics of a stock-market bubble.

There are many stories in this book of groups making bad

decisions, as well as groups making good ones. Why? Well, one reason is that this is the way the world works. The wisdom of crowds has a far more important and beneficial impact on our everyday lives than we recognize, and its implications for the future are immense. But in the present, many groups struggle to make even mediocre decisions, while others wreak havoc with their bad judgment. Groups work well under certain circumstances, and less well under others. Groups generally need rules to maintain order and coherence, and when they're missing or malfunctioning, the result is trouble. Groups benefit from members talking to and learning from each other, but too much communication, paradoxically, can actually make the group as a whole less intelligent. While big groups are often good for solving certain kinds of problems, big groups can also be unmanageable and inefficient. Conversely, small groups have the virtue of being easy to run, but they risk having too little diversity of thought and too much consensus. Finally, Mackay was right about the extremes of collective behavior: there are times—think of a riot, or a stock-market bubble—when aggregating individual decisions produces a collective decision that is utterly irrational. The stories of these kinds of mistakes are negative proofs of this book's argument, underscoring the importance to good decision making of diversity and independence by demonstrating what happens when they're missing.

Diversity and independence are important because the best collective decisions are the product of disagreement and contest, not consensus or compromise. An intelligent group, especially when confronted with cognition problems, does not ask its members to modify their positions in order to let the group reach a decision everyone can be happy with. Instead, it figures out how to use mechanisms—like market prices, or intelligent voting systems—to aggregate and produce collective judgments that represent not what any one person in the group thinks but rather, in some sense, what they all think. Paradoxically, the best way for a group to be smart is for each person in it to think and act as independently as possible.

V

I began this Introduction with an example of a group solving a simple problem: figuring out the weight of an ox. I'll end it with an example of a group solving an incredibly complex problem: locating a lost submarine. The differences between the two cases are immense. But the principle in each is the same.

In May 1968, the U.S. submarine *Scorpion* disappeared on its way back to Newport News after a tour of duty in the North Atlantic. Although the navy knew the sub's last reported location, it had no idea what had happened to the *Scorpion,* and only the vaguest sense of how far it might have traveled after it had last made radio contact. As a result, the area where the navy began searching for the *Scorpion* was a circle twenty miles wide and many thousands of feet deep. You could not imagine a more hopeless task. The only possible solution, one might have thought, was to track down three or four top experts on submarines and ocean currents, ask them where they thought the *Scorpion* was, and search there. But, as Sherry Sontag and Christopher Drew recount in their book *Blind Man's Bluff,* a naval officer named John Craven had a different plan.

First, Craven concocted a series of scenarios—alternative explanations for what might have happened to the *Scorpion.* Then he assembled a team of men with a wide range of knowledge, including mathematicians, submarine specialists, and salvage men. Instead of asking them to consult with each other to come up with an answer, he asked each of them to offer his best guess about how likely each of the scenarios was. To keep things interesting, the guesses were in the form of wagers, with bottles of Chivas Regal as prizes. And so Craven's men bet on why the submarine ran into trouble, on its speed as it headed to the ocean bottom, on the steepness of its descent, and so forth.

Needless to say, no one of these pieces of information could tell Craven where the *Scorpion* was. But Craven believed that if he put all the answers together, building a composite picture of how the *Scorpion* died, he'd end up with a pretty good idea of where it was. And that's exactly what he did. He took all the guesses, and used a formula called Bayes's theorem to estimate the *Scorpion*'s final location. (Bayes's theorem is a way of calculating how new information about an event changes your preexisting expectations of how likely the event was.) When he was done, Craven had what was, roughly speaking, the group's collective estimate of where the submarine was.

The location that Craven came up with was not a spot that any individual member of the group had picked. In other words, not one of the members of the group had a picture in his head that matched the one Craven had constructed using the information gathered from all of them. The final estimate was a genuinely collective judgment that the group as a whole had made, as opposed to representing the individual judgment of the smartest people in it. It was also a genuinely brilliant judgment. Five months after the *Scorpion* disappeared, a navy ship found it. It was 220 yards from where Craven's group had said it would be.

What's astonishing about this story is that the evidence that the group was relying on in this case amounted to almost nothing. It was really just tiny scraps of data. No one knew why the submarine sank, no one had any idea how fast it was traveling or how steeply it fell to the ocean floor. And yet even though no one in the group knew any of these things, the group as a whole knew them all.

PART I

THE WISDOM OF CROWDS

I

If, years hence, people remember anything about the TV game show *Who Wants to Be a Millionaire?*, they will probably remember the contestants' panicked phone calls to friends and relatives. Or they may have a faint memory of that short-lived moment when Regis Philbin became a fashion icon for his willingness to wear a dark blue tie with a dark blue shirt. What people probably won't remember is that every week *Who Wants to Be a Millionaire?* pitted group intelligence against individual intelligence, and that every week, group intelligence won.

Who Wants to Be a Millionaire? was a simple show in terms of structure: a contestant was asked multiple-choice questions, which got successively more difficult, and if she answered fifteen questions in a row correctly, she walked away with $1 million. The show's gimmick was that if a contestant got stumped by a question, she could pursue three avenues of assistance. First, she could have two of the four multiple-choice answers removed (so she'd have at least a fifty-fifty shot at the right response). Second, she could place a call to a friend or relative, a person whom, before the show, she had singled out as one of the smartest people she knew, and ask him or her for the answer. And third, she could poll the studio audience, which would immediately cast its votes by computer.

Everything we think we know about intelligence suggests that the smart individual would offer the most help. And, in fact, the "experts" did okay, offering the right answer—under pressure—almost 65 percent of the time. But they paled in comparison to the audiences. Those random crowds of people with nothing better to do on a weekday afternoon than sit in a TV studio picked the right answer 91 percent of the time.

Now, the results of *Who Wants to Be a Millionaire?* would never stand up to scientific scrutiny. We don't know how smart the experts were, so we don't know how impressive outperforming them was. And since the experts and the audiences didn't always answer the same questions, it's possible, though not likely, that the audiences were asked easier questions. Even so, it's hard to resist the thought that the success of the *Millionaire* audience was a modern example of the same phenomenon that Francis Galton caught a glimpse of a century ago.

As it happens, the possibilities of group intelligence, at least when it came to judging questions of fact, were demonstrated by a host of experiments conducted by American sociologists and psychologists between 1920 and the mid-1950s, the heyday of research into group dynamics. Although in general, as we'll see, the bigger the crowd the better, the groups in most of these early experiments—which for some reason remained relatively unknown outside of academia—were relatively small. Yet they nonetheless performed very well. The Columbia sociologist Hazel Knight kicked things off with a series of studies in the early 1920s, the first of which had the virtue of simplicity. In that study Knight asked the students in her class to estimate the room's temperature, and then took a simple average of the estimates. The group guessed 72.4 degrees, while the actual temperature was 72 degrees. This was not, to be sure, the most auspicious beginning, since classroom temperatures are so stable that it's hard to imagine a class's estimate being too far off base. But in the years that followed, far more convincing evidence emerged, as students and soldiers across America were subjected to a barrage of puzzles, intelligence tests, and word games. The sociologist Kate H. Gordon asked two hundred students to rank items by weight, and found that the group's "estimate" was 94 percent accurate, which was better than all but five of the individual guesses. In another experiment students were asked to look at ten piles of buckshot—each a slightly different size than the rest—that had been glued to a piece of white cardboard, and rank them by size. This time, the group's guess was 94.5 percent accurate. A classic demonstration of group intelligence is the jelly-beans-in-the-jar experiment, in which invariably the group's estimate is superior to the vast majority of the individual guesses. When finance professor Jack Treynor ran the experiment in his class with a jar that held 850 beans, the group estimate was 871. Only one of the fifty-six people in the class made a better guess.

There are two lessons to draw from these experiments. First, in most of them the members of the group were not talking to each other or working on a problem together. They were making individual guesses, which were aggregated and then averaged. This is exactly what Galton did, and it is likely to produce excellent results. (In a later chapter, we'll see how having members interact changes things, sometimes for the better, sometimes for the worse.) Second, the group's guess will not be better than that of every single person in the group each time. In many (perhaps most) cases, there will be a few people who do better than the group. This is, in some sense, a good thing, since especially in situations where there is an incentive for doing well (like, say, the stock market) it gives people reason to keep participating. But there is no evidence in these studies that certain people consistently outperform the group. In other words, if you run ten different jelly-bean-counting experiments, it's likely that each time one or two students will outperform the group. But they will not be the same students each time. Over the ten experiments, the group's performance will almost certainly be the best possible. The simplest way to get reliably good answers is just to ask the group each time.

A similarly blunt approach also seems to work when wrestling with other kinds of problems. The theoretical physicist Norman L. Johnson has demonstrated this using computer simulations of individual "agents" making their way through a maze. Johnson, who does his work at the Los Alamos National Laboratory, was interested in understanding how groups might be able to solve problems that individuals on their own found difficult. So he built a maze— one that could be navigated via many different paths, some shorter, and some longer—and sent a group of agents into the maze one by one. The first time through, they just wandered around, the way you would if you were looking for a particular café in a city where you'd never been before. Whenever they came to a turning point— what Johnson called a "node"—they would randomly choose to go right or left. Therefore some people found their way, by chance, to the exit quickly, others more slowly. Then Johnson sent the agents back into the maze, but this time he allowed them to use the information they'd learned on their first trip, as if they'd dropped bread crumbs behind them the first time around. Johnson wanted to know how well his agents would use their new information. Predictably enough, they used it well, and were much smarter the second time through. The average agent took 34.3 steps to find the exit the first time, and just 12.8 steps to find it the second.

The key to the experiment, though, was this: Johnson took the results of all the trips through the maze and used them to calculate what he called the group's "collective solution." He figured out what a majority of the group did at each node of the maze, and then plotted a path through the maze based on the majority's decisions. (If more people turned left than right at a given node, that was the direction he assumed the group took. Tie votes were broken randomly.) The group's path was just nine steps long, which was not only shorter than the path of the average individual (12.8 steps), but as short as the path that even the smartest individual had been able to come up with. It was also as good an answer as you could find. There was no way to get through the maze in fewer than nine steps, so the group had discovered the optimal solution. The obvious question that follows, though, is: The judgment of crowds may be good in laboratory settings and classrooms, but what happens in the real world?

II

At 11:38 AM on January 28, 1986, the space shuttle *Challenger* lifted off from its launch pad at Cape Canaveral. Seventy-four seconds later, it was ten miles high and rising. Then it blew up. The launch was televised, so news of the accident spread quickly. Eight minutes after the explosion, the first story hit the Dow Jones News Wire.

The stock market did not pause to mourn. Within minutes, investors started dumping the stocks of the four major contractors who had participated in the *Challenger* launch: Rockwell International, which built the shuttle and its main engines; Lockheed, which managed ground support; Martin Marietta, which manufactured the ship's external fuel tank; and Morton Thiokol, which built the solid-fuel booster rocket. Twenty-one minutes after the explosion, Lockheed's stock was down 5 percent, Martin Marietta's was down 3 percent, and Rockwell was down 6 percent.

Morton Thiokol's stock was hit hardest of all. As the finance professors Michael T. Maloney and J. Harold Mulherin report in their fascinating study of the market's reaction to the *Challenger* disaster, so many investors were trying to sell Thiokol stock and so few people were interested in buying it that a trading halt was called almost immediately. When the stock started trading again, almost an hour after the explosion, it was down 6 percent. By the end of the day, its decline had almost doubled, so that at market close, Thiokol's stock was down nearly 12 percent. By contrast, the stocks of the three other firms started to creep back up, and by the end of the day their value had fallen only around 3 percent.

What this means is that the stock market had, almost immediately, labeled Morton Thiokol as the company that was responsible for the *Challenger* disaster. The stock market is, at least in
theory, a machine for calculating the present value of all the "free
cash flow" a company will earn in the future. (Free cash flow is the
money that's left over after a company has paid all its bills and its
taxes, has accounted for depreciation, and has invested in the business. It's the money you'd get to take home and put in the bank if
you were the sole owner of the company.) The steep decline in
Thiokol's stock price—especially compared with the slight declines
in the stock prices of its competitors—was an unmistakable sign
that investors believed that Thiokol was responsible, and that the
consequences for its bottom line would be severe.

As Maloney and Mulherin point out, though, on the day of
the disaster there were no public comments singling out Thiokol as
the guilty party. While the *New York Times* article on the disaster
that appeared the next morning did mention two rumors that had
been making the rounds, neither of the rumors implicated Thiokol,
and the *Times* declared, "There are no clues to the cause of the accident."

Regardless, the market was right. Six months after the explosion, the Presidential Commission on the *Challenger* revealed that
the O-ring seals on the booster rockets made by Thiokol—seals
that were supposed to prevent hot exhaust gases from escaping—
became less resilient in cold weather, creating gaps that allowed
the gases to leak out. (The physicist Richard Feynman famously
demonstrated this at a congressional hearing by dropping an O-ring
in a glass of ice water. When he pulled it out, the drop in temperature had made it brittle.) In the case of the *Challenger,* the hot
gases had escaped and burned into the main fuel tank, causing the
cataclysmic explosion. Thiokol was held liable for the accident.
The other companies were exonerated.

In other words, within a half hour of the shuttle blowing up,
the stock market *knew* what company was responsible. To be sure,

this was a single event, and it's possible that the market's singling out of Thiokol was just luck. Or perhaps the company's business seemed especially susceptible to a downturn in the space program. Possibly the trading halt had sent a signal to investors to be wary. These all are important cautions, but there is still something eerie about what the market did. That's especially true because in this case the stock market was working as a pure weighing machine, undistorted by the factors—media speculation, momentum trading, and Wall Street hype—that make it a peculiarly erratic mechanism for aggregating the collective wisdom of investors. That day, it was just buyers and sellers trying to figure out what happened and getting it right.

How did they get it right? That's the question that Maloney and Mulherin found so vexing. First, they looked at the records of insider trades to see if Thiokol executives, who might have known that their company was responsible, had dumped stock on January 28. They hadn't. Nor had executives at Thiokol's competitors, who might have heard about the O-rings and sold Thiokol's stock short. There was no evidence that anyone had dumped Thiokol stock while buying the stocks of the other three contractors (which would have been the logical trade for someone with inside information). Savvy insiders alone did not cause that first-day drop in Thiokol's price. It was all those investors—most of them relatively uninformed—who simply refused to buy the stock.

But why did they not want Thiokol's stock? Maloney and Mulherin were finally unable to come up with a convincing answer to that question. In the end, they assumed that insider information was responsible for the fall in Thiokol's price, but they could not explain how. Tellingly, they quoted the Cornell economist Maureen O'Hara, who has said, "While markets appear to work in practice, we are not sure how they work in theory."

Maybe. But it depends on what you mean by "theory." If you strip the story down to its basics, after all, what happened that January day was this: a large group of individuals (the actual and potential shareholders of Thiokol's stock, and the stocks of its competitors) was asked a question—"How much less are these four companies worth now that the *Challenger* has exploded?"—that had an objectively correct answer. Those are conditions under which a crowd's average estimate—which is, dollar weighted, what a stock price is—is likely to be accurate. Perhaps someone did, in fact, have inside knowledge of what had happened to the O-rings. But even if no one did, it's plausible that once you aggregated all the bits of information about the explosion that all the traders in the market had in their heads that day, it added up to something close to the truth. As was true of those who helped John Craven find the *Scorpion,* even if none of the traders was sure that Thiokol was responsible, collectively they were certain it was.

The market was smart that day because it satisfied the four conditions that characterize wise crowds: diversity of opinion (each person should have some private information, even if it's just an eccentric interpretation of the known facts), independence (people's opinions are not determined by the opinions of those around them), decentralization (people are able to specialize and draw on local knowledge), and aggregation (some mechanism exists for turning private judgments into a collective decision). If a group satisfies those conditions, its judgment is likely to be accurate. Why? At heart, the answer rests on a mathematical truism. If you ask a large enough group of diverse, independent people to make a prediction or estimate a probability, and then average those estimates, the errors each of them makes in coming up with an answer will cancel themselves out. Each person's guess, you might say, has two components: information and error. Subtract the error, and you're left with the information.

Now, even with the errors canceled out, it's possible that a group's judgment will be bad. For the group to be smart, there has to be at least some information in the "information" part of the "information minus error" equation. (If you'd asked a large group of children to buy and sell stocks in the wake of the *Challenger* disaster, it's unlikely they would have picked out Thiokol as the culprit.) What is striking, though—and what makes a phrase like "the wisdom of crowds" meaningful—is just how much information a group's collective verdict so often contains. In cases like Francis Galton's experiment or the *Challenger* explosion, the crowd is holding a nearly complete picture of the world in its collective brain.

Perhaps this isn't surprising. After all, we are the products of evolution, and presumably we have been equipped to make sense of the world around us. But who knew that, given the chance, we can collectively make so *much* sense of the world. After all, think about what happens if you ask a hundred people to run a 100-meter race, and then average their times. The average time will not be better than the time of the fastest runners. It will be worse. It will be a mediocre time. But ask a hundred people to answer a question or solve a problem, and the average answer will often be at least as good as the answer of the smartest member. With most things, the average is mediocrity. With decision making, it's often excellence. You could say it's as if we've been programmed to be collectively smart.

III

Truly successful decision making, of course, demands more than just a picture of the world as it is. It demands in addition a picture of the world as it will (or least as it may) be. Any decision-making mechanism therefore has to be good under conditions of uncertainty. And what's more uncertain than the future? Group intelligence may be good at telling how many jelly beans are in a jar or remembering the year Nirvana released *Nevermind*. But how does it perform under conditions of true uncertainty, when the right answer is seemingly unknowable—because it hasn't happened yet?

Robert Walker's entire career depends on the answer to that

question. Walker is the sports book director at the Mirage Hotel and Casino in Las Vegas, which means that every week he fields thousands of bets in sports ranging from pro football to Ivy League basketball. For all those games, Walker has to offer a line (or point spread), which lets bettors know which team is favored to win and by how many points. The way the line works is simple. Say the Giants are favored this week by three and a half points over the Rams. If you bet on the Giants, they have to win by four points or more for you to win the bet. Conversely, if you bet on the Rams, they have to lose by three points or less (or win), for you to walk away with the casino's money. In other sports, bets are framed in terms of odds: if you bet on the favorite, you might have to put down $150 to get $100 back, while if you bet on the underdog, you'd have to lay down $75 to win $100.

As a bookmaker, Walker's job is not to try to pick what team will win. He leaves that to the gamblers, at least in theory. Instead, his job is to make sure that the gamblers bet roughly the same amount of money on one team as on the other. If he does that, then he knows that he will win half the bets he's taken in and lose the other half. Why would Walker be satisfied with just breaking even? Because bookies make more money on every bet they win than they lose on every bet they get wrong. If you place a point-spread bet with a bookie, you have to put up $11 to win $10. Imagine there are only two bettors, one who bets on the favorite and the other who bets on the underdog. Walker takes in $22 ($11 from each of them). He pays out $21 to the winner. The $1 he keeps is his profit. That slim advantage, which is known as the vigorish, or the vig, is what pays the bookie's bills. And the bookie keeps that advantage only when he avoids having too much money riding on one side of a bet.

To keep that from happening, Walker needs to massage the point spread so that bets keep coming in for both teams. "The line we want is the line that'll split the public, because that's when you start earning that vig," he said. In the week before the 2001 Super Bowl, for instance, the Mirage's opening line had the Baltimore Ravens favored by two and a half points. But soon after the line was posted, the Mirage booked a couple of early $3,000 bets on Baltimore. That's not much money, but it was enough to convince Walker to raise the point spread to three. If everyone wanted to bet on Baltimore, chances were the line wasn't right. So the line moved. The opening line is set by the bookmaker, but it shifts largely in response to what bettors do—much as stock prices rise and fall with investor demand.

In theory, you could set the opening line wherever, and simply allow it to adjust from there automatically, so that the point spread would rise or fall anytime there was a significant imbalance between the amounts wagered on each side. The Mirage would have no problem doing this; its computerized database tracks the bets as they come in. But bookies place a premium on making the opening line as accurate as possible, because if they set it badly they're going to get stuck taking a lot of bad bets. Once a line opens, though, it's out of the bookie's hands, and a game's point spread ends up representing bettors' collective judgment of what the final outcome of that game will be. As Bob Martin, who was essentially the country's oddsmaker in the 1970s, said, "Once you put a number on the board, it becomes public property."

The public, it turns out, is pretty smart. It does not have a crystal ball: point spreads only weakly predict the final scores of most NFL games, for instance. But it is very hard for even well-informed gamblers to beat the final spread consistently. In about half the games, favorites cover the spread, while in the other half underdogs beat the spread. This is exactly what a bookie wants to have happen. And there are no obvious mistakes in the market's judgment—like, say, home teams winning more than the crowd predicts they will, or road underdogs being consistently undervalued. Flaws in the crowd's judgment are found occasionally, but when they are they're typically like the one documented in a recent paper that found that in weeks fifteen, sixteen, and seventeen of the NFL season, home underdogs have historically been a good bet. So you have to search hard to outperform the betting crowd. Roughly three-quarters of the time, the Mirage's final line will be the most reliable forecast of the outcomes of NFL games that you can find.

The same is true in many other sports. Because sports betting is a kind of ready-made laboratory to study predictions and their outcomes, a host of academics have perused gambling markets to see how efficient—that is, how good at capturing all the available information—they are. The results of their studies are consistent: in general, in most major sports the market is relatively efficient. In some cases, the crowd's performance is especially good: in horse racing, for instance, the final odds reliably predict the race's order of finish (that is, the favorite wins most often, the horse with the second-lowest odds is the second-most-often winner, and so on) and also provide, in economist Raymond D. Sauer's words, "reasonably good estimates of the probability of winning." In other words, a three-to-one horse will win roughly a quarter of the time. There are exceptions: odds are less accurate in those sports and games where the betting market is smaller and less liquid (meaning that the odds can change dramatically thanks to only a few bets), like hockey or golf or small-college basketball games. These are often the sports where professional gamblers can make real money, which makes sense given that we know the bigger the group, the more accurate it becomes. And there are also some interesting quirks: in horse racing, for instance, people tend to bet on long shots slightly more often than they should and bet on favorites slightly less often than they should. (This seems to be a case of risk-seeking behavior: bettors, especially bettors who have been losing, would rather take a flyer on a long shot that offers the possibility of big returns than grind it out by betting on short-odds favorites.) But on the whole, if bettors aren't collectively foreseeing the future, they're doing the next best thing.

IV

Recently I decided I needed—*this minute!*—the exact text of Bill Murray's *Caddyshack* riff about toting the Dalai Lama's golf bag. The punch line of the riff is "So I got that going for me, which is nice" and the Dalai Lama, in Murray's telling, likes to say "Gunga galunga." So I went to Google, the Internet search engine, typed in "going for me" and "gunga," and hit the search button. A list of 695 Web pages came back. First on the list was an article from GolfOnline, which included the second half of the riff. That was okay, but third on the list was a Web site for something called the Penn State Soccer Club. The goalie, a guy named David Feist, had posted the entire monologue. The search took 0.18 seconds.

Then I needed to check out the Mulherin paper on the *Challenger* that I discuss above. I couldn't remember the author's name, so I typed in " 'stock market' challenger reaction": 2,370 pages came back. The first one was an article by *Slate*'s Daniel Gross about the Mulherin paper. The third was Mulherin's own Web site, with a link to his paper. That search—which, remember, did not include Mulherin's name—took 0.10 seconds. A few minutes later, my search for the lyrics to a Ramones song about Ronald Reagan visiting the Bitburg cemetery took 0.23 seconds, and the first item on the list had what I needed.

If you use the Internet regularly, these examples of Google's performance will not surprise you. This is what we have come to expect from Google: instantaneous responses with the exact page we need up high in the rankings. But if possible, it's worth letting yourself be a little amazed at what happened during those routine searches. Each time, Google surveyed billions of Web pages and picked exactly the pages that I would find most useful. The cumulative time for all the searches: about a minute and a half.

Google started in 1998, at a time when Yahoo! seemed to have a stranglehold on the search business—and if Yahoo! stumbled, then AltaVista or Lycos looked certain to be the last man standing. But within a couple of years, Google had become the default search engine for anyone who used the Internet regularly, simply because it was able to do a better job of finding the right page quickly. And the way it does that—and does it while surveying three billion Web pages—is built on the wisdom of crowds.

Google keeps the details of its technology to itself, but the core of the Google system is the PageRank algorithm, which was first defined by the company's founders, Sergey Brin and Lawrence Page, in a now-legendary 1998 paper called "The Anatomy of a Large-Scale Hypertextual Web Search Engine." PageRank is an algorithm—a calculating method—that attempts to let all the Web pages on the Internet decide which pages are most relevant to a particular search. Here's how Google puts it:

> PageRank capitalizes on the uniquely democratic characteristic of the web by using its vast link structure as an organizational tool. In essence, Google interprets a link from page A to page B as a vote, by page A, for page B. Google assesses a page's importance by the votes it receives. But Google looks at more than sheer volume of votes, or links; it also analyzes the page that casts the vote. Votes cast by pages that are themselves "important" weigh more heavily and help to make other pages "important."

In that 0.12 seconds, what Google is doing is asking the entire Web to decide which page contains the most useful information, and the page that gets the most votes goes first on the list. And that page, or the one immediately beneath it, more often than not is in fact the one with the most useful information.

Now, Google is a republic, not a perfect democracy. As the description says, the more people that have linked to a page, the more influence that page has on the final decision. The final vote is a "weighted average"—just as a stock price or an NFL point spread is—rather than a simple average like the ox-weighers' estimate. Nonetheless, the big sites that have more influence over the crowd's final verdict have that influence only because of all the votes that smaller sites have given them. If the smaller sites were giving the wrong sites too much influence, Google's search results would not be accurate. In the end, the crowd still rules. To be smart at the top, the system has to be smart all the way through.

V

If allowing people to bet on sporting events effectively creates a kind of machine that's good at predicting the outcome of those events, an obvious question follows: Wouldn't people betting on other kinds of events be equally good, as a group, at predicting them? Why confine ourselves to knowing what the chances are of Los Angeles beating Sacramento if there's a way we could know what the chances are of, say, George W. Bush beating Howard Dean?

We do have a well-established way of knowing what George W. Bush's chances are: the poll. If you want to know how people are going to vote, you just ask them. Polling is, relatively speaking, accurate. It has a solid methodology behind it, and is statistically rigorous. But there's reason to wonder if a market such as the betting market—one that allowed the people participating in it to rely on many different kinds of information, including but not limited to polls—might at the very least offer a competitive alternative to Gallup. That's why the Iowa Electronic Markets (IEM) project was created.

Founded in 1988 and run by the College of Business at the University of Iowa, the IEM features a host of markets designed to predict the outcomes of elections—presidential, congressional, gubernatorial, and foreign. Open to anyone who wants to participate, the IEM allows people to buy and sell futures "contracts" based on how they think a given candidate will do in an upcoming election. While the IEM offers many different types of contracts, two are most common. One is designed to predict the winner of an election. In the case of the California recall in 2003, for instance, you could have bought an "Arnold Schwarzenegger to win" contract, which would have paid you $1 when Schwarzenegger won. Had he lost, you would have gotten nothing. The price you pay for this kind of contract reflects the market's judgment of a candidate's chances of victory. If a candidate's contract costs 50 cents, it means, roughly speaking, that the market thinks he has a 50 percent chance of winning. If it costs 80 cents, he has an 80 percent chance of winning, and so on.

The other major kind of IEM contract is set up to predict what percentage of the final popular vote a candidate will get. In this case, the payoffs are determined by the vote percentage: if you'd bought a George W. Bush contract in 2000, you would have received 48 cents (he got 48 percent of the vote) when the election was over.

If the IEM's predictions are accurate, the prices of these different contracts will be close to their true values. In the market to predict election winners, the favorite should always win, and bigger favorites should win by bigger margins. Similarly, in the vote-share market, if George W. Bush were to end up getting 49 percent of the vote in 2004, then the price of a George W. Bush contract in the run-up to the election should be close to 49 cents.

So how has the IEM done? Well, a study of the IEM's performance in forty-nine different elections between 1988 and 2000 found that the election-eve prices in the IEM were, on average, off by just 1.37 percent in presidential elections, 3.43 percent in other U.S. elections, and 2.12 percent in foreign elections. (Those numbers are in absolute terms, meaning that the market would have been off by 1.37 percent if, say, it had predicted that Al Gore would get 48.63 percent of the vote when in reality he got 50 percent.) The IEM has generally outperformed the major national polls, and has been more accurate than them even months in advance of the actual election. Over the course of the presidential elections between 1988 and 2000, for instance, 596 different polls were released. Three-fourths of the time, the IEM's market price on the day each of those polls was released was more accurate. Polls tend to be very volatile, with vote shares swinging wildly up and down. But the IEM forecasts, though ever-changing, are considerably less volatile, and tend to change dramatically only in response to new information. That makes them more reliable as forecasts.

What's especially interesting about this is that the IEM isn't very big—there have never been more than eight hundred or so traders in the market—and it doesn't, in any way, reflect the makeup of the electorate as a whole. The vast majority of traders are men, and a disproportionate—though shrinking—number of them are from Iowa. So the people in the market aren't predicting their own behavior. But their predictions of what the voters of the country will do are better than the predictions you get when you ask the voters themselves what they're going to do.

The IEM's success has helped inspire other similar markets, including the Hollywood Stock Exchange (HSX), which allows people to wager on box-office returns, opening-weekend performance, and the Oscars. The HSX enjoyed its most notable success in March of 2000. That was when a team of twelve reporters from *The Wall Street Journal* assiduously canvassed members of the Academy of Motion Pictures Arts and Sciences in order to find out how they had voted. The Academy was not happy about this. The organization's president publicly attacked the *Journal* for trying to "scoop us before Oscar night," and the Academy urged members not to talk to reporters. But with the *Journal* promising anonymity, more than a few people—356, or about 6 percent of all members— disclosed how they had filled out their ballots. The Friday before the ceremony, the *Journal* published its results, forecasting the win-

ners in the six major Oscar categories—Best Picture, Best Director, Best Actor and Best Actress, Best Supporting Actor and Best
Supporting Actress. And when the envelopes were opened, the
Journal's predictions—much to the Academy's dismay—turned out
to be pretty much on target, with the paper picking five of the six
winners. The HSX, though, had done even better, getting all six of
the six right. In 2002, the exchange, perhaps even more impres-
sively, picked thirty-five of the eventual forty Oscar nominees.

The HSX's box-office forecasts are not as impressive or as accurate as the IEM's election forecasts. But Anita Elberse, a professor of marketing at Harvard Business School, has compared the
HSX's forecasts to other Hollywood prediction tools, and found
that the HSX's closing price the night before a movie opens is the
single best available forecast of its weekend box office. As a result,
the HSX's owner, Cantor Index Holdings, is now marketing its data
to Hollywood studios.

One of the interesting things about markets like the IEM and
the HSX is that they work fairly well without much—or any—
money at stake. The IEM is a real-money market, but the most you
can invest is $500, and the average trader has only $50 at stake. In
the HSX, the wagering is done entirely with play money. All the evidence we have suggests that people focus better on a decision
when there are financial rewards attached to it (which may help explain why the IEM's forecasts tend to be more accurate). But
David Pennock—a researcher at Overture who has studied these
markets closely—found that, especially for active traders in these
markets, status and reputation provided incentive enough to encourage a serious investment of time and energy in what is, after
all, a game.

As the potential virtues of these decision markets have become obvious, the range of subjects they cover has grown rapidly.
At the NewsFutures and TradeSports exchanges, people could bet,
in the fall of 2003, on whether or not Kobe Bryant would be con-
victed of sexual assault, on whether and when weapons of mass

destruction would be found in Iraq, and on whether Ariel Sharon would remain in power longer than Yasir Arafat. Ely Dahan, a professor at UCLA, has experimented with a classroom decision market in which students bought and sold securities representing a variety of consumer goods and services, including SUVs, ski resorts, and personal digital assistants. (In a real-life market of this kind, the value of a security might depend on the first-year sales of a particular SUV.) The market's forecasts were eerily similar to the predictions that conventional market research had made (but the classroom research was much cheaper). In the fall of 2003, meanwhile, MIT's *Technology Review* set up a site called Innovation Futures, where people could wager on future technological developments. And Robin Hanson, an economics professor at George Mason University who was one of the first to write about the possibility of using decision markets in myriad contexts, has suggested that such markets could be used to guide scientific research and even as a tool to help governments adopt better policies.

Some of these markets will undoubtedly end up being of little use, either because they'll fail to attract enough participants to make intelligent forecasts or because they'll be trying to predict the unpredictable. But given the right conditions and the right problems, a decision market's fundamental characteristics—diversity, independence, and decentralization—are guaranteed to make for good group decisions. And because such markets represent a relatively simple and quick means of transforming many diverse opinions into a single collective judgment, they have the chance to improve dramatically the way organizations make decisions and think about the future.

In that sense, the most mystifying thing about decision markets is how little interest corporate America has shown in them. Corporate strategy is all about collecting information from many different sources, evaluating the probabilities of potential outcomes, and making decisions in the face of an uncertain future. These are tasks for which decision markets are tailor-made. Yet companies have remained, for the most part, indifferent to this source of potentially excellent information, and have been surprisingly unwilling to improve their decision making by tapping into the collective wisdom of their employees. We'll look more closely at people's discomfort with the idea of the wisdom of crowds, but the problem is simple enough: just because collective intelligence is real doesn't mean that it will be put to good use.

A DECISION MARKET is an elegant and well-designed method for capturing the collective wisdom. But the truth is that the specific method that one uses probably doesn't matter very much. In this chapter, we've looked at a host of different ways of tapping into what a group knows: stock prices, votes, point spreads, pari-mutuel odds, computer algorithms, and futures contracts. Some of these methods seem to work better than others, but in the end there's nothing about a futures market that makes it inherently smarter than, say, Google or a pari-mutuel pool. These are all attempts to tap into the wisdom of the crowd, and that's the reason they work. The real key, it turns out, is not so much perfecting a particular method, but satisfying the conditions—diversity, independence, and decentralization—that a group needs to be smart. As we'll see in the chapters that follow, that's the hardest, but also perhaps the most interesting, part of the story.

2

THE DIFFERENCE DIFFERENCE MAKES:

WAGGLE DANCES, THE BAY OF PIGS, AND

THE VALUE OF DIVERSITY

I

In 1899, Ransom E. Olds opened the Olds Motor Works in Detroit, Michigan. Olds had been in the automobile business since the mid-1880s, when he built his first car, a steam-powered vehicle with three wheels. But success had remained elusive. After moving on to gasoline-powered cars, Olds started his own company in the early 1890s, but it floundered, leaving him nearly destitute. He was only able to start the Motor Works, in fact, by convincing a financier named Samuel Smith to put up nearly all the money. Olds got his company, but he also got a boss to whom he had to answer. This was a problem, because the two did not agree on what the Olds Motor Works should be making. Smith thought the company should cater to the high end of the market, building large, expensive cars with all the trimmings. Olds, though, was more intrigued by the possibility of building a car that could be marketed to the middle class. In 1900, the auto market was still minuscule—there were fewer than 15,000 cars on the road that year. But it seemed plausible that an invention as revolutionary as the car would be able to find a mass audience, if you could figure out a way to make one cheaply enough.

Olds couldn't commit himself to one idea, though. Instead, he dabbled, building eleven different prototypes in the company's first year, including electric-powered cars in addition to steamers and internal-combustion-powered vehicles. It was a strategy that seemed destined for failure. But in March of 1901, bad luck lent a helping hand. Olds's factory burned down, and all the prototypes went up in flames. All, that is, but one—which happened to be right near the door, and to be light enough that the lone man present could push it to safety. The prototype that survived, fortuitously enough, was the inexpensive, low-cost model that Olds had imagined could be sold to a much larger market. In the wake of the fire, Olds rushed the prototype into production. The vehicle he produced was known as the "curved-dash Olds," since the floor curved up to form the dashboard. In design, it was an ungainly thing, a horseless carriage, started by a seat-side crank and steered by a tiller. It had two forward gears, one reverse, and a small, single-cylinder engine. It won no points for style. But at $600, it was within the reach of many Americans.

Though Olds was an engineer, he turned out to be something of a marketing whiz, too. He concocted elaborate publicity stunts—like sending a young driver eight hundred miles cross-country in an Olds to the Manhattan Auto Show—that won the attention of the press and of auto dealers while demonstrating to a still-skeptical public that the automobile was not just a gimmick. He drove a souped-up Olds in the first race at Daytona Beach. And in 1903, the company sold 4,000 vehicles, more than any other U.S. manufacturer, while two years later it sold 6,500 cars. Olds, it turned out, had designed the first mass-produced automobile in American history.

Olds's success came in the face of fierce competition. In that first decade of the twentieth century, there were literally hundreds of companies trying to make automobiles. And because there was no firm definition of what a car should look like, or what kind of engine it should have, those companies offered a bewildering variety of vehicles, including the aforementioned steamers and battery-powered cars. The victory of the gasoline-powered engine was not a foregone conclusion. Thomas Edison, for instance, had designed a battery-powered vehicle, and in 1899 one sage had offered the prediction that "the whole of the United States will be sprinkled with electric changing stations." At one point, a third of all the cars on U.S. roads were electric-powered. Similarly, steam-powered engines were seen by many as the most logical way to propel a vehicle, since steam obviously worked so well in propelling trains and boats. In the early part of the decade, there were more than a hundred makers of steam-powered cars, and the most successful of these, the Stanley Steamer, became legendary for its speed—in 1905, it went 127 miles per hour—and the comfort of its ride.

As the decade wore on, though, the contenders began to fade. Electric-powered cars couldn't go far enough without a recharge. Steam-powered cars took a long time to heat up. More important, though, the makers of gasoline-powered cars were the first to invest heavily in mass-production techniques and to figure out a way to reach the mass market. Olds had been the first automaker to buy different parts from different manufacturers, instead of making them all itself. Cadillac became the first manufacturer successfully to use standardized components, which cut down on the time and cost of manufacturing. And Ford, of course, revolutionized the industry with the moving assembly line and a relentless focus on producing one kind of car as cheaply as possible. By the time of World War I, there were still more than a hundred automakers in America. But more than four hundred car companies had gone out of business or been acquired, including the Olds Motor Works, which had been bought by General Motors.

As for Olds himself, he never really got to enjoy the early success of his company since he left it after only a few years following a fight with Samuel Smith's sons. He eventually started a new car company called REO. But the moment had passed him by. What he had started, Henry Ford—who by World War I made almost half the cars in America—had finished. There was no more talk of steam- or electric-powered vehicles, and cars no longer came in a bewildering variety of shapes and sizes. Everyone knew what an automobile looked like. It looked like a Model T.

THE STORY OF THE early days of the U.S. auto industry is not an unusual one. In fact, if you look at the histories of most new industries in America, from the railroads to television to personal computers to, most recently, the Internet, you'll see a similar pattern. In all these cases, the early days of the business are characterized by a profusion of alternatives, many of them dramatically different from each other in design and technology. As time passes, the market winnows out the winners and losers, effectively choosing which technologies will flourish and which will disappear. Most of the companies fail, going bankrupt or getting acquired by other firms. At the end of the day, a few players are left standing and in control of most of the market.

This seems like a wasteful way of developing and selling new technologies. And, the experience of Google notwithstanding, there is no guarantee that at the end of the process, the best technology will necessarily win (since the crowd is not deciding all at once, but rather over time). So why do it this way?

For an answer, consider a hive of bees. Bees are remarkably efficient at finding food. According to Thomas Seeley, author of *The Wisdom of the Hive,* a typical bee colony can search six or more kilometers from the hive, and if there is a flower patch within two kilometers of the hive, the bees have a better-than-half chance of finding it. How do the bees do this? They don't sit around and have a collective discussion about where foragers should go. Instead, the hive sends out a host of scout bees to search the surrounding area. When a scout bee has found a nectar source that seems strong, he comes back and does a waggle dance, the intensity of which is shaped, in some way, by the excellence of the nectar supply at the site. The waggle dance attracts other forager bees, which follow the first forager, while foragers who have found less-good sites attract fewer followers and, in some cases, eventually abandon their sites entirely. The result is that bee foragers end up distributing themselves across different nectar sources in an almost perfect fashion, meaning that they get as much food as possible relative to the time and energy they put into searching. It is a collectively brilliant solution to the colony's food problem.

What's important, though, is the way the colony gets to that collectively intelligent solution. It does not get there by first rationally considering all the alternatives and then determining an ideal foraging pattern. It *can't* do this, because it doesn't have any idea what the possible alternatives—that is, where the different flower patches—are. So instead, it sends out scouts in many different directions and trusts that at least one of them will find the best patch, return, and do a good dance so that the hive will know where the food source is.

This is, it's important to see, different from the kind of problem solving that we looked at earlier. In the case of the ox-weighing experiment, or the location of the *Scorpion,* or the betting markets, or the IEM, the group's job was to decide among already defined choices or to solve a well-defined problem. In those cases, different members of the group could bring different pieces of information to bear on a problem, but the set of possible solutions was already, in a sense, determined. (Bush or Gore would become president; the Yankees or the Marlins would win the World Series.) In the case of problems like finding the most nectar-rich flower patches, though, the task is more complicated. It becomes a twofold process. First, uncover the possible alternatives. Then decide among them.

In the first stage of this process, the list of possible solutions is so long that the smart thing to do is to send out as many scout bees as possible. You can think of Ransom Olds and Henry Ford and the countless would-be automakers who tried and failed, then, as foragers. They discovered (in this case, by inventing) the sources of nectar—the gasoline-powered car, mass production, the moving assembly line—and then asked the crowd to render its verdict. You might even see Olds's publicity stunts as a kind of equivalent to the waggle dance.

One key to this approach is a system that encourages, and funds, speculative ideas even though they have only slim possibilities of success. Even more important, though, is diversity—not in a sociological sense, but rather in a conceptual and cognitive sense. You want diversity among the entrepreneurs who are coming up with the ideas, so you end up with meaningful differences among those ideas rather than minor variations on the same concept. But you also want diversity among the people who have the money, too. If one virtue of a decentralized economy is that it diffuses decision-making power (at least on a small scale) throughout the system, that virtue becomes meaningless if all the people with power are alike (or if, as we'll see in the next chapter, they become alike through imitation). The more similar they are, the more similar the ideas they appreciate will be, and so the set of new products and concepts the rest of us see will be smaller than possible. By contrast, if they are diverse, the chances that at least someone will take a gamble on a radical or unlikely idea obviously increases. Take the early days of radio, when three companies—American Marconi, NESCO, and De Forest Wireless Telegraphy—dominated the industry. American Marconi relied on investment banks to raise its capital from large private investors; NESCO was funded by two rich men from Pittsburgh; and De Forest Wireless Telegraphy was owned by small stockholders looking for a speculative gain. The variety of possible funding sources encouraged a variety of technological approaches.

Of course, even with diverse sources of funding, most endeavors will end up as failures. This was nicely expressed by Jeff Bezos, the CEO of Amazon, when he compared the Internet boom to the Cambrian explosion, which was the period in evolutionary history that saw the birth and the extinction of more species than any other period. The point is that you cannot, or so at least it seems, have one without the other. It's a familiar truism that governments can't, and therefore shouldn't try to, "pick winners." But the truth is that no system seems all that good at picking winners in advance. After all, tens of thousands of new products are introduced every year, and only a small fraction ever become successes. The steam-powered car, the picturephone, the Edsel, the Betamax, pen computing: companies place huge bets on losers all the time. What makes a system successful is its ability to recognize losers and kill them quickly. Or, rather, what makes a system successful is its ability to generate lots of losers and then to recognize them as such and kill them off. Sometimes the messiest approach is the wisest.

II

Generating a diverse set of possible solutions isn't enough. The crowd also has to be able to distinguish the good solutions from the bad. We've already seen that groups seem to do a good job of making such distinctions. But does diversity matter to the group? In other words, once you've come up with a diverse set of possible solutions, does having a diverse group of decision makers make a difference?

It does, in two ways. Diversity helps because it actually adds perspectives that would otherwise be absent and because it takes away, or at least weakens, some of the destructive characteristics of group decision making. Fostering diversity is actually more important in small groups and in formal organizations than in the kinds of larger collectives—like markets or electorates—that we've already talked about for a simple reason: the sheer size of most markets, coupled with the fact that anyone with money can enter them (you don't need to be admitted or hired), means that a certain level of diversity is almost guaranteed. Markets, for instance, are usually prima facie diverse because they're made up of people with different attitudes toward risk, different time horizons, different investing styles, and different information. On teams or in organizations, by contrast, cognitive diversity needs to be actively selected, and it's important to do so because in small groups it's easy for a few biased individuals to exert undue influence and skew the group's collective decision.

Scott Page is a political scientist at the University of Michigan who has done a series of intriguing experiments using computer-simulated problem-solving agents to demonstrate the positive effects of diversity. For instance, Page set up a series of groups of ten or twenty agents, with each agent endowed with a different set of skills, and had them solve a relatively sophisticated problem. Individually, some of the agents were very good at solving the problem while others were less effective. But what Page found was that a group made up of some smart agents and some not-so-smart agents almost always did better than a group made up just of smart agents. You could do as well or better by selecting a group randomly and letting it solve the problem as by spending a lot of time trying to find the smart agents and then putting them alone on the problem.

The point of Page's experiment is that diversity is, on its own, valuable, so that the simple fact of making a group diverse makes it better at problem solving. That doesn't mean that intelligence is irrelevant—none of the agents in the experiment were ignorant, and all the successful groups had some high-performing agents in them. But it does mean that, on the group level, intelligence alone is not enough, because intelligence alone cannot guarantee you different perspectives on a problem. In fact, Page speculates, grouping only smart people together doesn't work that well because the smart people (whatever that means) tend to resemble each other in what they can do. If you think about intelligence as a kind of toolbox of skills, the list of skills that are the "best" is relatively small, so that people who have them tend to be alike. This is normally a good thing, but it means that as a whole the group knows less than it otherwise might. Adding in a few people who know less, but have different skills, actually improves the group's performance.

This seems like an eccentric conclusion, and it is. It just happens to be true. The legendary organizational theorist James G.

March, in fact, put it like this: "The development of knowledge may depend on maintaining an influx of the naïve and the ignorant, and . . . competitive victory does not reliably go to the properly educated." The reason, March suggested, is that groups that are too much alike find it harder to keep learning, because each member is bringing less and less new information to the table. Homogeneous groups are great at doing what they do well, but they become progressively less able to investigate alternatives. Or, as March has famously argued, they spend too much time exploiting and not enough time exploring. Bringing new members into the organization, even if they're less experienced and less capable, actually makes the group smarter simply because what little the new members do know is not redundant with what everyone else knows. As March wrote, "[The] effect does not come from the superior knowledge of the average new recruit. Recruits are, on average, less knowledgeable than the individuals they replace. The gains come from their diversity."

III

The fact that cognitive diversity matters does not mean that if you assemble a group of diverse but thoroughly uninformed people, their collective wisdom will be smarter than an expert's. But if you can assemble a diverse group of people who possess varying degrees of knowledge and insight, you're better off entrusting it with major decisions rather than leaving them in the hands of one or two people, no matter how smart those people are. If this is difficult to believe—in the same way that March's assertions are hard to believe—it's because it runs counter to our basic intuitions about intelligence and business. Suggesting that the organization with the smartest people may not be the best organization is heretical, particularly in a business world caught up in a ceaseless "war for talent" and governed by the assumption that a few superstars can make the difference between an excellent and a mediocre company. Heretical or not, it's the truth: the value of expertise is, in many contexts, overrated.

Now, experts obviously exist. The play of a great chess player is qualitatively different from the play of a merely accomplished one. The great player sees the board differently, he processes information differently, and he recognizes meaningful patterns almost instantly. As Herbert A. Simon and W. G. Chase demonstrated in the 1970s, if you show a chess expert and an amateur a board with a chess game in progress on it, the expert will be able to re-create from memory the layout of the entire game. The amateur won't. Yet if you show that same expert a board with chess pieces irregularly and haphazardly placed on it, he will not be able to re-create the layout. This is impressive testimony to how thoroughly chess is imprinted on the minds of successful players. But it also demonstrates how limited the scope of their expertise is. A chess expert knows about chess, and that's it. We intuitively assume that intelligence is fungible, and that people who are excellent at one intellectual pursuit would be excellent at another. But this is not the case with experts. Instead, the fundamental truth about expertise is that it is, as Chase has said, "spectacularly narrow."

More important, there's no real evidence that one can become expert in something as broad as "decision making" or "policy" or "strategy." Auto repair, piloting, skiing, perhaps even management: these are skills that yield to application, hard work, and native talent. But forecasting an uncertain future and deciding the best course of action in the face of that future are much less likely to do so. And much of what we've seen so far suggests that a large group of diverse individuals will come up with better and more robust forecasts and make more intelligent decisions than even the most skilled "decision maker."

We're all familiar with the absurd predictions that business titans have made: Henry Warner of Warner Bros. pronouncing in 1927, "Who the hell wants to hear actors talk?," or Thomas Watson of IBM declaring in 1943, "I think there is a world market for maybe five computers." These can be written off as amusing anomalies, since over the course of a century, some smart people are bound to say some dumb things. What can't be written off, though, is the dismal performance record of most experts.

Between 1984 and 1999, for instance, almost 90 percent of mutual-fund managers underperformed the Wilshire 5000 Index, a relatively low bar. The numbers for bond-fund managers are similar: in the most recent five-year period, more than 95 percent of all managed bond funds underperformed the market. After a survey of expert forecasts and analyses in a wide variety of fields, Wharton professor J. Scott Armstrong wrote, "I could find no studies that showed an important advantage for expertise." Experts, in some cases, were a little better at forecasting than laypeople (although a number of studies have concluded that nonpsychologists, for instance, are actually better at predicting people's behavior than psychologists are), but above a low level, Armstrong concluded, "expertise and accuracy are unrelated." James Shanteau is one of the country's leading thinkers on the nature of expertise, and has spent a great deal of time coming up with a method for estimating just how expert someone is. Yet even he suggests that "experts' decisions are seriously flawed."

Shanteau recounts a series of studies that have found experts' judgments to be neither consistent with the judgments of other experts in the field nor internally consistent. For instance, the between-expert agreement in a host of fields, including stock picking, livestock judging, and clinical psychology, is below 50 percent, meaning that experts are as likely to disagree as to agree. More disconcertingly, one study found that the internal consistency of medical pathologists' judgments was just 0.5, meaning that a pathologist presented with the same evidence would, half the time, offer a different opinion. Experts are also surprisingly bad at what social scientists call "calibrating" their judgments. If your judgments are well calibrated, then you have a sense of how likely it is that your judgment is correct. But experts are much like normal people: they routinely overestimate the likelihood that they're right.

A survey on the question of overconfidence by economist Terrance Odean found that physicians, nurses, lawyers, engineers, entrepreneurs, and investment bankers all believed that they knew more than they did. Similarly, a recent study of foreign-exchange traders found that 70 percent of the time, the traders overestimated the accuracy of their exchange-rate predictions. In other words, it wasn't just that they were wrong; they also didn't have any idea how wrong they were. And that seems to be the rule among experts. The only forecasters whose judgments are routinely well calibrated are expert bridge players and weathermen. It rains on 30 percent of the days when weathermen have predicted a 30 percent chance of rain.

Armstrong, who studies expertise and forecasting, summarized the case this way: "One would expect experts to have reliable information for predicting change and to be able to utilize the information effectively. However, expertise beyond a minimal level is of little value in forecasting change." Nor was there evidence that even if most experts were not very good at forecasting, a few titans were excellent. Instead, Armstrong wrote, "claims of accuracy by a single expert would seem to be of no practical value." This was the origin of Armstrong's "seer-sucker theory": "No matter how much evidence exists that seers do not exist, suckers will pay for the existence of seers."

Again, this doesn't mean that well-informed, sophisticated analysts are of no use in making good decisions. (And it certainly doesn't mean that you want crowds of amateurs trying to collectively perform surgery or fly planes.) It does mean that however well-informed and sophisticated an expert is, his advice and predictions should be pooled with those of others to get the most out of him. (The larger the group, the more reliable its judgment will be.) And it means that attempting to "chase the expert," looking for the one man who will have the answers to an organization's problem, is a waste of time. We know that the group's decision will consistently be better than most of the people in the group, and that it will be better decision after decision, while the performance of human experts will vary dramatically depending on the problem they're asked to solve. So it is unlikely that one person, over time, will do better than the group.

Now, it's possible that a small number of genuine experts— that is, people who can consistently offer better judgments than those of a diverse, informed group—do exist. The investor Warren Buffett, who has consistently outperformed the S&P 500 Index since the 1960s, is certainly someone who comes to mind. The problem is that even if these superior beings do exist, there is no easy way to identify them. Past performance, as we are often told, is no guarantee of future results. And there are so many would-be experts out there that distinguishing between those who are lucky and those who are genuinely good is often a near-impossible task. At the very least, it's a job that requires considerable patience: if you wanted to be sure that a successful money manager was beating the market because of his superior skill, and not because of luck or measurement error, you'd need many years, if not decades, of data. And if a group is so unintelligent that it will flounder without the right expert, it's not clear why the group would be intelligent enough to recognize an expert when it found him.

We think that experts will, in some sense, identify themselves, announcing their presence and demonstrating their expertise by their level of confidence. But it doesn't work that way. Strangely, experts are no more confident in their abilities than average people are, which is to say that they are overconfident like everyone else, but no more so. Similarly, there is very little correlation between experts' self-assessment and their performance. Knowing and knowing that you know are apparently two very different skills.

If this is the case, then why do we cling so tightly to the idea that the right expert will save us? And why do we ignore the fact that simply averaging a group's estimates will produce a very good result? Richard Larrick and Jack B. Soll suggest that the answer is that we have bad intuitions about averaging. We assume averaging means dumbing down or compromising. When people are faced with the choice of picking one expert or picking pieces of advice from a number of experts, they try to pick the best expert rather than simply average across the group. Another reason, surely, is our assumption that true intelligence resides only in individuals, so that finding the right person—the right consultant, the right CEO—will make all the difference. In a sense, the crowd is blind to its own wisdom. Finally, we seek out experts because we get, as the writer Nassim Taleb asserts, "fooled by randomness." If there are enough people out there making predictions, a few of them are going to compile an impressive record over time. That does not mean that the record was the product of skill, nor does it mean that the record will continue into the future. Again, trying to find smart people will not lead you astray. Trying to find *the* smartest person will.

IV

In part because individual judgment is not accurate enough or consistent enough, cognitive diversity is essential to good decision making. The positive case for diversity, as we've seen, is that it expands a group's set of possible solutions and allows the group to conceptualize problems in novel ways. The negative case for diversity is that diversity makes it easier for a group to make decisions based on facts, rather than on influence, authority, or group allegiance. Homogeneous groups, particularly small ones, are often victims of what the psychologist Irving Janis called "groupthink." After a detailed study of a series of American foreign-policy fiascoes, including the Bay of Pigs invasion and the failure to anticipate Pearl Harbor, Janis argued that when decision makers are too much alike—in worldview and mind-set—they easily fall prey to groupthink. Homogeneous groups become cohesive more easily than diverse groups, and as they become more cohesive they also become more dependent on the group, more insulated from outside opinions, and therefore more convinced that the group's judgment on important issues must be right. These kinds of groups, Janis suggested, share an illusion of invulnerability, a willingness to rationalize away possible counterarguments to the group's position, and a conviction that dissent is not useful.

In the case of the Bay of Pigs invasion, for instance, the Kennedy administration planned and carried out its strategy without ever really talking to anyone who was skeptical of the prospects of success. The people who planned the operation were the same ones who were asked to judge whether it would be successful or not. The few people who voiced caution were quickly silenced. And, most remarkably, neither the intelligence branch of the CIA nor the Cuban desk of the State Department was consulted about the plan. The result was a bizarre neglect of some of the most elemental facts about Cuba in 1961, including the popularity of Fidel Castro, the strength of the Cuban army, and even the size of the island itself. (The invasion was predicated on the idea that 1,200 men could take over all of Cuba.) The administration even convinced itself that the world would believe the United States had nothing to do with the invasion, though American involvement was an open secret in Guatemala (where the Cuban exiles were being trained).

The important thing about groupthink is that it works not so much by censoring dissent as by making dissent seem somehow improbable. As the historian Arthur Schlesinger Jr. put it, "Our meetings took place in a curious atmosphere of assumed consensus." Even if at first no consensus exists—only the appearance of one—the group's sense of cohesiveness works to turn the appearance into reality, and in doing so helps dissolve whatever doubts members of the group might have. This process obviously works all the more powerfully in situations where the group's members already share a common mind-set. Because information that might represent a challenge to the conventional wisdom is either excluded or rationalized as obviously mistaken, people come away from discussions with their beliefs reinforced, convinced more than ever that they're right. Deliberation in a groupthink setting has the disturbing effect not of opening people's minds but of closing them. In that sense, Janis's work suggests that the odds of a homogeneous group of people reaching a good decision are slim at best.

One obvious cost of homogeneity is also that it fosters the palpable pressures toward conformity that groups often bring to bear on their members. This seems similar to the problem of groupthink, but it's actually distinct. When the pressure to conform is at work, a person changes his opinion not because he actually believes something different but because it's easier to change his opinion than to challenge the group. The classic and still definitive illustration of the power of conformity is Solomon Asch's experiment in which he asked groups of people to judge which of three lines was the same size as a line on a white card. Asch assembled groups of seven to nine people, one of them the subject and the rest (unbeknownst to the subject) confederates of the experimenter. He then put the subject at the end of the row of people, and asked each person to give his choice out loud. There were twelve cards in the experiment, and with the first two cards, everyone in the group identified the same lines. Beginning with the third card, though, Asch had his confederates begin to pick lines that were clearly not the same size as the line on the white card. The subject, in other words, sat there as everyone else in the room announced that the truth was something that he could plainly see was not true. Not surprisingly, this occasioned some bewilderment. The unwitting subjects changed the position of their heads to look at the lines from a different angle. They stood up to scrutinize the lines more closely. And they joked nervously about whether they were seeing things.

Most important, a significant number of the subjects simply went along with the group, saying that lines that were clearly shorter or longer than the line on the card were actually the same size. Most subjects said what they really thought most of the time, but 70 percent of the subjects changed their real opinion at least once, and a third of the subjects went along with the group at least half the time. When Asch talked to the subjects afterward, most of them stressed their desire to go along with the crowd. It wasn't that they really believed the lines were the same size. They were only willing to say they were in order not to stand out.

Asch went on, though, to show something just as important: while people are willing to conform even against their own better judgment, it does not take much to get them to stop. In one variant on his experiment, for instance, Asch planted a confederate who, instead of going along with the group, picked the lines that matched the line on the card, effectively giving the unwitting subject an ally. And that was enough to make a huge difference. Having even one other person in the group who felt as they did made the subjects happy to announce their thoughts, and the rate of conformity plummeted.

Ultimately, diversity contributes not just by adding different perspectives to the group but also by making it easier for individuals to say what they really think. As we'll see in the next chapter, independence of opinion is both a crucial ingredient in collectively wise decisions and one of the hardest things to keep intact. Because diversity helps preserve that independence, it's hard to have a collectively wise group without it.

3.

MONKEY SEE, MONKEY DO: IMITATION,

INFORMATION CASCADES,

AND INDEPENDENCE

I

In the early part of the twentieth century, the American naturalist William Beebe came upon a strange sight in the Guyana jungle. A group of army ants was moving in a huge circle. The circle was 1,200 feet in circumference, and it took each ant two and half hours to complete the loop. The ants went around and around the circle for two days until most of them dropped dead.

What Beebe saw was what biologists call a "circular mill." The mill is created when army ants find themselves separated from their colony. Once they're lost, they obey a simple rule: follow the ant in front of you. The result is the mill, which usually only breaks up when a few ants straggle off by chance and the others follow them away.

As Steven Johnson showed in his illuminating book *Emergence,* an ant colony normally works remarkably well. No one ant runs the colony. No one issues orders. Each individual ant knows, on its own, almost nothing. Yet the colony successfully finds food, gets all its work done, and reproduces itself. But the simple tools that make ants so successful are also responsible for the demise of the ants who get trapped in the circular mill. Every move an ant makes depends on what its fellow ants do, and an ant cannot act independently, which would help break the march to death.

So far in this book, I've assumed that human beings are not ants. In other words, I've assumed that human beings can be independent decision makers. Independence doesn't mean isolation, but it does mean relative freedom from the influence of others. If we are independent, our opinions are, in some sense, our own. We will not march to death in a circle just because the ants in front of us are.

This is important because a group of people—unlike a colony of ants—is far more likely to come up with a good decision if the people in the group are independent of each other. Independence is always a relative term, but the story of Francis Galton and the ox illustrates the point. Each fairgoer figured out his estimate of the weight of the ox on his own (with allowances made for kibitzing), relying on what economists call "private information." (Private information isn't just concrete data. It can also include interpretation, analysis, or even intuition.) And when you put all those independent estimates together, the combined guess was, as we've seen, near perfect.

Independence is important to intelligent decision making for two reasons. First, it keep the mistakes that people make from becoming correlated. Errors in individual judgment won't wreck the group's collective judgment as long as those errors aren't systematically pointing in the same direction. One of the quickest ways to make people's judgments systematically biased is to make them dependent on each other for information. Second, independent individuals are more likely to have new information rather than the same old data everyone is already familiar with. The smartest groups, then, are made up of people with diverse perspectives who are able to stay independent of each other. Independence doesn't imply rationality or impartiality, though. You can be biased and irrational, but as long you're independent, you won't make the group any dumber.

Now, the assumption of independence is a familiar one. It's intuitively appealing, since it takes the autonomy of the individual for granted. It's at the core of Western liberalism. And, in the form of what's usually called "methodological individualism," it underpins most of textbook economics. Economists usually take it as a given that people are self-interested. And they assume people arrive at their idea of self-interest on their own.

For all this, though, independence is hard to come by. We are autonomous beings, but we are also social beings. We want to learn from each other, and learning is a social process. The neighborhoods where we live, the schools we attend, and the corporations where we work shape the way we think and feel. As Herbert J. Simon once wrote, "A man does not live for months or years in a particular position in an organization, exposed to some streams of communication, shielded from others, without the most profound effects upon what he knows, believes, attends to, hopes, wishes, emphasizes, fears, and proposes."

Even while recognizing (how could they not?) the social nature of existence, economists tend to emphasize people's autonomy and to downplay the influence of others on our preferences and judgments. Sociologists and social-network theorists, by contrast, describe people as *embedded* in particular social contexts, and see influence as inescapable. Sociologists generally don't view this as a problem. They suggest it's simply the way human life is organized. And it may not be a problem for everyday life. But what I want to argue here is that the more influence a group's members exert on each other, and the more personal contact they have with each other, the less likely it is that the group's decisions will be wise ones. The more influence we exert on each other, the more likely it is that we will believe the same things and make the same mistakes. That means it's possible that we could become individually smarter but collectively dumber. The question we have to ask in thinking about collective wisdom, then, is: Can people make collectively intelligent decisions even when they are in constant, if erratic, interaction with each other?

II

In 1968, the social psychologists Stanley Milgram, Leonard Bickman, and Lawrence Berkowitz decided to cause a little trouble. First, they put a single person on a street corner and had him look up at an empty sky for sixty seconds. A tiny fraction of the passing pedestrians stopped to see what the guy was looking at, but most just walked past. Next time around, the psychologists put five skyward-looking men on the corner. This time, four times as many people stopped to gaze at the empty sky. When the psychologists put fifteen men on the corner, 45 percent of all passerbys stopped, and increasing the cohort of observers yet again made more than 80 percent of pedestrians tilt their heads and look up.

This study appears, at first glance, to be another demonstration of people's willingness to conform. But in fact it illustrated something different, namely the idea of "social proof," which is the tendency to assume that if lots of people are doing something or believe something, there must be a good reason why. This is different from conformity: people are not looking up at the sky because of peer pressure or a fear of being reprimanded. They're looking up at the sky because they assume—quite reasonably—that lots of people wouldn't be gazing upward if there weren't something to see. That's why the crowd becomes more influential as it becomes bigger: every additional person is proof that something important is happening. And the governing assumption seems to be that when things are uncertain, the best thing to do is just to follow along. This is actually not an unreasonable assumption. After all, if the group usually knows best (as I've argued it often does), then following the group is a sensible strategy. The catch is that if too many people adopt that strategy, it stops being sensible and the group stops being smart.

Consider, for instance, the story of Mike Martz, the head coach of the St. Louis Rams. Going into Super Bowl XXXVI, the Rams were fourteen-point favorites over the New England Patriots. St. Louis had one of the most potent offenses in NFL history, had led the league in eighteen different statistical categories, and had outscored their opponents 503 to 273 during the regular season. Victory looked like a lock.

Midway through the first quarter, the Rams embarked on their first big drive of the game, moving from their own twenty yard line to the Patriots' thirty-two. On fourth down, with three yards to go for a first down, Martz faced his first big decision of the game. Instead of going for it, he sent on field-goal kicker Jeff Wilkins, who responded with a successful kick that put the Rams up 3 to 0.

Six minutes later, Martz faced a similar decision, after a Rams drive stalled at the Patriots' thirty-four yard line. With St. Louis needing five yards for a first down, Martz again chose to send on the kicking team. This time, Wilkins's attempt went wide left, and the Rams came away with no points.

By NFL standards, Martz's decisions were good ones. When given the choice between a potential field goal and a potential first down, NFL coaches will almost always take the field goal. The conventional wisdom among coaches holds that you take points when you can get them. (We'll see shortly why "conventional wisdom" is not the same as "collective wisdom.") But though Martz's decisions conformed to the conventional wisdom, they were wrong.

Or so, at least, the work of David Romer would suggest. Romer is an economist at Berkeley who, a couple of years ago, decided to figure out exactly what the best fourth-down strategy actually was. Romer was interested in two different variations of that problem. First, he wanted to know when it made sense to go for a first down rather than punt or kick a field goal. And second, he wanted to know when, once you were inside your opponent's ten yard line, it made sense to go for a touchdown rather than kick a field goal. Using a mathematical technique called dynamic programming, Romer analyzed just about every game—seven hundred in all—from the 1998, 1999, and 2000 NFL seasons. When he was done, he had figured out the value of a first down at every single point on the field. A first-and-ten on a team's own twenty yard line was worth a little bit less than half a point—in other words, if a team started from its own twenty yard line fourteen times, on average it scored just one touchdown. A first-and-ten at midfield was worth about two points. A first-and-ten on its opponent's thirty yard line was worth three. And so on.

Then Romer figured out how often teams that went for a first down on fourth down succeeded. If you had a fourth-and-three on your opponent's thirty-two yard line, in other words, he knew how likely it was that you'd get a first down if you went for it. And he also knew how likely it was that you'd kick a field goal successfully. From there, comparing the two plays was simple: if a first down on your opponent's twenty-nine yard line was worth three points, and you had a 60 percent chance of getting the first down, then the expected value of going for it was 1.8 points ($3 \times .6$). A field goal attempt from the thirty-one yard line, on the other hand, was worth barely more than a single point. So Mike Martz should have gone for the first down.

The beauty of Romer's analysis was that it left nothing out. After all, when you try a fifty-two yard field goal, it isn't just the potential three points you have to take into account. You also have to consider the fact that if you fail, your opponents will take over at their own thirty-five yard line. Romer could tell you how many points that would cost you. Every outcome, in other words, could be compared to every other outcome on the same scale.

Romer's conclusions were, by NFL standards, startling. He argued that teams should pass up field goals and go for first downs far more often than they do. In fact, just about any time a team faced a fourth down needing three or fewer yards for a first, Romer recommended they go for it, and between midfield and the opponent's thirty yard line—right where the Rams were when Martz made his decisions—Romer thought teams should be even more aggressive. Inside your opponent's five yard line, meanwhile, you should always go for the touchdown.

Romer's conclusions were the kind that seem surprising at first and then suddenly seem incredibly obvious. Consider a fourth down on your opponent's two yard line. You can take a field goal, which is essentially a guaranteed three points, or go for a touchdown, which you will succeed at scoring only 43 percent of the time. Now, 43 percent of seven points is roughly three points, so the value of the two plays is identical. But that's not all you have to think about. Even if the touchdown attempt fails, your opponent will be pinned on its two yard line. So the smart thing to do is to go for it.

Or consider a fourth-and-three at midfield. Half the time you'll succeed, and half the time you'll fail, so it's a wash (since no matter what happens, either team will have the ball at the same place on the field). But the 50 percent of the time that you succeed, you'll gain an average of six yards, leaving you better off than your opponent is when you fail. So, again, aggressiveness makes sense.

Obviously there were things that Romer couldn't factor in, including, most notably, the impact of momentum on a team's play. And his numbers were averaged across the league as a whole, so individual teams would presumably need to do some adjusting to figure out their particular chances of success on fourth down. Even so, the analysis seems undeniable: coaches are being excessively cautious. And, as for Mike Martz, his two decisions in that Super Bowl game were about as bad as decisions get. Martz refused to go for a first down on the Patriots' thirty-two yard line when the Rams needed just three yards. Romer's calculations suggest that Martz would have been justified in going for a first down even if the Rams had needed nine yards (since at that place on the field, the chances of missing a field goal are high, and the field-position cost is slight). And that's with an average team. With an offense like the Rams', the value of going for it would presumably have been much higher. While it's impossible to say that any one (or two) decisions were responsible for the final outcome, it's not exactly surprising that the Rams lost that Super Bowl.

Again, though, Martz was not alone. Romer looked at all the first-quarter fourth-down plays in the three seasons he studied, and found 1,100 plays where the teams would have been better off going for it. Instead, they kicked the ball 992 times.

This is perplexing. After all, football coaches are presumably trying their best to win games. They are experts. They have an incentive to introduce competitive innovations. But they're not adopting a strategy that would help them win. It's possible, of course, that Romer is wrong. Football is a remarkably complex, dynamic game, in which it's hard to distinguish among skill, strategy, emotion, and luck, so there may be something important that his computer program is missing. But it's not likely. Romer's study suggests that the gains from being more aggressive on fourth down are so big that they can't be explained away as a fluke or a statistical artifact. Teams that became more aggressive on fourth down would unquestionably have a competitive edge. But most NFL coaches prefer to be cautious instead. The interesting question is: Why?

The answer, I think, has a lot to do with imitation and social proof and the limits of group thinking. First, and perhaps most important, playing it conservatively on fourth down is as close to a fundamental truth in professional football as you get. In the absence of hard evidence to the contrary, it's easier for individuals to create explanations to justify the way things are than to imagine how they might be different. If no one else goes for it, then that must mean that it doesn't make sense to go for it.

The imitative impulse is magnified by the fact that football—like most professional sports—is a remarkably clubby, insular institution. To be sure, there have been myriad genuine innovators in the game—including Martz himself—but in its approach to statistical analysis the game has been strangely hidebound. The pool of decision makers is not, in other words, particularly diverse. That means it is unlikely to come up with radical innovations, and even more unlikely to embrace them when they're proposed. To put it another way, the errors most football coaches make are correlated: they all point in the same direction. This is exactly the problem with most major-league baseball teams, too, as Michael Lewis documented so well in his book about the recent success of the Oakland A's, *Moneyball*. Billy Beane and Paul DePodesta, the brain trust of the A's, have been able to build a tremendously successful team for very little money precisely because they've rejected the idea of social proof, abandoning the game's conventional strategic and tactical wisdom in order to cultivate diverse approaches to player evaluation and development. (Similarly, the one current NFL coach who appears to have taken Romer's ideas seriously— and perhaps even used them in games—is the New England Patriots' Bill Belichick, whose penchant for rejecting the conventional wisdom has helped the Patriots win two Super Bowls in three years.)

Another factor shaping NFL coaches' caution may be, as Romer himself suggests, an aversion to risk. Going for it on fourth-and-two makes strategic sense, but it may not make psychological sense. After all, Romer's strategy means that teams would fail to score roughly half the time they were inside their opponent's ten yard line. That's a winning strategy in the long run. But it's still a tough ratio for a risk-averse person to accept. Similarly, even though punting on fourth down makes little sense, it at least limits disaster.

The risk-averse explanation makes additional sense if you think about the pressures that any community can bring to bear on its members. That doesn't mean that NFL coaches are forced to be conservative. It just means that when all of one's peers are following the exact same strategy, it's difficult to follow a different one, especially when the new strategy is more risky and failure will be public and inescapable (as it is for NFL coaches). Under those conditions, sticking with the crowd and failing small, rather than trying to innovate and run the risk of failing big, makes not just emotional but also professional sense. This is the phenomenon that's sometimes called *herding*. Just as water buffalo will herd together in the face of a lion, football coaches, money managers, and corporate executives often find the safety of numbers alluring—as the old slogan "No one ever got fired for buying IBM" suggests.

The striking thing about herding is that it takes place even among people who seem to have every incentive to think independently, like professional money managers. One classic study of herding, by David S. Scharfstein and Jeremy C. Stein, looked at the tendency of mutual-fund managers to follow the same strategies and herd into the same stocks. This is thoroughly perplexing. Money managers have jobs, after all, only because they've convinced investors that they can outperform the market. Most of them can't. And surely herding only makes a difficult task even harder, since it means the managers are mimicking the behavior of their competitors.

What Scharfstein and Stein recognized, though, was that mutual-fund managers actually have to do two things: they have to invest wisely, and they have to convince people that they're investing investing wisely, too. The problem is that it's hard for mutual-fund investors to know if their money manager is, in fact, investing their money wisely. After all, if you knew what investing wisely was, you'd do it yourself. Obviously you can look at performance, but we know that short-term performance is an imperfect indicator of skill at best. In any one quarter, a manager's performance may be significantly better or worse depending on factors that have absolutely nothing to do with his stock-picking or asset-allocation skills. So investors need more evidence that a mutual-fund manager's decisions are reasonable. The answer? Look at how a manager's style compares to that of his peers. If he's following the same strategy—

investing in the same kinds of stocks, allocating money to the same kinds of assets—then at least investors know he's not irrational. The problem, of course, is that this means that, all other things being equal, someone who bucks the crowd—by, say, following a contrarian strategy—is likely to be considered crazy.

This would not matter if investors had unlimited patience, because the difference between good and bad strategies would eventually show up in the numbers. But investors do not have unlimited patience, and even the smartest investor will fail a significant percentage of the time. It's much safer for a manager to follow the strategy that seems rational rather than the strategy that is rational. As a result, managers anxious to protect their jobs come to mimic each other. In doing so, they destroy whatever information advantage they might have had, since the mimicking managers are not really trading on their own information but are relying on the information of others. That shrinks not only the range of possible investments but also the overall intelligence of the market, since imitating managers aren't bringing any new information to the table.

III

Herders may think they want to be right, and perhaps they do. But for the most part, they're following the herd because that's where it's safest. They're assuming that John Maynard Keynes was right when he wrote, in *The General Theory of Employment, Interest and Money,* "Worldly wisdom teaches that it is better for reputation to fail conventionally than to succeed unconventionally." And yet there is the fact that the crowd is right much of the time, which means that paying attention to what others do should make you smarter, not dumber. Information isn't in the hands of one person. It's dispersed across many people. So relying on only your private information to make a decision guarantees that it will be less informed than it could be. Can you safely rely on the information of others? Does learning make for better decisions?

The answer is that it depends on how we learn. Consider the story of plank-road fever, which the economist Daniel B. Klein and the historian John Majewski uncovered a decade ago. In the first half of the nineteenth century, Americans were obsessed with what were then known as "internal improvements"—canals, railroads, and highways. The country was growing fast and commerce was booming, and Americans wanted to make sure that transportation—or rather the lack of it—didn't get in the way. In 1825, the Erie Canal was completed, linking New York City to Lake Erie via a 363-mile-long channel that cut travel time from the East Coast to the western interior in half and cut shipping costs by 90 percent. Within a few years, the first local rail lines were being laid, even as private companies were busy building private turnpikes all over the eastern part of the country.

There was a problem, though, that all this feverish building did not solve. Although the canals and railroads would do an excellent job of connecting major towns and cities (and of turning small villages into thriving commercial hubs merely by virtue of going through them), they made it no easier for people who lived outside of those towns—which is to say, most Americans—to get their goods to market, or for that matter to get from one small town to the next. There were local public roads, different stretches of which were maintained by individual villages (much as in a city people take care, at least in theory, of the patch of sidewalk in front of their apartment), but these roads were usually in pretty bad shape. "They had shallow foundations, if any, and were poorly drained," write Klein and Majewski. "Their surfaces were muddy ruts in wet weather, dusty ruts in dry; travel was slow and extremely wearing on vehicles and on the animals that drew them."

An engineer named George Geddes, though, believed he had uncovered a solution to this problem: the plank road. The plank road—which, as its name suggests, consisted of wooden planks laid over two lines of timber—had been introduced in Canada in the early 1840s, and after seeing evidence of its success there, Geddes was convinced it would work in the United States as well. There was no question that a plank road was superior to a rutted, muddy path. What wasn't clear was whether a plank road—which would, in most cases, be privately owned and supported by tolls—would last long enough to be cost-effective. Geddes believed that a typical road would last eight years, more than long enough to provide a reasonable return on investment, and so, in 1846, he convinced some of his fellow townsmen in Salina, New York, to charter a company to build the state's first plank road.

The road was a roaring success, and soon plank-road fever swept through first New York, then through the mid-Atlantic states and the Midwest. Geddes became a kind of spokesman for the industry, even as other promoters played a similar role in states across the country. Within a decade, there were 352 plank-road companies in New York, and more than a thousand in the United States as a whole.

Unfortunately, the whole business was built on an illusion. Plank roads did not last the eight years Geddes had promised (let alone the twelve years that other enthusiasts had suggested). As Klein and Majewski show, the roads' actual life span was closer to four years, which made them too expensive for companies to maintain. By the late 1850s, it was clear that the plank road was not a transportation panacea. And though a few roads—including a thirteen-mile stretch along what is now Route 27A in Jamaica, Queens—remained in operation until the 1880s, by the end of the Civil War almost all of them had been abandoned.

PLANK-ROAD FEVER WAS a vivid example of a phenomenon that economists call an "information cascade." The first Salina road was a success, as were those which were built in the years immediately following. People who were looking around for a solution to the problem of local roads had one ready-made at hand. As more people built plank roads, their legitimacy became more entrenched, and the desire to consider other solutions shrank. It was years before the fundamental weakness of the roads—they didn't last long enough—became obvious, and by that time plank roads were being built all over the country.

Why did this happen? The economists Sushil Bikhchandani, David Hirshleifer, and Ivo Welch, who offered the first real model of an information cascade, suggest that it works like this. Assume you have a large group of people, all of whom have the choice of going to either a new Indian restaurant or a new Thai place. The Indian restaurant is better (in an objective sense) than the Thai place. And each person in the group is going to receive, at some point, a piece of information about which restaurant is better. But the information is imperfect. Sometimes it will be wrong—that is, it will say the Thai place is better when it's not—and will guide a person in the wrong direction. So to supplement their own information, people will look at what others are doing. (The economists assume that everyone knows that everyone else has a piece of good information, too.)

The problem starts when people's decisions are not made all at once but rather in sequence, so that some people go to one of the two restaurants first and then everyone else follows in order. Remember, the information people have is imperfect. So if the first couple of people happen to get bad information, leading them to believe that the Thai restaurant is great, that's where they'll go. At that point, in the cascade model, everyone who follows assumes—even if they're getting information telling them to go to the Indian restaurant—that there's a good chance, simply because the Thai place is crowded, that it's better. So everyone ends up making the wrong decision, simply because the initial diners, by chance, got the wrong information.

In this case, a cascade is not the result of mindless trend-following, or conformity, or peer pressure. ("Everyone likes that new Britney Spears song, so I will, too!") People fall in line because they believe they're learning something important from the example of others. In the case of the plank roads, for instance, it wasn't simply that George Geddes was a smooth talker, or that townspeople across the country said, "We just have to have a new plank road because the town across the river has one." Plank-road fever spread because plank roads really seemed to be a better solution. They cut travel time between towns in half. You could ride on them in any kind of weather. And they allowed small farmers to expand the markets for their goods far beyond what had previously been possible. These were genuine improvements, and as more and more plank roads were built, the fact that those improvements were real and long lasting seemed increasingly plausible. Each new road that was built was in a sense telling people that plank roads worked. And each new road that was built made coming up with an alternative seem increasingly improbable.

The fundamental problem with an information cascade is that after a certain point it becomes rational for people to stop paying attention to their own knowledge—their private information—and to start looking instead at the actions of others and imitate them. (If everyone has the same likelihood of making the right choice, and everyone before you has made the same choice, then you should do what everyone else has done.) But once each individual stops relying on his own knowledge, the cascade stops becoming informative. Everyone thinks that people are making decisions based on what they know, when in fact people are making decisions based on what they think the people who came before them knew. Instead of aggregating all the information individuals have, the way a market or a voting system does, the cascade becomes a sequence of uninformed choices, so that collectively the group ends up making a bad decision—spending all that money on plank roads.

That original model is far from the only theory of how cascades work, of course. In *The Tipping Point,* for instance, Malcolm Gladwell offered a very different account, which emphasized the importance of particular kinds of individuals—what he called mavens, connectors, and salesmen—in spreading new ideas. In Bikhchandani, Hirshleifer, and Welch's model of cascades, everyone had as much private information as everyone else. The only thing that made the early adopters of a product more influential was the fact that they were early, and so their actions were the ones that everyone who came after them observed. In Gladwell's world, some people are far more influential than others, and cascades (he writes of them as epidemics) move via social ties, rather than being a simple matter of anonymous strangers observing each other's behavior. People are still looking for information, but they believe that the ones who have it are the mavens, connectors, and salesmen (each of whom has a different kind of information).

Do cascades exist? Without a doubt. They are less ubiquitous than the restaurant-going model suggests, since, as Yale economist Robert Shiller has suggested, people don't usually make decisions in sequence. "In most cases," Shiller writes, "many people independently choose their action based on their own signals, without observing the actions of others." But there are plenty of occasions when people do closely observe the actions of others before making their own decisions. In those cases, cascades are possible, even likely. That is not always a bad thing. For instance, one of the most important and valuable innovations in American technological history was made possible by the orchestrating of a successful information cascade. The innovation was the humble screw, and in the 1860s a man named William Sellers, who was the most prominent and respected machinist of his era at a time when the machine-tool industry was the rough equivalent of the technology industry in the 1990s, embarked on a campaign to get America to adopt a standardized screw, which happened to be of his own design. When Sellers started his campaign, every American screw had to be handmade by a machinist. This obviously limited the possibilities for mass production, but it also allowed the machinists to protect their way of life. In economic terms, after all, anything tailor-made has the advantage of locking in customers. If someone bought a lathe from a machinist, that person had to come back to the machinist for screw repairs or replacements. But if screws became interchangeable, customers would need the craftsmen less and would worry about the price more.

Sellers understood the fear. But he also believed that interchangeable parts and mass production were inevitable, and the screw he designed was meant to be easier, cheaper, and faster to produce than any other. His screws fit the new economy, where a premium was placed on speed, volume, and cost. But because of what was at stake, and because the machinist community was so tight-knit, Sellers understood that connections and influence would shape people's decisions. So over the next five years, he targeted influential users, like the Pennsylvania Railroad and the U.S. Navy, and he successfully created an air of momentum behind the screw. Each new customer made Sellers's eventual triumph seem more likely, which in turn made his eventual triumph more likely. Within a decade the screw was on its way to becoming a national standard. Without it, assembly-line production would have been difficult at best and impossible at worst. In a sense, Sellers had helped lay the groundwork for modern mass production.

Sellers's story is of a beneficial cascade. The screw's design was, by all accounts, superior to its chief competitor, a British screw. And the adoption of a standard screw was a great leap forward for the U.S. economy. But there is an unnerving idea at the heart of Sellers's story: if his screw was adopted because he used his influence and authority to start a cascade, we were just lucky that Sellers happened to design a good screw. If the machinists were ultimately following Sellers's lead, rather than acting on their own sense of which screw was better, it was pure chance that they got the answer right.

In other words, if most decisions to adopt new technologies or social norms are driven by cascades, there is no reason to think that the decisions we make are, on average, good ones. Collective decisions are most likely to be good ones when they're made by people with diverse opinions reaching independent conclusions, relying primarily on their private information. In cascades, none of these things are true. Effectively speaking, a few influential people—either because they happened to go first, or because they have particular skills and fill particular holes in people's social networks—determine the course of the cascade. In a cascade, people's decisions are not made independently, but are profoundly influenced—in some cases, even determined—by those around them.

We recently experienced perhaps the most disastrous information cascade in history, which was the bubble of the late 1990s in the telecommunications business. In the early days of the Internet, traffic was growing at the rate of 1,000 percent a year. Beginning in 1996 or so, that rate slowed dramatically (as one would expect). But no one noticed. The figure "1,000 percent" had become part of the conventional wisdom, and had inspired telecom companies to start investing tens, and eventually hundreds, of billions of dollars to build the capacity that could handle all that traffic. At the time, not investing seemed tantamount to suicide. Even if you had doubts about whether the traffic would ever materialize, everyone around you was insisting that it would. It wasn't until after the bubble burst, when most of the telecom companies were either bankrupt or on the verge of going out of business, that the conventional wisdom was seriously questioned and found wanting.

IV

So should we just lock ourselves up in our rooms and stop paying attention to what others are doing? Not exactly (although it is true that we would make better collective decisions if we all stopped taking only our friends' advice). Much of the time, imitation works.

At least in a society like America's, where things generally work pretty well without much top-down control, taking your cues from everyone else's behavior is an easy and useful rule of thumb. Instead of having to undertake complicated calculations before every action, we let others guide us. Take a couple of everyday examples from city life. On a cloudy day, if I'm unsure of whether or not to take an umbrella when I leave my apartment, the easiest solution— easier, even, than turning on the Weather Channel—is to pause a moment on the doorstep to see if the people on the street are carrying umbrellas. If most of them are, I do, too, and it's the rare time when this tactic doesn't work. Similarly, I live in Brooklyn, and I have a car, which I park on the street. Twice a week, I have to move the car by 11 AM because of street cleaning, and routinely, by 10:45 or so, every car on the street that's being cleaned has been moved. Occasionally, though, I'll come out of the house at 10:40 and find that all the cars are still on the street, and I'll know that that day street cleaning has been suspended, and I won't move my car. Now, it's possible that every other driver on the street has kept close track of the days on which street cleaning will be suspended. But I suspect that most drivers are like me: piggybacking, as it were, on the wisdom of others.

In a sense, imitation is a kind of rational response to our own cognitive limits. Each person can't know everything. With imitation, people can specialize and the benefits of their investment in uncovering information can be spread widely when others mimic them. Imitation also requires little top-down direction. The relevant information percolates quickly through the system, even in the absence of any central authority. And people's willingness to imitate is not, of course, unconditional. If I get a couple of tickets because of bad information, I'll soon make sure I know when I have to move my car. And although I don't think Milgram and his colleagues ever followed up with the people in their experiment who had stopped to look at the sky, one suspects that the next time they walked by a guy with his head craned upward, they didn't stop to see what he was looking at. In the long run, imitation has to be effective for people to keep doing it.

Mimicry is so central to the way we live that economist Herbert Simon speculated that humans were genetically predisposed to be imitation machines. And imitation seems to be a key to the transmission of valuable practices even among nonhumans. The most famous example is that of the macaque monkeys on the island of Koshima in Japan. In the early 1950s, a one-year-old female macaque named Imo somehow hit upon the idea of washing her sweet potatoes in a creek before eating them. Soon it was hard to find a Koshima macaque who wasn't careful to wash off her sweet potato before eating it. A few years later, Imo introduced another innovation. Researchers on the island occasionally gave the monkeys wheat (in addition to sweet potatoes). But the wheat was given to them on the beach, where it quickly became mixed with sand. Imo, though, realized that if you threw a handful of wheat and sand into the ocean, the sand would sink and the wheat would float. Again, within a few years most of her fellow macaques were hurling wheat and sand into the sea and reaping the benefits.

The Imo stories are interesting because they seem to be in stark contrast to the argument of this book. This was one special monkey who hit on the right answer and basically changed macaque "society." How, then, was the crowd wise?

The wisdom was in the decision to imitate Imo. As I suggested in the last chapter, groups are better at deciding between possible solutions to a problem than they are at coming up with them. Invention may still be an individual enterprise (although, as we'll see, invention has an inescapably collective dimension), but selecting among inventions is a collective one. Used well, imitation is a powerful tool for spreading good ideas fast—whether they be in culture, business, sports, or the art of wheat eating. At its best, you can see it as a way of speeding up the evolutionary process— the community can become more fit without the usual need for multiple generations of genetic winnowing. Scientists Robert Boyd and Peter J. Richerson have pioneered the study of the transmission of social norms, trying to understand how groups arrive at collectively beneficial conclusions. They've run a series of computerized simulations looking at the behavior of agents who are trying to discover which of two different behaviors is best suited to the environment they're living in. In the simulation, each agent can try out a behavior for himself and see what happens, but he can also observe the behavior of someone else who's already made a decision about which behavior is best. Boyd and Richerson found that under these circumstances, everyone benefits when a sizable percentage of the population imitates. But this is only true as long as people are willing to stop imitating and learn for themselves when the benefits of doing so become high enough. In other words, if people just keep following the lead of others regardless of what happens, the well-being of the group suffers. Intelligent imitation can help the group—by making it easier for good ideas to spread quickly—but slavish imitation hurts.

Distinguishing between the two kinds of imitation is, of course, not easy, since few people will admit that they're mindlessly conforming or herding. But it does seem clear that intelligent imitation depends on a couple of things: first, an initially wide array of options and information; and second, the willingness of at least some people to put their own judgment ahead of the group's, even when it's not sensible to do so.

Do such people exist? Actually they're a lot more common than you'd expect. One reason is that people are, in general, overconfident. They overestimate their ability, their level of knowledge, and their decision-making prowess. And people are more overconfident when facing difficult problems than when facing easy ones. This is not good for the overconfident decision makers themselves, since it means that they're more likely to choose badly. But it is good for society as a whole, because overconfident people are less likely to get sucked into a negative information cascade, and, in the right circumstances, are even able to break cascades. Remember that a cascade is kept going by people valuing public information more highly than their private information. Overconfident people don't do that. They tend to ignore public information and go on their gut. When they do so, they disrupt the signal that everyone else is getting. They make the public information seem less certain. And that encourages others to rely on themselves rather than just follow everyone else.

At the same time, even risk-averse people do not, for the most part, slavishly fall in line. For instance, in 1943 the sociologists Bryce Ryan and Neal Gross published a study of the way Iowa farmers adopted a new, more productive hybrid seed corn. In their study, which became the most influential study of innovation in history, Ryan and Gross found that most farmers didn't investigate the corn independently as soon as they heard about it, even though there was good information available that showed it increased yields by 20 percent. They waited until other farmers had success with it and then followed their example. So that suggests that a cascade was at work. But in fact, even after witnessing the success of their neighbors, the farmers did not seed their entire fields with the hybrid corn. Instead, they set aside a small part of a field and tested the corn for themselves first. Only after they were personally satisfied with it did they start using the corn exclusively. And it took nine years from the time the first farmer planted his field with the new corn to the time half of the farmers in the region were using it, which does not suggest a rash decision-making process.

Similarly, in a fascinating study of how farmers in India decided whether or not to adopt new high-yielding-variety crop strains during the Green Revolution of the late 1960s, Kaivan Munshi shows that rice farmers and wheat farmers made their decisions about new crops in very different ways. In the wheat-growing regions Munshi looked at, land conditions were relatively uniform, and the performance of a crop did not vary much from farm to farm. So if you were a wheat farmer and you saw that the new seeds substantially improved your neighbor's crop, then you could be confident that it would improve your crop as well. As a result, wheat farmers paid a great deal of attention to their neighbors, and made decisions based on their performance. In rice-growing regions, on the other hand, land conditions varied considerably, and there were substantial differences in how crops did from farm to farm. So if you were a rice farmer, the fact that your neighbor was doing well (or poorly) with the new crop didn't tell you much about what would happen on your land. As a result, rice farmers' decisions were not that influenced by their neighbors. Instead, rice farmers experimented far more with the new crop on their own land before deciding to adopt it. What's telling, too, is that even the wheat farmers did not use the new strains of wheat until after they could see how the early adopters' new crops did.

For farmers, choosing the right variety of corn or wheat is the most important decision they can make, so it's perhaps not surprising that they would make those decisions on their own, rather than simply mimicking those who came before them. And that suggests that certain products or problems are more susceptible to cascades than others. For instance, fashion and style are obviously driven by cascades, which we call fads, because when it comes to fashion, what you like and what everyone else likes are clearly wrapped up with each other. I like to dress a certain way, but it's hard to imagine that the way I like to dress is disconnected from the kind of impression I want to make, which in turn must have something to do with what other people like. The same might also be said, though less definitively, about cultural products (like TV shows) where part of why we watch the show is to talk about it with our friends, or even restaurants, since no one likes to eat in an empty restaurant. No one buys an iPod *because* other people have them—the way they might, in fact, go to a movie because other people are going—but many technology companies insist that information cascades (of the good kind, they would say) are crucial to their success, as early adopters spread the word of a new product's quality to those who come after. The banal but key point I'm trying to make is that the more important the decision, the less likely a cascade is to take hold. And that's obviously a good thing, since it means that the more important the decision, the more likely it is that the group's collective verdict will be right.

V

What makes information cascades interesting is that they are a form of aggregating information, just like a voting system or a market. And the truth is that they don't do a terrible job of aggregation. In classroom experiments, where cascades are easy to start and observe, cascading groups pick the better alternative about 30 percent of the time, which is better than any individual in the groups can do. The fundamental problem with cascades is that people's choices are made sequentially, instead of all at once. There are good reasons for this—some people are more cautious than others, some are more willing to experiment, some have more money than others. But roughly speaking, all of the problems that cascades can cause are the result of the fact that some people make their decisions before others. If you want to improve an organization's or an economy's decision making, one of the best things you can do is make sure, as much as possible, that decisions are made simultaneously (or close to it) rather than one after the other.

An interesting proof of this can be found in one of those very classroom experiments I just mentioned. This one was devised by economists Angela Hung and Charles Plott, and it involved the time-honored technique of having students draw colored marbles from urns. In this case, there were two urns. Urn A contained twice as many light marbles as dark ones. Urn B contained twice as many dark marbles as light ones. At the beginning of the experiment, the people in charge chose one of the two urns from which, in se-

quence, each volunteer drew a marble. The question the participants in the experiment had to answer was: Which urn was being
used? A correct answer earned them a couple of dollars.

To answer that question, the participants could rely on two
sources of information. First, they had the marble they had drawn
from the urn. If they drew a light marble, chances were that it was
from Urn A. If they drew a dark marble, chances are that it was
from Urn B. This was their "private information," because no one
was allowed to reveal what color marble they had drawn. All people revealed was their guess as to which urn was being used. This
was the second source of information, and it created a potential
conflict. If three people in front of you had guessed Urn B, but you
drew a light marble, would you still guess Urn A even though the
group thought otherwise?

Most of the time the student in that situation guessed Urn B,
which was the rational thing to do. And in 78 percent of the trials,
information cascades started. This was as expected. But then Hung
and Plott changed the rules. The students still drew their marbles
from the urn and made their decisions in order. But this time, instead of being paid for picking the correct answer, the students got
paid based on whether the group's collective answer—as decided
by majority vote—was the right one. The students' task shifted
from trying to do the best they could individually to trying to make
the group as smart as it could be.

This meant one thing had to happen: each student had to pay
more attention to his private information and less attention to
everyone else's. (Collective decisions are only wise, remember,
when they incorporate lots of different information.) People's private information, though, was imperfect. So by paying attention to
only his own information, a student was more likely to make a
wrong guess. But the group was more likely to be collectively right.
Encouraging people to make incorrect guesses actually made the
group as a whole smarter. And when it was the group's collective
accuracy that counted, people listened to their private information.

The group's collective judgment became, not surprisingly, significantly more accurate than the judgments of the cascading groups.

Effectively what Hung and Plott did in their experiment was remove (or at least reduce) the sequential element in the way people made decisions, by making previous choices less important to the decision makers. That's obviously not something that an economy as a whole can do very easily—we don't want companies to have to wait to launch products until the public at large has voted yea or nay. Organizations, on the other hand, clearly can and should have people offer their judgments simultaneously, rather than one after the other. On a deeper level, the success of the Hung and Plott experiment—which effectively forced the people in the group to make themselves independent—underscores the value and the difficulty of autonomy. One key to successful group decisions is getting people to pay much less attention to what everyone else is saying.

4

PUTTING THE PIECES TOGETHER:

THE CIA, LINUX, AND THE

ART OF DECENTRALIZATION

I

In April 1946, at a forum organized by the *New York Herald-Tribune*, General Wild Bill Donovan gave a speech entitled "Our Foreign Policy Needs a Central Intelligence Agency." During World War II, Donovan had been the head of the Office of Strategic Services, the United States' chief wartime intelligence organization, and once the war ended he became a loud public advocate for the creation of a more powerful peacetime version of the OSS. Before the war, the United States had divided intelligence-gathering responsibilities among the different military services. But the failure of any of those services to anticipate the attack on Pearl Harbor— despite what seemed, in retrospect, to be ample evidence that a major Japanese strike was in the works—had pointed up the system's limitations and suggested the need for a more comprehensive approach to intelligence gathering. So, too, did the prospect of conflict with the Soviet Union, which even in 1946 loomed as a real possibility, and the advent of new technologies—Donovan cited "the rocket, the atomic bomb, bacteriological warfare"—that made America's borders seem far from impregnable. In his April speech,

Donovan hit on all of these themes, arguing that what the United States needed was "a centralized, impartial, independent agency" to take charge of all of the country's intelligence operations.

Donovan's public speaking didn't do much for his own career, since his sharp criticisms alienated the intelligence community and probably doomed his chances of returning to government service. Nonetheless, in 1947, Congress passed the National Security Act and created the Central Intelligence Agency. As historian Michael Warner has put it, the goal of the law was to "implement the principles of unity of command and unity of intelligence." Fragmentation and division had left the United States vulnerable to surprise attack. Centralization and unity would keep it safe in the future.

In fact, though, the centralization of intelligence never happened. Although the CIA was initially the key player in the postwar period, as time passed the intelligence community became more fragmented than ever, divided into a kind of alphabet soup of agencies with overlapping responsibilities and missions, including not just the CIA but also the National Security Agency, the National Imagery and Mapping Agency, the National Reconnaissance Office, the Defense Intelligence Agency, and the intelligence arms of each of the three major military services. In theory, the director of the CIA was in charge of the U.S. intelligence community as a whole, but in practice he exercised very little supervision over these agencies, and most of the money for intelligence operations came from the Department of Defense. In addition, the FBI—which was responsible for domestic law enforcement—operated almost completely outside the orbit of this intelligence community, even though information about foreign terrorists operating inside the United States would obviously be of interest to the CIA. In place of the centralized repository of information and analysis that Donovan had envisioned, the U.S. intelligence community evolved into a collection of virtually autonomous, decentralized groups, all working toward the same broad goal—keeping the United States safe from attack—but in very different ways.

Until September 11, 2001, the flaws of this system were over-looked. The intelligence community had failed to anticipate the 1993 bombing of the World Trade Center and the 1998 bombings of the U.S. embassy in Kenya and the USS *Cole* in Yemen. But not until September 11 did the failure of U.S. intelligence gathering come to seem undeniable. The Congressional Joint Inquiry into the attacks found that the U.S. intelligence community had "failed to capitalize on both the individual and collective significance of available information that appears relevant to the events of September 11." Intelligence agencies "missed opportunities to disrupt the September 11th plot," and allowed information to pass by unnoticed that, if appreciated, would have "greatly enhanced its chances of uncovering and preventing" the attacks. It was, in other words, Pearl Harbor all over again.

The congressional inquiry was unquestionably a classic example of Monday-morning quarterbacking. Given the sheer volume of information that intelligence agencies process, it's hardly surprising that a retrospective look at the data they had on hand at the time of the attack would uncover material that seemed relevant to what happened on September 11. That doesn't necessarily mean the agencies could have been realistically expected to recognize the relevance of the material beforehand. In her classic account of the intelligence failures at Pearl Harbor, *Warning and Decision,* Roberta Wohlstetter shows how many signals there were of an impending Japanese attack, but suggests that it was still unreasonable to expect human beings to have picked the right signals out from "the buzzing and blooming confusion" that accompanied them. Strategic surprise, Wohlstetter suggests, is an intractable problem to solve. And if a massive Japanese naval attack comprising hundreds of planes and ships and thousands of men was difficult to foresee, how much harder would it have been to predict a terrorist attack involving just nineteen men?

And yet one has to wonder. Given the almost complete failure of the intelligence community to anticipate any of four major terrorist attacks from 1993 through 2001, is it not possible that or-ganizing the intelligence community differently would have, at the very least, improved its chances of recognizing what the Joint In-quiry called "the collective significance" of the data it had on hand? Predicting the actual attacks on the World Trade Center and the Pentagon may have been impossible. But coming up with a rea-sonable, concrete estimate of the likelihood of such an attack may not have been.

That, at least, was the conclusion that Congress reached: bet-ter processes would have produced a better result. In particular, they stressed the lack of "information sharing" between the various agencies. Instead of producing a coherent picture of the threats the United States faced, the various agencies produced a lot of local-ized snapshots. The sharpest critic of the agencies' work, Senator Richard Shelby, argued that the FBI in particular was crippled by its "decentralized organizational structure," which "left information-holdings fragmented into largely independent fief-doms." And the intelligence community as a whole was hurt by a failure to put the right information in the hands of the right people. What needed to be done, Shelby suggested, was to abolish the fief-doms and return to the idea for which Bill Donovan had argued half a century ago. One agency, which could stand "above and in-dependent from the disputatious bureaucracies," needed to be put in charge of U.S. intelligence. Decentralization had led the United States astray. Centralization would put things right.

II

In challenging the virtues of decentralization, Shelby was challeng-ing an idea that in the past fifteen years has seized the imagination of businessmen, academics, scientists, and technologists every-where. In business, management theories like reengineering advo-cated replacing supervisors and managers with self-managed teams that were responsible for solving most problems on their own, while more utopian thinkers deemed the corporation itself outmoded. In physics and biology, scientists paid increasing attention to self-organizing, decentralized systems—like ant colonies or beehives—which, even without a center, proved robust and adaptable. And social scientists placed renewed emphasis on the importance of social networks, which allow people to connect and coordinate with each other without a single person being in charge. Most important, of course, was the rise of the Internet—in some respects, the most visible decentralized system in the world—and of corollary technologies like peer-to-peer file sharing (exemplified by Napster), which offered a clear demonstration of the possibilities (economic, organizational, and more) that decentralization had to offer.

The idea of the wisdom of crowds also takes decentralization as a given and a good, since it implies that if you set a crowd of self-interested, independent people to work in a decentralized way on the same problem, instead of trying to direct their efforts from the top down, their collective solution is likely to be better than any other solution you could come up with. American intelligence agents and analysts were self-interested, independent people working in a decentralized way on roughly the same problem (keeping the country safe). So what went wrong? Why did those agents not produce a better forecast? Was decentralization really the problem?

BEFORE WE ANSWER THAT question, we need to answer a simpler one first: What do we mean by "decentralization," anyway? It's a capacious term, and in the past few years it's been tossed around more freely than ever. Flocks of birds, free-market economies, cities, peer-to-peer computer networks: these are all considered examples of decentralization. Yet so, too, in other contexts, are the American public-school system and the modern corporation. These systems are dramatically different from each other, but they do have this in common: in each, power does not fully reside in one central location, and many of the important decisions are made by individuals based on their own local and specific knowledge rather than by an omniscient or farseeing planner.

In terms of decision making and problem solving, there are a couple of things about decentralization that really matter. It fosters, and in turn is fed by, specialization—of labor, interest, attention, or what have you. Specialization, as we've known since Adam Smith, tends to make people more productive and efficient. And it increases the scope and the diversity of the opinions and information in the system (even if each individual person's interests become more narrow).

Decentralization is also crucial to what the economist Friedrich Hayek described as tacit knowledge. Tacit knowledge is knowledge that can't be easily summarized or conveyed to others, because it is specific to a particular place or job or experience, but it is nonetheless tremendously valuable. (In fact, figuring out how to take advantage of individuals' tacit knowledge is a central challenge for any group or organization.) Connected with this is the assumption that is at the heart of decentralization, namely that the closer a person is to a problem, the more likely he or she is to have a good solution to it. This practice dates back to ancient Athens, where decisions about local festivals were left up to the *demes,* as opposed to the Athenian assembly, and regional magistrates handled most nonserious crimes. It can also be seen in Exodus, where Moses' father-in-law counseled him to judge only in "great matter[s]" and to leave all other decisions to local rulers.

Decentralization's great strength is that it encourages independence and specialization on the one hand while still allowing people to coordinate their activities and solve difficult problems on the other. Decentralization's great weakness is that there's no guarantee that valuable information which is uncovered in one part of the system will find its way through the rest of the system. Sometimes valuable information never gets disseminated, making it less useful than it otherwise would be. What you'd like is a way for in-

dividuals to specialize and to acquire local knowledge—which increases the total amount of information available in the system—
while also being able to aggregate that local knowledge and private
information into a collective whole, much as Google relies on the
local knowledge of millions of Web-page operators to make Google
searches ever-smarter and ever-quicker. To accomplish this, any
"crowd"—whether it be a market, a corporation, or an intelligence
agency—needs to find the right balance between the two impera-
tives: making individual knowledge globally and collectively useful
(as we know it can be), while still allowing it to remain resolutely
specific and local.

III

In 1991, Norwegian hacker Linus Torvalds created his own version
of the Unix operating system, dubbing it Linux. He then released
the source code he had written to the public, so everyone out
there—well, everyone who understood computer code—could see
what he had done. More important, he attached a note that read,
"If your efforts are freely distributable, I'd like to hear from you, so
I can add them to the system." It was a propitious decision. As one
history of Linux points out: "Of the first ten people to download
Linux, five sent back bug fixes, code improvements, and new features." Over time, this improvement process became institutionalized, as thousands of programmers, working for free, contributed
thousands of minor and major fixes to the operating system, making Linux ever-more reliable and robust.

Unlike Windows, which is owned by Microsoft and worked
on only by Microsoft employees, Linux is owned by no one. When
a problem arises with the way Linux works, it only gets fixed if
someone, on his own, offers a good solution. There are no bosses
ordering people around, no organizational charts dictating people's
responsibilities. Instead, people work on what they're interested in

and ignore the rest. This seems like—in fact, it is—a rather hap-hazard way to solve problems. But so far at least, it has been remarkably effective, making Linux the single most important chal-lenger to Microsoft.

Linux is clearly a decentralized system, since it has no formal organization and its contributors come from all over the world. What decentralization offers Linux is diversity. In the traditional corporate model, top management hires the best employees it can, pays them to work full-time, generally gives them some direction about what problems to work on, and hopes for the best. That is not a bad model. It has the great virtue of making it easy to mobi-lize people to work on a particular problem, and it also allows com-panies to get very good at doing the things they know how to do. But it also necessarily limits the number of possible solutions that a corporation can come up with, both because of mathematical re-ality (a company has only so many workers, and they have only so much time) and because of the reality of organizational and bu-reaucratic politics. Linux, practically speaking, doesn't worry much about either. Surprisingly, there seems to be a huge supply of pro-grammers willing to contribute their efforts to make the system better. That guarantees that the field of possible solutions will be immense. There's enough variety among programmers, and there are enough programmers, that no matter what the bug is, someone is going to come up with a fix for it. And there's enough diversity that someone will recognize bugs when they appear. In the words of open-source guru Eric Raymond, "Given enough eyeballs, all bugs are shallow."

In the way it operates, in fact, Linux is not all that different from a market, as we saw in Chapter 2 on diversity. Like a bee colony, it sends out lots of foragers and assumes that one of them will find the best route to the flower fields. This is, without a doubt, less efficient than simply trying to define the best route to the field or even picking the smartest forager and letting him go. After all, if hundreds or thousands of programmers are spending their time trying to come up with a solution that only a few of them are going to find, that's many hours wasted that could be spent doing something else. And yet, just as the free market's ability to generate lots of alternatives and then winnow them down is central to its continued growth, Linux's seeming wastefulness is a kind of strength (a kind of strength that for-profit companies cannot, fortunately or unfortunately, rely on). You can let a thousand flowers bloom and then pick the one that smells the sweetest.

IV

So who picks the sweetest-smelling one? Ideally, the crowd would. But here's where striking a balance between the local and the global is essential: a decentralized system can only produce genuinely intelligent results if there's a means of aggregating the information of everyone in the system. Without such a means, there's no reason to think that decentralization will produce a smart result. In the case of the experiment with which this book opened, that aggregating mechanism was just Frances Galton counting the votes. In the case of the free market, that aggregating mechanism is obviously price. The price of a good reflects, imperfectly but effectively, the actions of buyers and sellers everywhere, and provides the necessary incentive to push the economy where the buyers and sellers want it to go. The price of a stock reflects, imperfectly but effectively, investors' judgment of how much a company is worth. In the case of Linux, it is the small number of coders, including Torvalds himself, who vet every potential change to the operating-system source code. There are would-be Linux programmers all over the world, but eventually all roads lead to Linus.

Now, it's not clear that the decision about what goes into Linux's code needs to be or should be in the hands of such a small group of people. If my argument in this book is right, a large group of programmers, even if they weren't as skilled as Torvalds and his lieutenants, would do an excellent job of evaluating which code was worth keeping. But set that aside. The important point here is that if the decision were not being made by someone, Linux itself would not be as successful as it is. If a group of autonomous individuals tries to solve a problem without any means of putting their judgments together, then the best solution they can hope for is the solution that the smartest person in the group produces, and there's no guarantee they'll get that. If that same group, though, has a means of aggregating all those different opinions, the group's collective solution may well be smarter than even the smartest person's solution. Aggregation—which could be seen as a curious form of centralization—is therefore paradoxically important to the success of decentralization. If this seems dubious, it may be because when we hear centralization we think "central planners," as in the old Soviet Union, and imagine a small group of men—or perhaps just a single man—deciding how many shoes will be made today. But in fact there's no reason to confuse the two. It's possible, and desirable, to have collective decisions made by decentralized agents.

Understanding when decentralization is a recipe for collective wisdom matters because in recent years the fetish for decentralization has sometimes made it seem like the ideal solution for every problem. Obviously, given the premise of this book, I think decentralized ways of organizing human effort are, more often than not, likely to produce better results than centralized ways. But decentralization works well under some conditions and not very well under others. In the past decade, it's been easy to believe that if a system is decentralized, then it must work well. But all you need to do is look at a traffic jam—or, for that matter, at the U.S. intelligence community—to recognize that getting rid of a central authority is not a panacea. Similarly, people have become enamored of the idea that decentralization is somehow *natural* or *automatic*, perhaps because so many of our pictures of what decentralization looks like come from biology. Ants, after all, don't need to do anything special to form an ant colony. Forming ant colonies is inherent in their biology. The same is not, however, true of human beings. It's hard to make real decentralization work, and hard to keep it going, and easy for decentralization to become disorganization.

A good example of this was the performance of the Iraqi military during the U.S.–Iraq war in 2003. In the early days of the war, when Iraqi fedayeen paramilitaries had surprised U.S. and British troops with the intensity of their resistance, the fedayeen were held up as an example of a successful decentralized group, which was able to flourish in the absence of any top-down control. In fact, one newspaper columnist compared the fedayeen to ants in an ant colony, finding their way to a "good" solution while communicating only with the soldiers right next to them. But after a few days, the idea that the fedayeen were mounting a meaningful, organized resistance vanished, as it became clear that their attacks were little more than random, uncoordinated assaults that had no connection to what was happening elsewhere in the country. As one British commander remarked, it was all tactics and no strategy. To put it differently, the individual actions of the fedayeen fighters never added up to anything bigger, precisely because there was no method of aggregating their local wisdom. The fedayeen were much like ants—following local rules. But where ants who follow their local rules actually end up fostering the well-being of the colony, soldiers who followed their local rules ended up dead. (It may be, though, that once the actual war was over, and the conflict shifted to a clash between the occupying U.S. military and guerrillas using hit-and-run terrorist tactics, the absence of aggregation became less important, since the goal was not to defeat the United States in battle, but simply to inflict enough damage to make staying seem no longer worth it. In that context, tactics may have been enough.)

The irony is that the true decentralized military in the U.S.–Iraq war was the U.S. Army. American troops have always been given significantly more initiative in the field than other armies, as the military has run itself on the "local knowledge is good" theory. But in recent years, the army has dramatically reinvented itself. Today, local commanders have considerably greater latitude to act, and sophisticated communications systems mean that collectively wise strategies can emerge from local tactics. Commanders at the top are not isolated from what's happening in the field, and their decisions will inevitably reflect, in a deep sense, the local knowledge that field commanders are acquiring. In the case of the invasion of Baghdad for instance, the U.S. strategy adapted quickly to the reality of Iraq's lack of strength, once local commanders reported little or no resistance. This is not to say, as some have suggested, that the military has become a true bottom-up organization. The chain of command remains essential to the way the military works, and all battlefield action takes place within a framework defined by what's known as the Commander's Intent, which essentially lays out a campaign's objectives. But increasingly, successful campaigns may depend as much on the fast aggregation of information from the field as on preexisting, top-down strategies.

V

When it comes to the problems of the U.S. intelligence community before September 11, the problem was not decentralization. The problem was the *kind* of decentralization that the intelligence community was practicing. On the face of it, the division of labor between the different agencies makes a good deal of sense. Specialization allows for a more fine-grained appreciation of information and greater expertise in analysis. And everything we know about decision making suggests that the more diverse the available perspectives on a problem, the more likely it is that the final decision will be smart. Acting Defense Intelligence Agency director Lowell Jacoby suggested precisely this in written testimony before Congress, writing, "Information considered irrelevant noise by one

set of analysts may provide critical clues or reveal significant relationships when subjected to analytic scrutiny by another."

What was missing in the intelligence community, though, was
any real means of aggregating not just information but also judgments. In other words, there was no mechanism to tap into the collective wisdom of National Security Agency nerds, CIA spooks,
and FBI agents. There was decentralization but no aggregation, and
therefore no organization. Richard Shelby's solution to the problem—creating a truly central intelligence agency—would solve the
organization problem, and would make it easier for at least one
agency to be in charge of all the information. But it would also
forego all the benefits—diversity, local knowledge, independence—that decentralization brings. Shelby was right that information needed to be shared. But he assumed that someone—or a
small group of someones—needed to be at the center, sifting
through the information, figuring out what was important and what
was not. But everything we know about cognition suggests that a
small group of people, no matter how intelligent, simply will not be
smarter than the larger group. And the best tool for appreciating
the collective significance of the information that the intelligence
community had gathered was the collective wisdom of the intelligence community. Centralization is not the answer. But aggregation is.

There were and are a number of paths the intelligence community could follow to aggregate information without adopting a
traditional top-down organization. To begin with, simply linking the
computer databases of the various agencies would facilitate the
flow of information while still allowing the agencies to retain their
autonomy. Remarkably, two years after September 11, the government still did not have a single unified "watch list" that drew on
data from all parts of the intelligence community. In some sense,
quite simple, almost mechanical steps would have allowed the intelligence community to be significantly smarter.

Other, more far-reaching possibilities were available, too, and in fact some within the intelligence community tried to investigate them. The most important of these, arguably, was the FutureMAP program, an abortive plan to set up decision markets—much like those of the IEM—that would have, in theory, allowed analysts from different agencies and bureaucracies to buy and sell futures contracts based on their expectations of what might happen in the Middle East and elsewhere. FutureMAP, which got its funding from the Defense Advanced Research Projects Agency (DARPA), had two elements. The first was a set of internal markets, which would have been quite small (perhaps limited to twenty or thirty people), and open only to intelligence analysts and perhaps a small number of outside experts. These markets might actually have tried to predict the probability of specific events (like, presumably, terrorist attacks), since the traders in them would have been able to rely on, among other things, classified information and hard intelligence data in reaching their conclusions. The hope was that an internal market would help circumvent the internal politics and bureaucratic wrangling that have indisputably had a negative effect on American intelligence gathering, in no small part by shaping the kinds of conclusions analysts feel comfortable reaching. In theory, at least, an internal market would have placed a premium not on keeping one's boss or one's agency happy (or on satisfying the White House) but rather on offering the most accurate forecast. And since it would have been open to people from different agencies, it might have offered the kind of collective judgment that the intelligence community has found difficult to make in the past decade.

The second part of FutureMAP was the so-called Policy Analysis Market (PAM), which in the summer of 2003 became the object of a firestorm of criticism from appalled politicians. The idea behind PAM was a simple one (and similar to the idea behind the internal markets): just as the IEM does a good job of forecasting election results and other markets seem to do a good job of forecasting the future, a market centered on the Middle East might provide intelligence that otherwise would be missed.

What distinguished PAM from the internal market was that it was going to be open to the public, and that it seemed to offer the possibility of ordinary people profiting from terrible things happening. Senators Ron Wyden and Byron Dorgan, who were the leaders of the effort to kill PAM, denounced it as "harebrained," "offensive," and "useless." The public, at least those who heard about PAM before it was unceremoniously killed, seemed equally appalled.

Given the thesis of this book, it will not surprise you to learn that I think PAM was potentially a very good idea. The fact that the market was going to be open to the public did not mean that its forecasts would be more inaccurate. On the contrary, we've seen that even when traders are not necessarily experts, their collective judgment is often remarkably good. More to the point, opening the market to the public was a way of getting people whom the American intelligence community might not normally hear from— whether because of patriotism, fear, or resentment—to offer up information they might have about conditions in the Middle East.

From the perspective of Shelby's attack on the intelligence community, PAM, like the internal markets, would have helped break down the institutional barriers that keep information from being aggregated in a single place. Again, since traders in a market have no incentive other than making the right prediction—that is, there are no bureaucratic or political factors influencing their decisions—and since they have that incentive to be right, they are more likely to offer honest evaluations instead of tailoring their opinions to fit the political climate or satisfy institutional demands.

Senator Wyden dismissed PAM as a "fairy tale" and suggested that DARPA would be better off putting its money into "real world" intelligence. But the dichotomy was a false one. No one suggested replacing traditional intelligence gathering with a market. PAM was intended to be simply another way of collecting information. And in any case, if PAM had, in fact, been a "fairy tale," we would have known it soon enough. Killing the project ensured only that we would have no idea whether decision markets might have something to add to our current intelligence efforts.

The hostility toward PAM, in any case, had little to do with how effective it would or would not be. The real problem with it, Wyden and Dorgan made clear, was that it was "offensive" and "morally wrong" to wager on potential catastrophes. Let's admit there's something viscerally ghoulish about betting on an assassination attempt. But let's also admit that U.S. government analysts ask themselves every day the exact same questions that PAM traders would have been asking: How stable is the government of Jordan? How likely is it the House of Saud will fall? Who will be the head of the Palestinian Authority in 2005? If it isn't immoral for the U.S. government to ask these questions, it's hard to see how it's immoral for people outside the U.S. government to ask them.

Nor should we have shied from the prospect of people profiting from predicting catastrophe. CIA analysts, after all, don't volunteer their services. We pay them to predict catastrophes, as we pay informants for valuable information. Or consider our regular economy. The entire business of a life-insurance company is based on betting on when people are going to die (with a traditional life-insurance policy, the company is betting you'll die later than you think you will, while with an annuity it's betting you'll die sooner). There may be something viscerally unappealing about this, but most of us understand that it's necessary. This is, in some sense, what markets often do: harness amorality to improve the collective good. If the price of better intelligence was simply having our sensibilities bruised, that doesn't seem like too high a price to have paid. And surely letting people wager on the future was less morally problematic than many of the things our intelligence agencies have done and continue to do to get information. If PAM would actually have made America's national security stronger, it would have been morally wrong not to use it.

There were serious problems that the market would have had to overcome. Most notably, if the market was accurate, and the Department of Defense acted on its predictions to stop, say, a coup in Jordan, that action would make the traders' predictions false and thereby destroy the incentives to make good predictions. A well-designed market would probably have to account for such U.S. interventions, presumably by making the wagers conditional on U.S. action (or, alternatively, traders would start to factor the possibility of U.S. action into their prices). But this would be a problem only if the market was in fact making good predictions. Had PAM ever become a fully liquid market, it would probably also have had the same problems other markets sometimes have, like bubbles and gaming. But it is not necessary to believe that markets work perfectly to believe that they work well.

More important, although most of the attention paid to PAM focused on the prospect of people betting on things like the assassination of Arafat, the vast majority of the "wagers" that PAM traders would have been making would have been on more mundane questions, such as the future economic growth of Jordan or how strong Syria's military was. At its core, PAM was not meant to tell us what Hamas was going to do next week or to stop the next September 11. Instead, it was meant to give us a better sense of the economic health, the civil stability, and the military readiness of Middle Eastern nations, with an eye on what that might mean for U.S. interests in the region. That seems like something about which the aggregated judgment of policy analysts, would-be Middle Eastern experts, and businessmen and academics from the Middle East itself (the kind of people who would likely have been trading on PAM) would have had something valuable to say.

We may yet find out if they do, because in the fall of 2003, NetExchange, the company that had been responsible for setting up PAM, announced that in 2004, a new, revised Policy Analysis Market (this one without government involvement of any sort) would be opened to the public. NetExchange was careful to make clear that the goal of the market would not be to predict terrorist incidents but rather to forecast broader economic, social, and military trends in the region. So perhaps the promise of PAM will actually get tested against reality, instead of being dismissed out of hand. It also seems plausible, and even likely, that the U.S. intelligence community will eventually return to the idea of using internal prediction markets—limited to analysts and experts—as a means of aggregating dispersed pieces of information and turning them into coherent forecasts and policy recommendations. Perhaps that would mean that the CIA would be running what Senators Wyden and Dorgan scornfully called "a betting parlor." But we know one thing about betting markets: they're very good at predicting the future.

5

SHALL WE DANCE?: COORDINATION IN A

COMPLEX WORLD

I

No one has ever paid more attention to the streets and sidewalks of New York City than William H. Whyte. In 1969, Whyte—the author of the sociological classic *The Organization Man*—got a grant to run what came to be known as the Street Life Project, and spent much of the next sixteen years simply watching what New Yorkers did as they moved through the city. Using time-lapse cameras and notebooks, Whyte and his group of young research assistants compiled a remarkable archive of material that helped explain how people used parks, how they walked on busy sidewalks, and how they handled heavy traffic. Whyte's work, which was eventually published in his book *City*, was full of fascinating ideas about architecture, urban design, and the importance to a city of keeping street life vibrant. It was also a paean to the urban pedestrian. "The pedestrian is a social being," Whyte wrote. "He is also a transportation unit, and a marvelously complex and efficient one." Pedestrians, Whyte showed, were able, even on crowded sidewalks, to move surprisingly fast without colliding with their neighbors. In fact, they were often at their best when the crowds were at their biggest. "The good pedestrian," Whyte wrote, "usually walks slightly to one side, so that he is looking over the shoulder of the person ahead. In this position he has the maximum choice and the person ahead is in a sense running interference for him."

New Yorkers mastered arts like "the simple pass," which involved slowing ever so slightly in order to avoid a collision with an oncoming pedestrian. They platooned at crosswalks as a protection against traffic. In general, Whyte wrote, "They walk fast and they walk adroitly. They give and they take, at once aggressive and accommodating. With the subtlest of motions they signal their intentions to one another." The result was that "At eye level, the scene comes alive with movement and color—people walking quickly, walking slowly, skipping up steps, weaving in and out in crossing patterns, accelerating and retarding to match the moves of others. There is a beauty that is beguiling to watch."

What Whyte saw—and made us see—was the beauty of a well-coordinated crowd, in which lots of small, subtle adjustments in pace and stride and direction add up to a relatively smooth and efficient flow. Pedestrians are constantly anticipating each other's behavior. No one tells them where or when or how to walk. Instead, they all decide for themselves what they'll do based on their best guess of what everyone else will do. And somehow it usually works out well. There is a kind of collective genius at play here.

It is, though, a different kind of genius from the one represented by the NFL point spread or Google. The problem that a crowd of pedestrians is "solving" is fundamentally different from a problem like "Who will win the Giants–Rams game, and by how much?" The pedestrian problem is an example of what are usually called *coordination problems*. Coordination problems are ubiquitous in everyday life. What time should you leave for work? Where do we want to eat tonight? How do we meet our friends? How do we allocate seats on the subway? These are all coordination problems. So, too, are many of the fundamental questions that any economic system has to answer: Who will work where? How much should my factory produce? How can we make sure that people get the goods and services they want? What defines a coordination problem is that to solve it, a person has to think not only about what he believes the right answer is but also about what other people think the right answer is. And that's because what each person does affects and depends on what everyone else will do, and vice versa.

One obvious way of coordinating people's actions is via authority or coercion. An army goose-stepping in a parade is, after all, very well-coordinated. So, too, are the movements of workers on an old-fashioned assembly line. But in a liberal society, authority (which includes laws or formal rules) has only limited reach over the dealings of private citizens, and that seems to be how most Americans like it. As a result many coordination problems require bottom-up, not top-down, solutions. And at the heart of all of them is the same question: How can people voluntarily—that is, without anyone telling them what to do—make their actions fit together in an efficient and orderly way?

It's a question without an easy answer, though this does not mean that no answer exists. What is true is that coordination problems are less amenable to clear, definitive solutions than are many of the problems we've already considered. Answers, when they can be found, are often good rather than optimal. And those answers also often involve institutions, norms, and history, factors that both shape a crowd's behavior and are also shaped by it. When it comes to coordination problems, independent decision making (that is, decision making which doesn't take the opinions of others into account) is pointless—since what I'm willing to do depends on what I think you're going to do, and vice versa. As a result, there's no guarantee that groups will come up with smart solutions. What's striking, though, is just how often they do.

II

Consider, to begin with, this problem. There's a local bar that you like. Actually, it's a bar that lots of people like. The problem with the bar is that when it's crowded, no one has a good time. You're planning on going to the bar Friday night. But you don't want to go if it's going to be too crowded. What do you do?

To answer the question, you need to assume, if only for the sake of argument, that everyone feels the way you do. In other words, the bar is fun when it's not crowded, but miserable when it is. As a result, if everyone thinks the bar will be crowded on Friday night, then few people will go. The bar, therefore, will be empty, and anyone who goes will have a good time. On the other hand, if everyone thinks the bar won't be crowded, everyone will go. Then the bar will be packed, and no one will have a good time. (This problem was captured perfectly, of course, by Yogi Berra, when he said of Toots Shor's nightclub: "No one goes there anymore. It's too crowded.") The trick, of course, is striking the right balance, so that every week enough—but not too many—people go.

There is, of course, an easy solution to this problem: just invent an all-powerful central planner—a kind of über-doorman— who tells people when they can go to the bar. Every week the central planner would issue his dictate, banning some, allowing others in, thereby ensuring that the bar was full but never crowded. Although this solution makes sense in theory, it would be intolerable in practice. Even if central planning of this sort were possible, it would represent too great an interference with freedom of choice. We want people to be able to go to a bar if they want, even if it means that they'll have a bad time. Any solution worth talking about has to respect people's right to choose their own course of action, which means that it has to emerge out of the collective mix of all the potential bargoers' individual choices.

In the early 1990s, the economist Brian Arthur tried to figure out whether there really was a satisfying solution to this problem. He called the problem the "El Farol problem," after a local bar in Santa Fe that sometimes got too crowded on nights when it featured Irish music. Arthur set up the problem this way: If El Farol is less than 60 percent full on any night, everyone there will have fun. If it's more than 60 percent full, no one will have fun. There-fore, people will go only if they think the bar will be less than 60 percent full; otherwise, they stay home.

How does each person decide what to do on any given Friday? Arthur's suggestion was that since there was no obvious answer, no solution you could deduce mathematically, different people would rely on different strategies. Some would just assume that the same number of people would show up at El Farol this Friday as showed up last Friday. Some would look at how many people showed up the last time they'd actually been in the bar. (Arthur assumed that even if you didn't go yourself, you could find out how many people had been in the bar.) Some would use an average of the last few weeks. And some would assume that this week's attendance would be the opposite of last week's (if it was empty last week, it'll be full this week).

What Arthur did next was run a series of computer experi-ments designed to simulate attendance at El Farol over the period of one hundred weeks. (Essentially, he created a group of computer agents, equipped them with the different strategies, and let them go to work.) Because the agents followed different strategies, Arthur found, the number who ended up at the bar fluctuated sharply from week to week. The fluctuations weren't regular, but were random, so that there was no obvious pattern. Sometimes the bar was more than 60 percent full three or four weeks in a row, while other times it was less than 60 percent full four out of five weeks. As a result, there was no one strategy that a person could follow and be sure of making the right decision. Instead, strategies worked for a while and then had to be tossed away.

The fluctuations in attendance meant that on some Friday nights El Farol was too crowded for anyone to have fun, while on other Fridays people stayed home who, had they gone to the bar, would have had a good time. What was remarkable about the ex-periment, though, was this: during those one hundred weeks, the bar was—on average—exactly 60 percent full, which is precisely what the group as a whole wanted it to be. (When the bar is 60 percent full, the maximum number of people possible are having a good time, and no one is having a bad time.) In other words, even in a case where people's individual strategies depend on each other's behavior, the group's collective judgment can be good.

A few years after Arthur first formulated the El Farol problem, engineers Ann M. Bell and William A. Sethares took a different approach to solving it. Arthur had assumed that the would-be bargoers would adopt diverse strategies in trying to anticipate the crowd's behavior. Bell and Sethares's bargoers, though, all followed the same strategy: if their recent experiences at the bar had been good, they went. If their recent experiences had been bad, they didn't.

Bell and Sethares's bargoers were therefore much less sophisticated than Arthur's. They didn't worry much about what the other bargoers might be thinking, and they did not know—as Arthur's bargoers did—how many people were at El Farol on the nights when they didn't show up. All they really knew was whether they'd recently enjoyed themselves at El Farol or not. If they'd had a good time, they wanted to go back. If they'd had a bad time, they didn't. You might say, in fact, that they weren't worrying about coordinating their behavior with the other bargoers at all. They were just relying on their feelings about El Farol.

Unsophisticated or not, this group of bargoers produced a different solution to the problem than Arthur's bargoers did. After a certain amount of time had passed—giving each bargoer the experience he needed to decide whether to go back to El Farol—the group's weekly attendance settled in at just below 60 percent of the bar's capacity, just a little bit worse than that ideal central planner would have done. In looking only to their own experience, and not worrying about what everyone else was going to do, the bargoers came up with a collectively intelligent answer, which suggests that even when it comes to coordination problems, independent thinking may be valuable.

There was, though, a catch to the experiment. The reason the group's weekly attendance was so stable was that the group quickly divided itself into people who were regulars at El Farol and people who went only rarely. In other words, El Farol started to look a lot like *Cheers*. Now, this wasn't a bad solution. In fact, from a utilitarian perspective (assuming everyone derived equal pleasure from going to the bar on any given night), it was a perfectly good one. More than half the people got to go to El Farol nearly every week, and they had a good time while they were there (since the bar was only rarely crowded). And yet it'd be hard to say that it was an ideal solution, since a sizable chunk of the group rarely went to the bar and usually had a bad time when they did.

The truth is that it's not really obvious (at least not to me) which solution—Arthur's or Sethares and Bell's—is better, though both of them seem surprisingly good. This is the nature of coordination problems: they are very hard to solve, and coming up with any good answer is a triumph. When what people want to do depends on what everyone else wants to do, every decision affects every other decision, and there is no outside reference point that can stop the self-reflexive spiral. When Francis Galton's fairgoers made their guesses about the ox's weight, they were trying to evaluate a reality that existed outside the group. When Arthur's computer agents made their guesses about El Farol, though, they were trying to evaluate a reality that their own decisions would help construct. Given those circumstances, getting even the average attendance right seems miraculous.

III

In 1958, the social scientist Thomas C. Schelling ran an experiment with a group of law students from New Haven, Connecticut. He asked the students to imagine this scenario: You have to meet someone in New York City. You don't know where you're supposed to meet, and there's no way to talk to the other person ahead of time. Where would you go?

This seems like an impossible question to answer well. New York is a very big city, with lots of places to meet. And yet a majority of the students chose the very same meeting place: the information booth at Grand Central Station. Then Schelling complicated the problem a bit. You know the date you're supposed to meet the other person, he said. But you don't know what time you're supposed to meet. When will you show up at the information booth? Here the results were even more striking. Just about all the students said they would show up at the stroke of noon. In other words, if you dropped two law students at either end of the biggest city in the world and told them to find each other, there was a very good chance that they'd end up having lunch together.

Schelling replicated this outcome in a series of experiments in which an individual's success depended on how well he coordinated his response with those of others. For instance, Schelling paired people up and asked them to name either "heads" or "tails," with the goal being to match what their partners said. Thirty-six of forty-two people named "heads." He set up a box of sixteen squares, and asked people to check one box (you got paid if everyone in the group checked the same box). Sixty percent checked the top left box. Even when the choices were seemingly infinite, people did a pretty good job of coordinating themselves. For instance, when asked the question: "Name a positive number," 40 percent of the students chose "one."

How were the students able to do this? Schelling suggested that in many situations, there were salient landmarks or "focal points" upon which people's expectations would converge. (Today these are known as "Schelling points.") Schelling points are important for a couple of reasons. First, they show that people can find their way to collectively beneficial results not only without centralized direction but also without even talking to each other. As Schelling wrote, "People can often concert their intentions and expectations with others if each knows that the other is trying to do the same." This is a good thing because conversation isn't always possible, and with large groups of people in particular it can be difficult or inefficient. (Howard Rheingold's book *Smart Mobs*, though, makes a convincing case that new mobile technologies—from cell phones to mobile computing—make it much easier for large collections of people to communicate with each other and so coordinate their activities.) Second, the existence of Schelling points suggests that people's experiences of the world are often surprisingly similar, which makes successful coordination easier. After all, it would not be possible for two people to meet at Grand Central Station unless Grand Central represented roughly the same thing to both of them. The same is obviously true of the choice between "heads" and "tails." The reality Schelling's students shared was, of course, cultural. If you put pairs of people from Manchuria down in the middle of New York City and told them to meet each other, it's unlikely any of them would manage to meet. But the fact that the shared reality is cultural makes it no less real.

IV

Culture also enables coordination in a different way, by establishing norms and conventions that regulate behavior. Some of these norms are explicit and bear the force of law. We drive on the right-hand side of the road because it's easier to have a rule that everyone follows rather than to have to play the guessing game with oncoming drivers. Bumping into a fellow pedestrian at the crosswalk is annoying, but smashing into an oncoming Mercedes-Benz is quite another thing. Most norms are long-standing, but it also seems possible to create new forms of behavior quickly, particularly if doing so solves a problem. The journalist Jonathan Rauch, for instance, relates this story about an experience Schelling had while teaching at Harvard: "Years ago, when he taught in a second-floor classroom at Harvard, he noticed that both of the building's two narrow stairwells—one at the front of the building, the other at the rear—were jammed during breaks with students laboriously jostling past one another in both directions. As an experiment, one day he asked his 10:00 AM class to begin taking the front stairway up and the back one down. 'It took about three days,' Schelling told me, 'before the nine o'clock class learned you should always come up the front stairs and the eleven o'clock class always came down the back stairs'—without, so far as Schelling knew, any explicit instruction from the ten o'clock class. 'I think they just forced the accommodation by changing the traffic pattern,' Schelling said." Here again, someone could have ordered the students to change their behavior, but a slight tweak allowed them to reach the good solution on their own, without forcing anyone to do anything.

Conventions obviously maintain order and stability. Just as important, though, they reduce the amount of cognitive work you have to put in to get through the day. Conventions allow us to deal with certain situations without thinking much about them, and when it comes to coordination problems in particular, they allow groups of disparate, unconnected people to organize themselves with relative ease and an absence of conflict.

Consider a practice that's so basic that we don't even think of it as a convention: first-come, first-served seating in public places. Whether on the subway or a bus or in a movie theater, we assume that the appropriate way to distribute seats is according to when people arrive. A seat belongs, in some sense, to the person occupying it. (In fact, in some places—like movie theaters—as long as a person has established his or her ownership of a seat, he or she can leave it, at least for a little while, and be relatively sure no one will take it.)

This is not necessarily the best way to distribute seats. It takes no account, for instance, of how much a person wants to sit down. It doesn't ensure that people who would like to sit together will be able to. And it makes no allowances—in its hard and fast form—for mitigating factors like age or illness. (In practice, of course, people do make allowances for these factors, but only in some places. People will give up a seat on the subway to an elderly person, but they're unlikely to do the same with a choice seat in a movie theater, or with a nice spot on the beach.) We could, in theory, take all these different preferences into account. But the amount of work it would require to figure out any ideal seating arrangement would far outweigh whatever benefit we would derive from a smarter allocation of seats. And, in any case, flawed as the first-come, first-served rule may be, it has a couple of advantages. To begin with, it's easy. When you get on a subway, you don't have to think strategically or worry about what anyone else is thinking. If there's an open seat and you want to sit down, you take it. Otherwise you stand. Coordination happens almost without anyone thinking about it. And the convention allows people to concentrate on other, presumably more important things. The rule doesn't need coercion to work, either. And since people get on and off the train randomly, everyone has as good a chance of finding a seat as anyone else.

Still, if sitting down really matters to you, there's no law preventing you from trying to circumvent the convention by, for instance, asking someone to give up his seat. So in the 1980s, the social psychologist Stanley Milgram decided to find out what would happen if you did just that. Milgram suggested to a class of graduate students that they ride the subway and simply ask people, in a courteous but direct manner, if they could have their seats. The students laughed the suggestion away, saying things like, "A person could get killed that way." But one student agreed to be the guinea pig. Remarkably, he found that half of the people he asked gave up their seats, even though he provided no reason for his request.

This was so surprising that a whole team of students fanned out on the subway, and Milgram himself joined in. They all reported similar results: about half the time, just asking convinced people to give up their seat. But they also discovered something else: the hard part of the process wasn't convincing the people, it was mustering the courage to ask them in the first place. The graduate students said that when they were standing in front of a subject, "they felt anxious, tense, and embarrassed." Much of the time, they couldn't even bring themselves to ask the question and they just moved on. Milgram himself described the whole experience as "wrenching." The norm of first-come, first-served was so ingrained that violating it required real labor.

The point of Milgram's experiment, in a sense, was that the most successful norms are not just externally established and maintained. The most successful norms are internalized. A person who has a seat on the subway doesn't have to defend it or assert her right to the seat because, for the people standing, it would be more arduous to contest that right.

Even if internalization is crucial to the smooth workings of conventions, it's also the case that external sanctions are often needed. Sometimes, as in the case of traffic rules, those sanctions are legal. But usually the sanctions are more informal, as Milgram discovered when he studied what happened when people tried to cut into a long waiting line. Once again, Milgram sent his intrepid graduate students out into the world, this time with instructions to jump lines at offtrack betting parlors and ticket counters. About half the time the students were able to cut the line without any problems. But in contrast to the subway—where, when people refused to give up their seat they generally just said no or even refused to answer—when people did try to stop the line cutting, their reaction was more vehement. Ten percent of the time they took some kind of physical action, sometimes going so far as to shove the intruder out of the way (though usually they just tapped or pulled on their shoulders). About 25 percent of the time they verbally protested and refused to let the jumper in. And 15 percent of the time the intruder just got dirty looks and hostile stares.

Interestingly, the responsibility for dealing with the intruder fell clearly on the shoulders of the person in front of whom the intruder had stepped. Everyone in line behind the intruder suffered when he cut the line, and people who were two or three places behind would sometimes speak up, but in general the person who was expected to act was the one who was closest to the newcomer. (Closest, but behind: people in front of the intruder rarely said anything.) Again, this was not a formal rule, but it made a kind of intuitive sense. Not only did the person immediately behind the intruder suffer most from the intrusion, but it was also easiest for him to make a fuss without disrupting the line as a whole.

That fear of disruption, it turns out, has a lot to do with why it's easier to cut a line, even in New York, than you might expect. Milgram, for one, argued that the biggest impediment to acting against line jumpers was the fear of losing one's place in line. The line is, like the first-come, first-served rule, a simple but effective mechanism for coordinating people, but its success depends upon everyone's willingness to respect the line's order. Paradoxically, this sometimes means letting people jump in front rather than risk wrecking the whole queue. That's why Milgram saw an ability to tolerate line jumpers as a sign of the resilience of a queue, rather than of its weakness.

A queue is, in fact, a good way of coordinating the behavior of individuals who have gathered in a single location in search of goods or a service. The best queues assemble everyone who's waiting into a single line, with the person at the head of the line being served first. The phalanx, which you often see in supermarkets, with each checkout counter having its own line, is by contrast a recipe for frustration. Not only do the other lines always seem shorter than the one you're in—which there's a good chance they are, since the fact that you're in this line, and not that one, makes it likely that this one is longer—but studies of the way people perceive traffic speed suggest that you're likely to do a bad job of estimating how fast your line is moving relative to everyone else's. The phalanx also makes people feel responsible for the speed with which they check out, since it's possible that if they'd picked a different line, they would have done better. As with strategizing about the subway seat, this is too much work relative to the payoff. The single-file queue does have the one disadvantage of being visually more intimidating than the phalanx (since everyone's packed into a single line), but on average everyone will be served faster in a single queue. If there's an intelligent way to wait in line, that's it. (One change to convention that would make sense would be to allow people to sell their places in line, since that would let the placeholders trade their time for money—a good trade for them—and people with busy jobs to trade money for time—also a good trade. But this would violate the egalitarian ethos that governs the queue.)

At the beginning of this chapter, I suggested that in liberal societies authority had only limited reach over the way citizens dealt with each other. In authority's stead, certain conventions—voluntarily enforced, as Milgram showed, by ordinary people—play an essential role in helping large groups of people to coordinate their behavior with each other without coercion, and without requiring too much thought or labor. It would seem strange to deny that there is a wisdom in that accomplishment, too.

V

Convention may play an important role in everyday social life. But in theory it should be irrelevant to economic life and to the way companies do business. Corporations, after all, are supposed to be maximizing their profits. That means their business practices and their strategic choices should be rationally determined, not shaped by history or by unwritten cultural rules. And yet the odd thing is that convention has a profound effect on economic life and on the way companies do business. Convention helps explain why companies rarely cut wages during a recession (it violates workers' expectations and hurts morale), preferring instead to lay people off. It explains why the vast majority of sharecropping contracts split the proceeds from the farm fifty-fifty, even though it would be logical to tailor the split to the quality of the farm and the soil. Convention has, as we've already seen, a profound effect on strategy and on player evaluation in professional sports. And it helps explain why every major car company releases its new models for the year in September, even though there would presumably be less competition if each company released its cars in different months.

Convention is especially powerful, in fact, in the one part of the economy that you might expect it to have little sway: pricing. Prices are, after all, the main vehicle by which information gets transmitted from buyers to sellers and vice versa, so you'd think companies would want prices to be as rational and as responsive to consumer demand as possible. More practically, getting the price right (at least for companies that aren't in pure competitive markets) is obviously key to maximizing profits. But while some companies—like American Airlines, which it's been said changes prices 500,000 times a day, and Wal-Mart, which has made steady price-cutting into a religion—have made intelligent pricing key to their businesses, many companies are positively cavalier about prices, setting them via guesswork or by following simple rules of thumb. In a fascinating study of the pricing history of thirty-five major American industries between 1958 and 1992, for instance, the economist Robert Hall found that there was essentially no connection between increases in demand and increases in price, which suggests that companies decided on the price they were going to charge and charged that price regardless of what happened. Clothing retailers, for instance, generally apply a simple markup rule: charge 50 percent more than the wholesale price (and then discount like mad if the items don't sell). And until recently, the record industry blithely insisted that consumers were actually indifferent to prices, insisting that it sold as many CDs while charging $17 per disk as it would if it charged $12 or $13 a disk.

One of the more perplexing examples of the triumph of convention over rationality are movie theaters, where it costs you as much to see a total dog that's limping its way through its last week of release as it does to see a hugely popular film on opening night. Most of us can't remember when it was done differently, so the practice seems only natural. But from an economic perspective, it makes little sense. In any given week, some movies will be playing to packed houses, while others will be playing to vacant theaters. Typically, when demand is high and supply is low, companies should raise prices, and when demand is low and supply is high, they should lower prices. But movie theaters just keep charging the same price for all of their products, no matter how popular or unpopular.

Now, there's a good reason for theaters not to charge more for popular movies. Theaters actually make most of their money on concessions, so they want as many people as possible coming through the door. The extra couple of dollars they'd make by charging $12.50 instead of $10 for the opening weekend of *Spider Man 2* is probably not worth the risk of forgoing a sellout, especially since in the first few weeks of a movie's run the theaters get to keep only 25 percent or so of the box-office revenue. (The movie studios claim the rest.) But the same can't be said for charging less for movies that are less popular. After all, if theaters make most of their money on concessions, and their real imperative is to get people into the theater, then there's no logic to charging someone $10 to see Cuba Gooding Jr. in *Snow Dogs* in its fifth week of release. Just as retail stores mark down inventory to move it, theaters could mark down movies to lure more customers.

So why don't they? Theaters offer a host of excuses. First, they insist (as the music industry once did) that moviegoers don't care about price, so that slashing prices on less-popular films won't bring in any more business. This is something you hear about cultural products in general but that is, on its face, untrue. It's an especially strange argument to make about the movies, when we know that millions of Americans who won't shell out $8 to see a not-so-great flick in the theater will happily spend $3 or $4 to watch the same movie on their twenty-seven-inch TV. In 2002, Americans spent $1 billion more on video rentals than on movies in the theaters. That year, the most popular video rental in the country was *Don't Say a Word*, a Michael Douglas thriller that earned a mediocre $55 million at the box office. Clearly, there were lots of people who thought *Don't Say a Word* wasn't worth $9 but was worth $4, which suggests that there is a lot of cash being spent at Blockbuster that theater owners could be claiming instead.

Theater owners also worry that marking down movies would confuse customers and alienate the movie studios, which don't want their products priced as if they're second-rate. Since theaters have to cut separate deals every time they want to show a movie, keeping the studios happy is important. But whether a studio is willing to admit that its movie is second-rate has no impact on its second-rateness. And if annoying a few studio execs is the price of innovation, one would think theater chains would be willing to pay it. After all, fashion designers are presumably annoyed when they see their suits and dresses marked down 50 percent during a Saks Fifth Avenue sale. But Saks still does it, as do Nordstrom and Barneys, and the designers still do business with them.

In the end, though, economic arguments may not be enough to get the theaters to abandon the one-price-fits-all model—a model that the theaters themselves discard when it comes to the difference between showing a movie during the day and seeing one at night (matinees are cheaper than evening shows), but that they cling to when it comes to the difference between *Finding Nemo* and *Gigli* (for which they charge the same price). The theaters' unwillingness to change is not a well-considered approach to profit maximization and more a testament to the power of custom and convention. Prices are uniform today because that's how they were done back in the days when Hollywood made two different kinds of movies: top-of-the-line features and B movies. Those films played in different kinds of theaters at different times, and where people lived and when they saw a movie affected how much they paid. But tickets to all A-list movies cost the same (with the occasional exception, actually, of a big event film, like *My Fair Lady,* which played in theaters with reserved seating and cost more). Today, there are no B movies. Every film a studio puts out is considered top-of-the-line, so they're all priced the same. It is true that this ensures customers remain unconfused. But as the economists Liran Einav and Barak Orbach have written, it also means that movie theaters "deny the law of supply and demand." They've uncoordinated themselves with moviegoers.

VI

A giant flock of starlings moves purposefully through the African sky, keeping its shape and speed while sweeping smoothly around a tree. From above, a bird of prey dives into the flock. As the starlings scatter, the flock seems to explode around the predator, but it quickly reassembles itself. As the frustrated predator dives again and again, the flock breaks up, re-forms, breaks up, re-forms, its motion creating an indecipherable but beautiful pattern. In the process, the hawk becomes disoriented, since no individual starling ever stays in the same place, even though the flock as a whole is never divided for long.

From the outside, the flock's movements appear to be the result of the workings of one mind, guiding the flock to protect itself. At the very least, the starlings appear to be acting in concert with each other, pursuing an agreed-upon strategy that gives each of them a better chance to survive. But neither of these is true. Each starling is acting on its own, following four rules: 1) stay as close to the middle as possible; 2) stay two to three body lengths away from your neighbor; 3) do not bump into any other starling; and 4) if a hawk dives at you, get out of the way. No starling knows what the other birds are going to do. No starling can command another bird to do anything. The rules alone allow the flock to keep moving in the right direction, to resist predators and to regroup when divided.

It's safe to say that anyone who's interested in group behavior is enamored of flocking birds. Of all the hundreds of books published in the past decade on how groups self-organize without direction from above, few have omitted a discussion of bird flocks (or schools of fish). The reason is obvious: a flock is a wonderful example of a social organization that accomplishes its goals and solves problems in a bottom-up fashion, without leaders and without having to follow complex algorithms or complicated rules. Watching a flock move through the air, you get a sense of what the economist Friedrich Hayek liked to term "spontaneous order." It's a biologically programmed spontaneity—starlings don't decide to follow these rules, they just do. But it is spontaneity for all that. No plans are made. The flock just moves.

You can see something similar—albeit much less beautiful—the next time you go to your local supermarket looking for a carton of orange juice. When you get there, the juice will be waiting, though you didn't tell the grocer you would be coming. And there will probably be, over the next few days, as much orange juice in the freezer as the store's customers want, even though none of them told the grocer they were coming, either. The juice you buy will have been packaged days earlier, after it was made from oranges that were picked weeks earlier, by people who don't even know you exist. The players in that chain—shopper, grocer, wholesaler, packager, grower—may not be acting on the basis of formal rules, like the starlings, but they are using local knowledge, like the starlings, and they are making decisions not on the basis of what's good for everyone but rather on the basis of what's good for themselves. And yet, without anyone leading them or directing them, people—most of them not especially rational or farsighted—are able to coordinate their economic activities.

Or so we hope. At its core, after all, what is the free market? It's a mechanism designed to solve a coordination problem, arguably the most important coordination problem: getting resources to the right places at the right cost. If the market is working well, products and services go from the people who can produce them most cheaply to the people who want them most fervently. What's mysterious is that this is supposed to happen without any one person seeing the whole picture of what the market is doing, and without anyone knowing in advance what a good answer will look like. (Even the presence of big corporations in the market doesn't change the fact that everyone in a market has only a partial picture of what's going on.) So can this work? Can people with only partial knowledge and limited calculating abilities actually get resources to the right place at the right price, just by buying and selling?

VII

In January 1956, the economist Vernon L. Smith decided to use his classroom as a laboratory to answer that exact question. Today this would hardly be surprising. Economists routinely use classroom experiments to test out economic hypotheses and to try to understand how human behavior affects the way markets work. But fifty years ago, the idea was a radical one. Economics was a matter of proving mathematical theorems or of analyzing real-world markets. The assumption was that lab tests could tell you nothing interesting about the real world. In fact, in all the economic literature, there were hardly any accounts of classroom experiments. The most famous had been written by Harvard professor Edward Chamberlin, who every year set up a simulated market that allowed his students to trade among themselves. One of those students, as it happened, was Vernon Smith.

The experiment Smith set up was, by modern standards, uncomplicated. He took a group of twenty-two students, and made half of them buyers and half of them sellers. Then he gave each seller a card that indicated the lowest price at which she'd be willing to sell, and gave each buyer a card that indicated the highest price at which she'd be willing to buy. In other words, if you were a seller and you got a card that said $25, you'd be willing to accept any offer of $25 or more. You'd look for a higher price, since the difference would be your profit. But if you had to, you'd be willing to sell for $25. The reverse was true for buyers. A buyer with a card that said $20 would try to pay as little as possible, but if necessary she'd be willing to shell out the double sawbuck. With that information, Smith was able to construct the class's supply-and-demand curves (or "schedules") and to figure out therefore at what price they would meet.

Once all the students had their cards and the rules had been explained, Smith let them start trading among themselves. The market Smith set up was what's called a double auction, which is much like a typical stock market. Buyers and sellers called out bids and asks publicly, and anyone who wanted to accept a bid or ask would shout out his response. The successful trades were recorded on a blackboard at the front of the room. If you were a buyer whose card said $35, you might start bidding by shouting out "Six dollars!" If no one accepted the bid, then you'd presumably raise it until you were able to find someone to accept your price.

Smith was doing this experiment for a simple reason. Economic theory predicts that if you let buyers and sellers trade with each other, the bids and asks will quickly converge on a single price, which is the price where supply and demand meet, or what economists call the "market-clearing price." What Smith wanted to find out was whether economic theory fit reality.

It did. The offers in the experimental market quickly converged on one price. They did so even though none of the students wanted this result (buyers wanted prices to be lower, sellers wanted prices to be higher), and even though the students didn't know anything except the prices on their cards. Smith also found that the student market maximized the group's total gain from trading. In other words, the students couldn't have done any better had someone with perfect knowledge told them what to do.

In one sense these results could be thought of as unsurprising. In fact, when Smith submitted a paper based on his experiment to the *Journal of Political Economy*, an ardently pro-market academic journal which was run by economists at the University of Chicago, the paper was rejected at first, because from the editors' perspective all Smith had done was prove that the sun rose in the east. (The journal eventually did publish the paper, even though four referee judgments on it had come back negative.) After all, ever since Adam Smith economists had been arguing that markets did an excellent job of allocating resources. And in the 1950s, the economists Kenneth J. Arrow and Gerard Debreu had proved that, under certain conditions, the workings of the free market actually led to an optimal allocation of resources. So why were Smith's experiments so important?

They were important because they demonstrated that markets could work well even when real people were trading in them. Arrow and Debreu's proof of the efficiency of markets—which is called the general equilibrium theorem—was beautiful in its perfection. It depicted an economy in which every part fit together and in which there was no possibility of error. The problem with the proof was that no real market could fulfill its conditions. In the Arrow-Debreu world, every buyer and seller has complete information, meaning that every one of them knows what all the other buyers and sellers are willing to pay or to sell for, and they know that everyone else knows that they know. All the buyers and sellers are perfectly rational, meaning that they have a clear sense of how to maximize their own self-interest. And every buyer and seller has access to a complete set of contracts that cover every conceivable state of the world, which means that they can insure themselves against any eventuality.

But no market is like this. Human beings don't have complete information. They have private, limited information. It may be valuable information and it may be accurate (or it may be useless and false), but it is always partial. Human beings aren't perfectly rational either. They may want, for the most part, to maximize their self-interest, but they aren't always sure how to do that, and they're often willing to settle for less-than-perfect outcomes. And contracts are woefully incomplete. So while Arrow-Debreu was an invaluable tool—in part because it provided a way of measuring what an ideal outcome would look like—as a demonstration of the wisdom of markets, it didn't prove that real-world markets could be efficient.

Smith's experiment showed that they could, that even imperfect markets populated by imperfect people could still produce near-ideal results. The people in Smith's experiments weren't always exactly sure of what was going on. Many of them saw the experience of trading as chaotic and confusing. And they described their own decisions not as the result of a careful search for just the right choice but rather as the best decisions they could come up with at the time. Yet while relying only on their private information, they found their way to the right outcome.

In the four decades since Smith published the results of that first experiment, they have been replicated hundreds, if not thousands, of times, in ever more complex variations. But the essential conclusion of those early tests—that, under the right conditions, imperfect humans can produce near-perfect results—has not been challenged.

Does this mean that markets always lead to the ideal outcome? No. First of all, even though Smith's students were far from ideal decision makers, the classroom was free of the imperfections that characterize most markets in the real world (and which, of course, make business a lot more interesting than it is in economics textbooks). Second, Smith's experiments show that there's a real difference between the way people behave in consumer markets (like, say, the market for televisions) and the way people behave in asset markets (like, say, the market for stocks). When they're buying and selling "televisions," the students arrive at the right solution very quickly. When they're buying and selling "stocks," the results are much more volatile and erratic. Third, Smith's experiments—like the Arrow-Debreu equations—can't tell us anything about whether or not markets produce socially, as opposed to economically, optimal outcomes. If wealth is unevenly distributed before people start to trade in a market, it's not going to be any more evenly distributed afterward. A well-functioning market will make everyone better off than they were when trading began—but better off compared to what they were, not compared to anyone else. On the other hand, better off is better off.

Regardless, what's really important about the work of Smith and his peers is that it demonstrates that people who can be, as he calls them, "naïve, unsophisticated agents," can coordinate themselves to achieve complex, mutually beneficial ends even if they're not really sure, at the start, what those ends are or what it will take to accomplish them. As individuals, they don't know where they're going. But as part of a market, they're suddenly able to get there, and fast.

6.

SOCIETY DOES EXIST: TAXES, TIPPING,

TELEVISION, AND TRUST

I

In the summer of 2002, a great crime was perpetrated against the entire nation of Italy. Or so at least tens of millions of Italian soccer fans insisted after the country's national team was knocked out of the World Cup by upstart South Korea. The heavily favored Italians had scored an early goal against the Koreans and had clung to their 1–0 lead for most of the game, before yielding a late equalizer and then an overtime goal that sent them packing. The Italian performance had been mediocre at best. But the team was victimized by a couple of very bad officiating decisions, including one that disallowed a goal. Had those decisions gone the other way, it's likely Italy would have won.

The Italian fans, of course, blamed the referee, an Ecuadorean named Byron Moreno, for the defeat. Strikingly, though, they did not blame Moreno for being incompetent (which he was). Instead, they blamed him for being criminal. In the fans' minds, their team had been the victim of something more sinister than just bad officiating. Instead, the Italians had fallen prey to a global conspiracy—perhaps orchestrated by FIFA, soccer's governing body—designed to keep them from their just desserts. Moreno had been the point man for the conspiracy. And he had carried out his orders perfectly.

The Milan daily *Corriere della Sera,* for instance, protested against a system in which "referees . . . are used as hitmen." *La Gazzetta dello Sport* editorialized, "Italy counts for nothing in those places where they decide the results and put together million-dollar deals." A government minister declared, "It seemed as if they just sat around a table and decided to throw us out." And Francesco Totti, one of the stars of the Italian team, captured the conspiratorial mood best when he said, "This was a desired elimination. By who? I don't know—there are things greater than me but the feeling is that they wanted us out." In the weeks that followed the game, no proof of an anti-Italian cabal or of Moreno's supposed chicanery surfaced (despite the best efforts of the Italian papers). But the fans remained unwavering in their conviction that dark forces had united to destroy Italy's ambitions.

To an outside observer, the accusations of corruption seemed crazy. Honest referees make bad decisions all the time. What reason was there to believe that Moreno was any different? But to anyone familiar with Italian soccer the accusations were completely predictable. That's because in Italian soccer, corruption is assumed to be the natural state of affairs. Every year, the Italian soccer season is marred by weekly charges of criminality and skulduggery. Teams routinely claim that individual refs have been bought off, and request that particular referees not be assigned to their games. Refereeing is front-page news. Every Monday night, a TV show called *Biscardi's Trial* devotes two and a half hours to dissecting officiating mistakes and lambasting the officials for favoritism.

The effect of all this on actual Italian soccer games is not good. Although the players are among the very best in the world, the games are often halting, foul-ridden affairs repeatedly delayed by playacting, whining players more interested in working the refs than anything else. Defeat is never accepted as the outcome of a fair contest. And even victory is marred by the thought that perhaps backroom machinations were responsible for it.

So what does Italian soccer have to do with collective decision making and problem solving? Well, although the teams in a soccer game are trying to defeat each other, and therefore have competing interests, the teams also have a common interest: namely, making sure that the games are entertaining and compelling for the fans. The more interesting the games are, the more likely it is that people will come, the greater ticket sales and TV ratings will be, and the higher team profits and player salaries will be. When two soccer teams play each other, then, they're not just competing. They're also, at least in theory, working together—along with the officials—in order to produce an entertaining game. And this is precisely what the Italian teams are unable to do. Because neither side can be sure that its efforts will be fairly rewarded, the players devote an inordinate amount of time to protecting their own interests. Energy, time, and attention that would be better spent improving the quality of play instead goes into excoriating, monitoring, and trying to manipulate the referees. And the manipulation feeds on itself. Even if most players would rather be honest, they realize that they'd only be asking to be exploited. As Gennaro Gattuso, a winger for European champions AC Milan, said in October of 2003, "The system prevents you from telling the truth and being yourself." Hardly anyone likes the system the way it is, but no one can change it.

What Italian soccer is failing to do, then, is come up with a good solution to what I'll call here a *cooperation* problem. Cooperation problems often look something like coordination problems, because in both cases a good solution requires people to take what everyone else is doing into account. But if the mechanism is right, coordination problems can be solved even if each individual is single-mindedly pursuing his self-interest—in fact, in the case of price, that's what coordination seems to require. To solve cooperation problems—which include things like keeping the sidewalk free of snow, paying taxes, and curbing pollution—the members of a group or a society need to do more. They need to adopt a broader definition of self-interest than the myopic one that maximizing profits in the short term demands. And they need to be able to trust those around them, because in the absence of trust the pursuit of myopic self-interest is the only strategy that makes sense. How does this happen? And does it make a difference when it does?

11

In September 2003, Richard Grasso, who was then the head of the New York Stock Exchange, became the first CEO in American history to get fired for making too much money. Grasso had run the NYSE since 1995, and by most accounts he had done a good job. He was aggressively self-promoting, but he did not appear to be incompetent or corrupt. But when the news broke that the NYSE was planning to give Grasso a lump-sum payment of $139.5 million—made up of retirement benefits, deferred pay, and bonuses—the public uproar was loud and immediate, and in the weeks that followed, the calls for Grasso's removal grew deafening. When the NYSE's board of directors (the very people, of course, who had agreed to pay him the $139.5 million in the first place) asked Grasso to step down, it was because the public's outrage had made it impossible to keep him around.

Why was the public so outraged? After all, they did not have to foot the bill for Grasso's millions. The NYSE was spending its own money. And complaining about Grasso's windfall didn't make anyone else any better off. He had already been paid, and the NYSE wasn't going to take the money it had promised him and give it to charity or invest it more wisely. From an economist's point of view, in fact, the public reaction seemed deeply irrational. Economists have traditionally assumed, reasonably, that human beings are basically self-interested. This means a couple of (perhaps obvious) things. First, faced with different choices (of products, services, or simply courses of action), a person will choose the one that benefits her personally. Second, her choices will not depend on what anyone else does. But with the possible exception of business columnists, no one who expressed outrage over how much Dick Grasso made reaped any concrete benefits from their actions, making it irrational to invest time and energy complaining about him. And yet that's exactly what people did. So the question again is: Why?

The explanation for people's behavior might have something to do with an experiment called the "ultimatum game," which is perhaps the most well-known experiment in behavioral economics. The rules of the game are simple. The experimenter pairs two people with each other. (They can communicate with each other, but otherwise they're anonymous to each other.) They're given $10 to divide between them, according to this rule: One person (the proposer) decides, on his own, what the split should be (fifty-fifty, seventy-thirty, or whatever). He then makes a take-it-or-leave-it offer to the other person (the responder). The responder can either accept the offer, in which case both players pocket their respective shares of the cash, or reject it, in which case both players walk away empty-handed.

If both players are rational, the proposer will keep $9 for himself and offer the responder $1, and the responder will take it. After all, whatever the offer, the responder should accept it, since if he accepts he gets some money and if he rejects, he gets none. A rational proposer will realize this and therefore make a lowball offer.

In practice, though, this rarely happens. Instead, lowball offers—anything below $2—are routinely rejected. Think for a moment about what this means. People would rather have nothing than let their "partners" walk away with too much of the loot. They will give up free money to punish what they perceive as greedy or selfish behavior. And the interesting thing is that the proposers anticipate this—presumably because they know they would act the same way if they were in the responder's shoes. As a result, the proposers don't make many low offers in the first place. The most common offer in the ultimatum game, in fact, is $5.

Now, this is a long way from the "rational man" picture of human behavior. The players in the ultimatum game are not choosing what's materially best for them, and their choices are clearly completely dependent on what the other person does. People play the ultimatum game this way all across the developed world: cross-national studies of players in Japan, Russia, the United States, and France all document the same phenomenon. And increasing the size of the stakes doesn't seem to matter much either. Obviously, if the proposer were given the chance to divide $1 million, the responder wouldn't turn down $100,000 just to prove a point. But the game has been played in countries, like Indonesia, where the possible payoff was equal to three days' work, and responders still rejected lowball offers.

It isn't just humans who act this way, either. In a study that was fortuitously released the day Richard Grasso stepped down, primatologists Sarah F. Brosnan and Frans B. M. de Waal showed that female capuchin monkeys are also offended by unfair treatment. The capuchins had been trained to give Brosnan a granite pebble in exchange for food. The pay, as it were, was a slice of cucumber. The monkeys worked in pairs, and when they were both rewarded with cucumbers, they exchanged rock for food 95 percent of the time. This idyllic market economy was disrupted, though, when the scientists changed the rules, giving one capuchin a delicious grape as a reward while still giving the other a cucumber slice. Confronted with this injustice, the put-upon capuchins often refused to eat their cucumbers, and 40 percent of the time stopped trading entirely. Things only got worse when one monkey was given a grape in exchange for doing nothing at all. In that case, the other monkey often tossed away her pebble, and trades took place only 20 percent of the time. In other words, the capuchins were willing to give up cheap food—after all, a cucumber slice for a pebble seems like a good deal—simply to express their displeasure at their comrades' unearned riches. Presumably if they'd been given the chance to stop their comrades from enjoying those riches—as the players in the ultimatum game were—the capuchins would have gladly taken it.

Capuchins and humans alike, then, seem to care whether rewards are, in some sense, "fair." That may seem like an obvious thing to worry about, but it's not. If the monkey thought a rock for a cucumber slice was a reasonable trade and was happy to make it before she saw her comrade get a grape, she should be happy to make the trade afterward, too. After all, her job hasn't gotten any harder, nor is the cucumber any less tasty. (Or if it is, that's because she's obsessed with what her neighbor's getting.) So her feelings about the deal should stay the same. Similarly, the responders in the ultimatum game are being offered money for what amounts to a few minutes of "work," which mostly consists of answering "yes" or "no." Turning down free money is not something that, in most circumstances, makes sense. But people are willing to do it in order to make sure that the distribution of resources is fair.

Does this mean people think that, in an ideal world, everyone would have the same amount of money? No. It means people think that, in an ideal world, everyone would end up with the amount of money they deserved. In the original version of the ultimatum game; only luck determines who gets to be the proposer and who gets to be the responder. So the split, people feel, should be fairly equal. But people's behavior in the game changes quite dramatically when the rules are changed. In the most interesting version of the ultimatum game, for instance, instead of assigning the proposer role randomly, the researchers made it seem as if the proposers had earned their positions by doing better on a test. In those experiments, proposers offered significantly less money, yet not a single offer was rejected. People apparently thought that a proposer who merited his position deserved to keep more of the wealth.

Put simply, people (and capuchins) want there to be a reasonable relationship between accomplishment and reward. That's what was missing in Grasso's case. He was getting too much for having done too little. Grasso seems to have been good at his job. But he was not irreplaceable: no one thought the NYSE would fall apart once he was gone. More to the point, the job was not a $140 million job. (What job is?) In terms of complexity and sophistication, it bore no resemblance to, say, running Merrill Lynch or Goldman Sachs. Yet Grasso was being paid as much as many Wall Street CEOs, who are themselves heftily overcompensated.

The impulse toward fairness that drove Grasso from office is a cross-cultural reality, but culture does have a major effect on what counts as fair. American CEOs, for instance, make significantly more money than European or Japanese CEOs, and salary packages that would send the Germans to the barricades barely merit a moment's notice in the United States. More generally, high incomes by themselves don't seem to bother Americans much—even though America has the most unequal distribution of income in the developed world, polls consistently show that Americans care much less about inequality than Europeans do. In fact, a 2001 study by economists Alberto Alesina, Rafael di Tella, and Robert MacCulloch found that in America the people whom inequality bothers most are the rich. One reason for this is that Americans are far more likely to believe that wealth is the result of initiative and skill, while Europeans are far more likely to attribute it to luck. Americans still think, perhaps inaccurately, of the United States as a relatively mobile society, in which it's possible for a working-class kid to become rich. The irony is that Grasso himself was a working-class kid who made good. But even for Americans, apparently, there is a limit to how good you can make it.

There's no doubt the indignation at Grasso's retirement package was, in an economic sense, irrational. But like the behavior of the ultimatum game responders, the indignation was an example of what economists Samuel Bowles and Herbert Gintis call "strong reciprocity," which is the willingness to punish bad behavior (and reward good behavior) even when you get no personal material benefits from doing so. And, irrational or not, strong reciprocity is, as Bowles and Gintis term it, a "prosocial behavior," because it pushes people to transcend a narrow definition of self-interest and do things, intentionally or not, that end up serving the common good. Strong reciprocators are not altruists. They are not rejecting lowball offers, or hounding Dick Grasso, because they love humanity. They're rejecting lowball offers because the offers violate their individual sense of what a just exchange would be. But the effect is the same as if they loved humanity: the group benefits. Strong reciprocity works. Offers in the ultimatum game are usually quite equitable, which is what they should be given the way the resources are initially set up. And whenever the NYSE thinks about hiring a CEO, it will presumably be more rigorous in figuring out how much he's actually worth. Individually irrational acts, in other words, can produce a collectively rational outcome.

III

The mystery that the idea of prosocial behavior may help resolve is the mystery of why we cooperate at all. Societies and organizations work only if people cooperate. It's impossible for a society to rely on law alone to make sure citizens act honestly and responsibly. And it's impossible for any organization to rely on contracts alone to make sure that its managers and workers live up to their obligations. So cooperation typically makes everyone better off. But for each individual, it's rarely rational to cooperate. It always makes more sense to look after your own interests first and then live off everyone else's work if they are silly enough to cooperate. So why don't most of us do just that?

The classic and canonical explanation of why people cooperate was offered by political scientist Robert Axelrod, who argued in the 1980s that cooperation is the result of repeated interactions with the same people. As Axelrod put it in his classic *The Evolution of Cooperation*, "The foundation of cooperation is not really trust, but the durability of the relationship . . . Whether the players trust each other or not is less important in the long run than whether the conditions are ripe for them to build a stable pattern of cooperation with each other." People who repeatedly deal with each other over time recognize the benefits of cooperation, and they do not try to take advantage of each other, because they know if they do, the other person will be able to punish them. The key to cooperation is what Axelrod called "the shadow of the future." The promise of our continued interaction keeps us in line. Successful cooperation, Axelrod argued, required that people start off by being nice—that is, by being willing to cooperate—but that they had to be willing to punish noncooperative behavior as soon as it appeared. The best approach was to be "nice, forgiving, and retaliatory."

Those rules seem completely sensible, and are probably a good description of the way most people in a well-functioning society deal with those they know. But there's something unsatisfying, as Axelrod himself now seems to recognize, about the idea that cooperation is simply the product of repeated interactions with the same people. After all, we often act in a prosocial fashion even when there is no obvious payoff for ourselves. Look at the ultimatum game again. It is a one-shot game. You don't play it with the same person more than once. The responders who turned down lowball offers were therefore not doing so in order to teach the proposer to treat them better. And yet they still punished those whom they thought were acting unfairly, which suggests that the "shadow of the future" alone cannot explain why we cooperate.

The interesting thing, ultimately, isn't that we cooperate with those we know and do business with regularly. The interesting thing is that we cooperate with strangers. We donate to charities. We buy things off eBay sight unseen. People sign on to Kazaa and upload songs for others to download, even though they reap no benefit from sharing those songs and doing so means letting strangers have access to their computers' hard drives. These are all, in the strict sense, irrational things to do. But they make all of us (well, aside from the record companies) better off. It may be, in the end, that a good society is defined more by how people treat strangers than by how they treat those they know.

Consider tipping. It's understandable that people tip at restaurants that they frequent regularly: tipping well may get them better service or a better table, or it may just make their interactions with the waiters more pleasant. But, for the most part, people tip even at restaurants that they know they'll never return to, and at restaurants in cities thousands of miles away from their homes. In part, this is because people don't want to run the risk of being publicly reprimanded for not tipping or undertipping. But mostly, it's because we accept that tipping is what you are supposed to do when you go to a restaurant, because tips are the only way that waiters and waitresses can make a living. And we accept this even though it means that we end up voluntarily giving money to strangers whom we may never see again. The logic of this whole arrangement is debatable (as Mr. Pink asked in *Reservoir Dogs,* why do we tip people who do certain jobs and not even think of tipping people who do other jobs?). But given that logic, tipping, and especially tipping strangers, is a resolutely prosocial behavior, and one that the shadow of the future alone cannot explain.

Why are we willing to cooperate with those we barely know? I like Robert Wright's answer, which is that over time, we have learned that trade and exchange are games in which everyone can end up gaining, rather than zero-sum games in which there's always a winner and a loser. But the "we" here is, of course, ill defined, since different cultures have dramatically different ideas about trust and cooperation and the kindness of strangers. In the next section, I want to argue that one of the things that accounts for those differences is something that is rarely associated with trust or cooperation: capitalism.

IV

In eighteenth- and early-nineteenth-century Britain, a sizable chunk of the nation's economy was run by members of the religious sect known as the Quakers. Quakers owned more than half of the country's ironworks. They were key players in banking (both Barclays and Lloyds were Quaker institutions). They dominated consumer businesses such as chocolate and biscuits. And they were instrumental in facilitating the transatlantic trade between Britain and America.

Initially, Quaker success was built around the benefits Quakers got from trading with each other. Because they dissented from the English state religion, members of the sect were barred from the professions, and as a result they gravitated toward business. When Quakers went looking for credit or for trade, they found it easy to partner with fellow believers. Their common faith facilitated trust, allowing a Quaker tradesman in London to ship goods across the ocean and be certain that he would be paid when they arrived in Philadelphia.

Quaker prosperity did not go unnoticed in the outside world. Quakers were well-known already for their personal emphasis on absolute honesty, and as businessmen they were famously rigorous and careful in their record keeping. They also introduced innovations like fixed prices, which emphasized transparency over sharp dealing. Soon, people outside the sect began to seek Quakers as trading partners, suppliers, and sellers. And as Quaker prosperity grew, people drew a connection between that prosperity and the sect's reputation for reliability and trustworthiness. Honesty, it started to seem, paid.

In the wake of the orgy of corruption in which American businesses indulged during the stock-market bubble of the late 1990s, the idea that trustworthiness and good business might go together sounds woefully naïve. Certainly one interpretation of these scandals is that they were not aberrations but the inevitable by-product of a system that plays to people's worst impulses: greed, cynicism, and selfishness. This argument sounds plausible, if only because capitalist rhetoric so often stresses the virtue of greed and the glories of what "Chainsaw" Al Dunlap, the legendarily ruthless, job-cutting CEO, liked to call "mean business." But this popular image of capitalism bears only slight resemblance to its reality. Over centuries, in fact, the evolution of capitalism has been in the direction of more trust and transparency, and less self-regarding behavior. Not coincidentally, this evolution has brought with it greater productivity and economic growth.

That evolution did not take place because capitalists are naturally good people. Instead it took place because the benefits of trust—that is, of being trusting and of being trustworthy—are potentially immense, and because a successful market system teaches people to recognize those benefits. At this point, it's been well demonstrated that flourishing economies require a healthy level of trust in the reliability and fairness of everyday transactions. If you assumed every potential deal was a rip-off or that the products you were buying were probably going to be lemons, then very little business would get done. More important, the costs of the transactions that did take place would be exorbitant, since you'd have to do enormous work to investigate each deal and you'd have to rely on the threat of legal action to enforce every contract. For an economy to prosper, what's needed is not a Pollyannaish faith in the good intentions of others—caveat emptor remains an important truth—but a basic confidence in the promises and commitments that people make about their products and services. As the economist Thomas Schelling has put it: "One has only to consider the enormous frustration of conducting foreign aid in an underdeveloped country, or getting a business established there, to realize what an extraordinary economic asset is a population of honest conscientious people."

Establishing that confidence has been a central part of the history of capitalism. In the medieval period, people trusted those within their particular ethnic or provincial group. Historian Avner Greif has shown how the Moroccan traders known as the Maghribi built a trading system across the Mediterranean in the eleventh century by creating a system of collective sanctions to punish those who violated their commercial codes. Trade between groups, meanwhile, depended on rules that applied to the group as a whole. If one Genoese trader ripped off someone in France, all Genoese traders paid the price. This may not have been exactly fair, but it had the virtue of creating conditions under which inter-state trading could flourish, since it compelled trading communities to enforce internal discipline to encourage fair dealing. On the flip side of this, merchant guilds—most notably the German Hanseatic League—protected their members against unfair treatment from city-states by imposing collective trade embargoes against cities that seized merchant property.

As the Quaker example suggests, intragroup trust remained important for centuries. For that matter, it remains important to-day—look at the success of ethnic Chinese businessmen in countries across Southeast Asia. But in England, at least, contract law evolved to emphasize individual responsibility for agreements and, more important, the idea of that responsibility began to take hold among businessmen more generally. As one observer said in 1717, "To support and maintain a man's private credit, 'tis absolutely necessary that the world have a fixed opinion of the honesty and integrity, as well as ability of a person." And Daniel Defoe, around the same time, wrote, "An honest tradesman is a jewel indeed, and is valued wherever he is found."

Still, Defoe's very emphasis on how valuable people found an honest businessman is probably evidence that there weren't many honest businessmen. And the Quakers, after all, became known for their reliability precisely because it seemed exceptional. It's certainly true that the benefits of honesty and the relationship between trust and healthy commerce were recognized. Adam Smith, in *The Wealth of Nations*, wrote, "when the greater part of people are merchants they always bring probity and punctuality into fashion," while Montesquieu wrote of the way commerce "polishes and softens" men. But it wasn't until the nineteenth century—not, coincidentally, the moment when capitalism as we know it flowered—that trust became, in a sense, institutionalized. As the historian Richard Tilly has shown in his study of business practices in Germany and Britain, it was during the 1800s that businessmen started to see that honesty might actually be profitable. In America, as John Mueller shows in his wonderful book *Capitalism, Democracy, and Ralph's Pretty Good Grocery*, P. T. Barnum—whom we all know as the victimizer of suckers—in fact pioneered modern ideas of customer service, while around the same time John Wanamaker was making fixed retail prices a new standard. And the end of the nineteenth century saw the creation of independent institutions like the Underwriters Laboratory and the Better Business Bureau, all of which were intended to foster a general climate of trust in everyday transactions. On Wall Street, meanwhile, J. P. Morgan built a lucrative business on the idea of trust. In the late nineteenth century, investors (particularly foreign investors) who had been burned by shady or shaky railroad investments were leery of putting more money into America. The presence of a Morgan man on the board of directors of a company came to be considered a guarantee that a firm was reliable and solid.

At the heart of this shift was a greater emphasis on the accumulation of capital over the long run as opposed to merely short-term profit, an emphasis that has been arguably a defining characteristic of modern capitalism. As Tilly writes, businessmen started to see "individual transactions as links in a larger chain of profitable business ventures," instead of just "one-time opportunities to be exploited to the utmost." If your prosperity in the long run depended on return business, on word-of-mouth recommendations, and on ongoing relationships with suppliers and partners, fair dealing became more valuable. The lubrication of commerce that trust provides became more than desirable. It became necessary.

What was most important about this new concept of trust was that it was, in some sense, impersonal. Previously, trust had been the product primarily of a personal or in-group relationship—I trust this guy because I know him or because he and I belong to the same sect or clan—rather than a more general assumption upon which you could do business. Modern capitalism made the idea of trusting people with whom you had "no prior personal ties" seem reasonable, if only by demonstrating that strangers would not, as a matter of course, betray you. This helped trust become woven into the basic fabric of everyday business. Buying and selling no longer required a personal connection. It could be driven instead by the benefits of mutual exchange.

The impersonality of capitalism is usually seen as one of its unfortunate, if inescapable, costs. In place of relationships founded on blood or affection, capitalism creates relationships founded solely on what Marx called the "money nexus." But, in this case, impersonality was a virtue. One of the fundamental problems with trust is that it usually flourishes only where there are what sociologists call "thick relationships"—relationships of family or clan or neighborhood. But these kinds of relationships are impossible to maintain with many people at once and they are incompatible with the kind of scope and variety of contacts that a healthy modern economy (or a healthy modern society) needs to thrive. In fact, thick relationships can often be inimical to economic growth, since they foster homogeneity and discourage open market exchange in favor of personalized trading. Breaking with the tradition of defining trust in familial or ethnic terms was therefore essential. As the economist Stephen Knack writes, "The type of trust that should be unambiguously beneficial to a nation's economic performance is trust between strangers, or more precisely between two randomly selected residents of a country. Particularly in large and mobile societies where personal knowledge and reputation effects are limited, a sizeable proportion of potentially mutually beneficial transactions will involve parties with no prior personal ties."

As with much else, though, this relationship between capitalism and trust is usually invisible, simply because it's become part of the background of everyday life. I can walk into a store anywhere in America to buy a CD player and be relatively certain that whatever product I buy—a product that, in all likelihood, will have been made in a country nine thousand miles away—will probably work pretty well. And this is true even though I may never walk into that store again. At this point, we take both the reliability of the store and my trust in that reliability for granted. But in fact they're remarkable achievements.

This sense of trust could not exist without the institutional and legal framework that underpins every modern capitalist economy. Consumers rarely sue businesses for fraud, but businesses know that the possibility exists. And if contracts between businesses are irrelevant, it's hard to understand why corporate lawyers are so well paid. But the measure of success of laws and contracts is how rarely they are invoked. And, as Stephen Knack and Philip Keefer write, "Individuals in higher-trust societies spend less to protect themselves from being exploited in economic transactions. Written contracts are less likely to be needed, and they do not have to specify every possible contingency." Or, as Axelrod quotes a purchasing agent for a Midwestern business as saying, "If something comes up you get the other man on the telephone and deal with the problem. You don't read legalistic contract clauses at each other if you ever want to do business again."

Trust begins there, as it does in Axelrod's model, because of the shadow of the future. All you really trust is that the other person will recognize his self-interest. But over time, that reliance on his own attention to his self-interest becomes something more. It becomes a general sense of reliability, a willingness to cooperate (even in competition) because cooperation is the best way to get things done. What Samuel Bowles and Herbert Gintis call prosociality becomes stronger because prosociality works.

Now, I realize how improbable this sounds. Markets, we know, foster selfishness and greed, not trust and fairness. But even if you find the history unconvincing, there is this to consider: in the late 1990s, under the supervision of Bowles, twelve field researchers—including eleven anthropologists and one economist—went into fifteen "small-scale" societies (essentially small tribes that were, to varying degrees, self-contained) and got people to play the kinds of games in which experimental economics specializes. The societies included three that depended on foraging for survival, six that used slash-and-burn techniques, four nomadic herding groups, and two small agricultural societies. The three games the people were asked to play were the three standards of behavioral economics: the ultimatum game (which you just read about), the public-goods game (in which if everyone contributes, everyone goes away significantly better off, while if only a few people contribute, then the others can free ride off their effort), and the dictator game, which is similar to the ultimatum game except that the responder can't say no to the proposer's offer. The idea behind all these games is that they can be played in a purely rational manner, in which case the player protects himself against loss but forgoes the possibility of mutual gain. Or they can be played in a prosocial manner, which is what most people do.

In any case, what the researchers found was that in every single society there was a significant deviation from the purely rational strategy. But the deviations were not all in the same direction, so there were significant differences between the cultures. What was remarkable about the study, though, was this: the higher the degree to which a culture was integrated with the market, the greater the level of prosociality. People from more market-oriented societies made higher offers in the dictator game and the ultimatum game, cooperated in the public-goods game, and exhibited strong reciprocity when they had the chance. The market may not teach people to trust, but it certainly makes it easier for people to do so.

V

The social benefits of trust and cooperation are, at this point, relatively unquestioned. But they do create a problem: the more people trust, the easier they are for others to exploit. And if trust is the most valuable social product of market interactions, corruption is its most damaging. Over the centuries, market societies have developed mechanisms and institutions that are supposed to limit corruption, including auditors, rating agencies, third-party analysts, and, as we've seen, even Wall Street banks. And they have relied, as well, on the idea that companies and individuals will act honestly—if not generously—because doing so is the best way to ensure long-term financial success. In addition, in the twentieth century a relatively elaborate regulatory apparatus emerged that was supposed to protect consumers and investors. These systems work well most of the time. But sometimes they don't, and when they don't, things come apart, as they did in the late 1990s.

The stock-market bubble of the late nineties created a perfect breeding ground for corruption. In the first place, it wiped away, almost literally, the shadow of the future for many corporate executives. CEOs who knew that their companies' future cash flow could never justify their outrageously inflated stock prices also knew that the future was therefore going to be less lucrative than the present. Capitalism is healthiest when people believe that the long-term benefits of fair dealing outweigh the short-term benefits of sharp dealing. In the case of the executives at companies like Enron and

Tyco, though, the short-term gains from self-interested and corrupt behavior were so immense—because they had so many stock options, and because their boards of directors paid them no attention—that any long-term considerations paled by comparison. In the case of Dennis Kozlowski, the CEO of Tyco, for instance, it's hard to see how he could have made $600 million honestly if he had stayed CEO of Tyco. But dishonestly, it was remarkably easy. Investors should have understood that the rules of the game had changed, and that the incentives for CEOs to keep their promises, or to worry about the long-term health of their businesses, had effectively disappeared. But they didn't, and because they were so intoxicated with their bull-market gains, they also stopped doing the due diligence that even trusting investors are supposed to do.

At the same time, the mechanisms and institutions that were supposed to limit corruption ended up facilitating corruption rather than stopping it. The business of Wall Street and the accounting industry is supposed to be to distinguish between the trustworthy and the trustworthless, just as the Underwriters Laboratory distinguishes between safe and dangerous electrical equipment. If Goldman Sachs underwrites a stock offering for a company, it's saying that the company has real value, as is Merrill Lynch when one of its analysts issues a buy recommendation. If the New York Stock Exchange lists a company, it's attesting to the fact that the firm is not a fly-by-night operation. And when Ernst and Young signs off on an audit, it's telling us that we can trust that company's numbers.

We are willing to believe Ernst and Young when it says this because its entire business seems to depend on its credibility. If the Underwriters Laboratory started affixing its UL mark to lamps that electrocuted people, pretty soon it wouldn't have a business. In the same way, if Ernst and Young tells us to trust a company that turns out to be cooking the books, people should stop working with Ernst and Young. As Alan Greenspan has said of accountants, "The market value of their companies rest[s] on the integrity of their operations." So accountants don't have to be saints to be useful. In theory, self-interest alone will compel them to do a good job of separating the white hats from the black. But this theory only works if the firms that don't do a good job are actually punished for their failure. And in the late nineties, they weren't. The Nasdaq listed laughable companies. White-shoe firms such as Goldman Sachs underwrote them. The accountants wielded their rubber stamps. (Between 1997 and 2000, seven hundred companies were forced to restate their earnings. In 1981, just three companies did.) But none of these institutions paid a price in the marketplace for such derelictions of duty. They got more business, not less. In the late nineties, Arthur Andersen was the auditor of record in accounting disasters like Waste Management and Sunbeam. Yet investors chose not to look skeptically at companies, such as WorldCom and Enron, that continued to use Andersen. In effect, investors stopped watching the watchmen, and so the watchmen stopped watching, too. In a world in which not all capitalists are Quakers, trust but verify remains a useful byword.

VI

In five thousand American homes, there are television sets that are rather different from your standard Sony. These sets have been wired by Nielsen Media Research with electronic monitoring devices called "people meters." The people meters are designed to track, in real time, two things: what TV shows are being watched and, just as important, who is watching them. Every person in a "people-meter family" is given a unique code, which they're supposed to use to log in each time they sit down to watch television. That way, Nielsen—which downloads the data from the people meters every night—is able to know that Mom and Dad like *CSI*, while their college-age daughter prefers *Alias*.

Nielsen, of course, wants that information because advertisers crave demographic data. Pepsi may be interested to hear that 22 million people watched a particular episode of *Friends*. But what it really cares about is how many people aged eighteen to twenty-four watched the episode. The people meter is the only technology that can tell Pepsi what it wants to know. So, when the major TV networks sell national advertising, it's the people-meter data that they rely on. Five thousand families determine what ads Americans see and, indirectly, what programs they watch.

There is, of course, something inherently troubling about this. Can five thousand really speak for 120 million? But Nielsen works hard to ensure that its families are a reasonable match, in demographic terms, for the country as a whole. And while the people meters are hardly flawless—over time, people become less religious about logging in—they have one great advantage over most ways of gathering information: they track what people actually did watch, not what they remember watching or say they watched. All in all, Nielsen's numbers are probably more accurate than your average public-opinion poll.

The trouble with people meters is that there are only five thousand of them, and they are scattered across the country. So while Nielsen's daily ratings provide a relatively accurate picture of what the country as a whole is watching, they can't tell you anything about what people in any particular city are watching.

That matters because not all the ads you see on prime-time television are national ads. In fact, a sizable percentage of them are local. And local advertisers like demographic information as much as national advertisers do. If you own a health club in Fort Wayne, Indiana, you'd like to know what Tuesday prime-time show eighteen- to thirty-four-year-olds in Fort Wayne watch. But the people meters can't tell you.

The major networks have tried to solve this problem with what's known as "sweeps." Four times a year—in February, May, July, and November—Nielsen sends out 2.5 million paper diaries to randomly selected people in almost every TV market in the country and asks them to record, for a week, what programs they watch. Nielsen also collects information on all the people who fill out diaries, so that at the end of each sweeps month it's able to produce demographic portraits of the country's TV markets. The networks' local stations—the affiliates—and local advertisers then use the information from those diaries to negotiate ad rates for the months ahead.

What's curious about this system is that it's lasted so long—sweeps have been around since the early days of television—even though its flaws are so obvious and so profound. To begin with, there's no guarantee sweeps ratings are accurate. The lower the response rate to a random survey, the greater the chance of error, and the sweeps system has a remarkably low response rate—only 30 percent or so of the diaries that Nielsen distributes are filled out. That helps create what's called "cooperator bias," which means that the people who cooperate with the survey may not watch the same programs as people who don't. (In fact, they almost certainly don't.) And the low-tech nature of the diaries creates problems, too. People don't fill out the diaries as they're actually watching TV. Like most of us, they procrastinate and fill out the diaries at the end of the week. So what people record will be what they remember watching, which may not match what they did watch. People are more likely to remember high-profile shows, so the diary system inflates network ratings while deflating the ratings of smaller cable networks. The diaries are also no good at chronicling the restless viewing habits of channel surfers.

Even if the diaries were accurate, though, they wouldn't be able to tell advertisers or the networks what people are really watching most of the time. That's because network programming during sweeps months has almost nothing in common with network programming during the other eight months of the year. Because sweeps matter so much to local stations, the networks are forced into what's called "stunt" programming. They pack sweeps months with one-time specials, expensive movies, and high-profile guest appearances. February 2003, for instance, became the month of Michael Jackson on network television, with ABC, NBC, and Fox all spending millions of dollars on shows about the bizarre pop singer. And that same month saw the long-awaited (at least by a few) climaxes to the unreality-TV sagas *The Bachelorette* and *Joe Millionaire*. The networks also have to air only new episodes of their best shows. During sweeps months, no reruns are allowed.

Stunt programming is bad for almost everyone: the advertisers, the networks, and the viewers. Advertisers, after all, are paying prices based on ratings that reflect stunt programming. Allen Banks, executive media director at Saatchi and Saatchi, North America, has called sweeps "a sham, a subterfuge." "The picture they give you is anything but typical of what's going on the rest of the year," he has said. Some advertisers do try to account for the impact of sweeps when buying ad time, but since in most local markets sweeps represent the only hard data they have, the numbers still end up being disproportionately important.

For the networks, meanwhile, sweeps months mean that much of their best—in the loose sense of the word—programming will be wasted in head-to-head competition. During sweeps month, in any given hour there may be two or three shows worth watching (if you really like television). But viewers can only watch one of those shows. Had the networks been able to air those shows at different times instead of against each other, the total number of people who watched them would have been much higher. By pitting their best shows against each other, the networks actually shrink their total viewership. In the same vein, sweeps are bad for TV viewers because they guarantee a paucity of new and interesting programming in non-sweeps months. If you're a connoisseur of lurid spectacle, your cup runneth over in November. But in January, you will be drowning in a sea of reruns.

Sweeps, then, are not very good at measuring who's watching what; they force advertisers to pay for unreliable and unrepresentative data; and they limit the number of viewers the networks can reach over the course of a year. Everyone in television knows this, and believes that the industry would be much better off with a different way of measuring local viewership. But even though there is a better alternative available—namely, Nielsen's people meters—everyone in television continues to participate in the sweeps system and play by its rules. This raises an obvious question: Why would so many people acquiesce in such a dumb system?

The immediate answer is that it's too expensive to change. People meters are costly to install and even more costly to keep running, since they're always on. Wiring every local market with people meters would cost . . . well, it's not exactly clear, since Nielsen refuses to release any data on how expensive the people meters are. But at the very least, if you wanted to wire thousands of homes in each of the country's 210 TV markets, you'd likely be talking at least nine figures. That's a lot more than the paper diaries—which people fill out for free—cost, even with the postage included.

Still, even $1 billion isn't that much money in the context of the TV and advertising industries as a whole. Every year something like $25 billion in ad money is spent on the basis of sweeps data, which means that $25 billion is almost certainly being misspent. The networks, meanwhile, spend hundreds of millions of dollars every year during sweeps that could certainly be better spent elsewhere, while they also pay a price for the suicidal competition that sweeps creates. So it seems likely that investing in people-meter technology—or something like it—would be the collectively intelligent thing to do, and would leave the networks and the advertisers much better off.

The problem is that even though most of the players in the TV business would be better off if they got rid of sweeps, no single player would be better off enough to justify spending the money on an alternative. Local advertisers in Sioux Falls, for instance, would obviously like it if they knew that the ratings of the CBS affiliate in Sioux Falls were really accurate. But local advertisers in Sioux Falls don't spend enough money to make it worth their while to invest in people meters for the town. And ABC might prefer not to have to stunt program, but it doesn't get much direct economic benefit from a more accurate local-rating system.

One obvious answer would be for everyone to pitch in and fix the system. But that strategy collides with the stinging critique of the possibility of cooperation that the sociologist Mancur Olson offered in his 1965 book, *The Logic of Collective Action*. Olson focused his work around the dilemma that interest groups, like the American Medical Association, faced in trying to get individual members to participate. Since all doctors benefited from the AMA's lobbying efforts, but no one doctor's effort made much of a difference in the success or failure of those efforts, Olson thought that no doctors would voluntarily participate. The only answer, he argued, was for the groups to offer members other benefits—like health insurance or, in the case of the AMA, its medical journal—that gave them an incentive to join. Even then, Olson suggested that it would be difficult at best to get people to do things like write a letter to Congress or attend a rally. For the individual, it would always make more sense to let someone else do the work. Similarly, if the group of networks and stations and advertisers were to act, everyone in the business—including those who did nothing—would reap the benefits. So everyone has an incentive to sit on their hands, wait for someone else to do something, and free ride. Since everyone wants to be a free rider, nothing gets done.

As we've seen, it's not clear that Olson's critique is as universally applicable as it was once thought to be. Groups do cooperate. People do contribute to the common good. But the fact that people will contribute to the common good doesn't mean that businesses necessarily will. The kind of enlightened self-interest that can lead people to cooperate requires an ability to think about the long term. Corporations are, perhaps because investors encourage them to be, myopic. And in any case, the way the TV industry is organized makes the networks and advertisers more susceptible to the collective-action trap than they otherwise would be.

The way Nielsen ratings are paid for exacerbates the problem. Since sweeps data is valuable to both the affiliates and the advertisers, you might imagine that the cost would be split between them. In fact, though, the affiliates pay 90 percent of the cost of collecting and analyzing the sweeps diaries, and since the one who pays is the one who has the power, the affiliates dictate what happens to sweeps. As it turns out, they're the only players in television who like sweeps. The diary system, after all, favors recognizable names and networks, which means it inflates the affiliates' ratings at the expense of smaller stations. The affiliates don't pay any of the hundreds of millions of dollars the networks spend on sweeps programming. They just reap the benefits. As for the negative effect that sweeps has on viewership in the other eight months of the year, the affiliates don't really care about those months, since their ratings aren't being tracked then. It's only a little bit of an overstatement, in fact, to say that the only shows the affiliates care about are those that air in February, May, July, and November. Far from wanting to use people meters, the affiliates are actively hostile to them. In fact, when Nielsen introduced people meters into Boston in 2002, not a single affiliate signed up for the service. The stations decided that no ratings would be better than the people-meter numbers.

As much as the persistence of sweeps testifies to the problem of collective action, it also demonstrates the perils of allowing a single self-interested faction to dictate a group's decision. If funding a reliable local-ratings system was something that historically the networks and advertisers had helped pay for, they might actually have had some leverage when it came to revamping the system. Instead, they're effectively dancing to the affiliates' tune.

All in all, it's a grim picture, even if you leave out *Joe Million-*

aire and Michael Jackson's face. It is a picture that's going to change—as cable becomes important, the paper-diary system looks more and more like a relic, and in 2003 Nielsen announced that it would go ahead and roll out people meters in the country's top-ten television markets. But what remains striking is that a multibillion-dollar industry has been stuck for a long time with a backward, inaccurate technology because the major players could not figure out how to cooperate. If successful solutions to cooperation problems are often, as in the case of the uprising against Richard Grasso, the result of individually irrational acts producing collectively rational results, the failure to solve cooperation problems is often the result of the opposite phenomenon. On their own, all the key players in the TV industry have been smart. But together, they've been dumb.

VII

When he opened the Guardian Bank and Trust Company in the Cayman Islands in 1986, John Mathewson had no experience, not many clients, and only a cursory knowledge of how banks really worked. But, in his own peculiar way, he was a visionary. What Mathewson understood was that there were many American citizens with lots of money that they did not want the Internal Revenue Service to know anything about, and that these Americans would pay hefty sums if Mathewson could keep their money safe from the prying eyes of the IRS.

So Mathewson obliged them. He showed his clients how to set up shell corporations. He never reported any of the deposits he received to the IRS. And he gave his clients debit cards that allowed them to access their Guardian accounts from anywhere in the United States. Mathewson charged hefty fees for his services— $8,000 to set up an account, $100 for each transaction—but no one seemed to mind. At its peak, Guardian had $150 million in deposits and two thousand clients.

In 1995, Mathewson left the Caymans after a dispute with a government official, and moved to San Antonio to enjoy his retirement. It didn't last long. Within a few months, he was arrested for money laundering. Mathewson was an old man. He did not want to go to prison. And he had something valuable to trade for his freedom: the encrypted records of all the depositors who had put money into Guardian Trust. So he cut a deal. He pled guilty (and was sentenced to five years' probation and five hundred hours of community service). And he told the government everything he knew about tax cheats.

The most interesting information Mathewson had to offer was that offshore banks were no longer catering only to drug dealers and money launderers. Instead, these banks served many Americans who had earned their money honestly but simply didn't want to pay taxes on it. As Mathewson told a Senate panel in 2000, "Most of [Guardian's] clients were legitimate business people and professionals." A typical Mathewson client was someone like Mark Vicini, a New Jersey entrepreneur who ran a computer company called Micro Rental and Sales. Vicini was, by all accounts, a respected member of his community. He put his relatives through college. He gave generously to charities. And, between 1991 and 1994, Vicini sent $9 million to the Caymans, $6 million of which he never mentioned to the IRS. This saved him $2.1 million in unpaid taxes. (It also eventually earned him a five-month stint in federal prison, where he was sent after pleading guilty to tax evasion.)

Mathewson's clients were not alone, either. In fact, the nineties saw a boom in tax evasion. By the end of the decade, two million Americans had credit cards from offshore banks. Fifteen years earlier, almost none did. Promoters, who often used the Internet to push their scams, advertised "layered trusts," "offshore asset protection trusts," and "constitutional pure trusts." A small but obstinate (and obtuse) group of tax evaders advised people that they didn't have to pay their taxes because the income tax had never actually been passed by Congress. And old standbys—keeping two sets of books, incorporating yourself as a charity or a church and then writing off all your expenses as charitable contributions—stayed alive. All these schemes did have an important downside: they were illegal. But rough estimates suggested that they were costing the United States as much as $200 billion a year by the end of the decade.

The vast majority of Americans never experimented with any of these schemes. They continued to pay their taxes honestly, and they continued to tell pollsters that cheating on your taxes was wrong. But there's little doubt that the proliferation of these schemes—and the perception that many of them were successful—made average Americans more skeptical of the fairness of the tax system. Adding to those doubts was the ever-increasing complexity of the tax system, which made it more difficult to know what your fair share of taxes really was, and the 1990s boom in corporate tax shelters, which was responsible for what the Treasury Department called, in 1999, "an unacceptable and growing level of tax avoidance." The title of a 2001 *Forbes* article on the tax system captured what more than a few Americans were wondering about themselves: ARE YOU A CHUMP?

Why did this matter? Because tax paying is a classic example of a cooperation problem. Everyone reaps benefits from the services that taxes fund. You get a military that protects you, schools that educate not only your children but the children of others (whom you need to become productive citizens so that they will grow up to support you in your old age), free roads, police and fire protection, and fundamental research in science and technology. You also get a lot of other stuff you perhaps don't want, too, but for most people the benefits must outweigh the costs, or else taxes would be lower than they are. The problem is that you can reap the benefits of all these things whether or not you actually pay taxes. Most of the goods that the government provides are what economists call nonexcludable goods—meaning, as the name suggests, that it's not possible to allow some people to enjoy the goods while excluding others. If a national missile defense system is ever built, it will protect your house whether or not you've ever paid taxes. Once I-95 was built, anyone could travel on it. So even if you think government spending is a good thing from a purely self-interested perspective, you have an incentive to avoid chipping in your fair share. Since you get the goods whether or not you personally pay for them, it's rational for you to free ride. But if most people free ride, then the public goods disappear. It's Mancur Olson's theory all over again.

We may not normally think of taxpaying as a matter of cooperation, but at its core that's what it comes down to. Taxpaying is obviously different from, say, being a member of an interest group in one important sense: not paying your taxes is against the law. But the truth is that if you cheat on your taxes, the chances that you'll get caught have historically been pretty slim. In 2001, for instance, the IRS audited only 0.5 percent of all returns. In purely economic terms, it may actually be rational to cheat. So a healthy tax system requires something more than law. Ultimately, a healthy tax system requires people to pay their taxes voluntarily (if grudgingly). Paying taxes is individually costly but collectively beneficial. But the collective benefits only materialize if everyone takes part.

Why do people take part? In other words, why, in countries like the United States where the rate of tax compliance is relatively high, do people pay taxes? The answer has something to do with the same principle that we saw at work in the story of Richard Grasso: reciprocity. Most people will participate as long as they believe that everyone else is participating, too. When it comes to taxes, Americans are what historian Margaret Levi calls "contingent consenters." They're willing to pay their fair share of taxes, but only as long as they think that others are doing so, too, and only as long as they believe that people who don't pay their taxes have a good chance of being caught and punished. "When people start to feel that the policeman is asleep, and when they think others are breaking the law and getting away with it, they start to feel like they're

THE WISDOM OF CROWDS 139

being taken advantage of," says Michael Graetz, a law professor at Yale. People want to do the right thing, but no one wants to be a sucker.

Consider the results of public-goods experiments that the economists Ernst Fehr and Simon Gächter have run. The experiments work like this. There are four people in a group. Each has twenty tokens, and the game will last four rounds. On each round, a player can either contribute tokens to the public pot, or keep them for himself. If a player invests a token, it costs him money. He invests one token, and he personally earns only 0.4 tokens. But every other member in the group gets 0.4 tokens, too. So the group as a whole gets 1.6 tokens for every one that's invested. The point is this: if everyone keeps their money and invests nothing, they each walk away with twenty tokens. If everyone invests all their money, they each walk away with thirty-two tokens. The catch, of course, is that the smartest strategy ordinarily will be to invest nothing yourself and simply free ride off everyone else's contributions. But if everyone does that, there will be no contributions.

As with the ultimatum game, the public-goods games are played in a similar fashion throughout the developed world. Most people do not act selfishly at first. Instead, most contribute about half their tokens to the public pot. But as each round passes, and people see that others are free riding, the rate of contribution drops. By the end, 70 to 80 percent of the players are free riding, and the group as a whole is much poorer than it would otherwise be.

Fehr and Gächter suggest that people in general fall into one of three categories. Twenty-five percent or so are selfish—which is to say they are rational, in the economic sense—and always free ride. (That's close to the same percentage of people who make low-ball offers in the ultimatum game.) A small minority are altruists, who contribute heavily to the public pot from the get-go and continue to do so even as others free ride. The biggest group, though, are the conditional consenters. They start out contributing at least some of their wealth, but watching others free ride makes them far less likely to keep putting money in. By the end of most public-goods games, almost all the conditional consenters are no longer cooperating.

The key to the system, then, is making sure the conditional consenters keep cooperating, and the way to do that is to make sure they don't feel like suckers. Fehr and Gächter tweaked the public-goods game to demonstrate: this time, at the end of every round, they revealed what each person had or had not contributed to the public pot, which made the free riders visible to everyone else. Then they offered people the opportunity to punish the free riders. For the price of a third of a token, you could take one token away from the free rider. Two things happened as a result. First, people spent money to punish the evildoers—even though, again, it was economically irrational for them to do so. Second, the free riders shaped up and started contributing their fair share. In fact, even during the last rounds of these games, when there was no reason to keep contributing (since no punishment could be inflicted), people continued to chip in.

When it comes to solving the collective problem of how to get people to pay their taxes, then, there are three things that matter. The first is that people have to trust, to some extent, their neighbors, and to believe that they will generally do the right thing and live up to any reasonable obligations. The political science professor John T. Scholz has found that people who are more trusting are more likely to pay their taxes and more likely to say that it's wrong to cheat on them. Coupled with this, but different from it, is trust in the government, which is to say trust that the government will spend your tax dollars wisely and in the national interest. Not surprisingly, Scholz has found that people who trust the government are happier (or at least less unhappy) about paying taxes.

The third kind of trust is the trust that the state will find and punish the guilty, and avoid punishing the innocent. Law alone cannot induce cooperation, but it can make cooperation more likely to succeed. If people think that free riders—people not paying taxes but still enjoying all the benefits of living in the United States—will be caught, they'll be happier (or at least less unhappy) about paying taxes. And they'll also, not coincidentally, be less likely to cheat. So the public image of the IRS can have a profound impact on the way conditional consenters behave. Mark Matthews, head of the agency's Criminal Investigative Division, was keenly aware that the success of criminal investigations was measured not just by the number of criminals caught but also by the public impact of its work. "There is a group of people that could be tempted by these scams, a group that could let aggressive tax planning become too aggressive. We need to convince them before that happens that it doesn't make sense," Matthews said. "A huge part of the agency's mission is making sure that people believe the system works."

Getting people to pay taxes is a collective problem. We know what the goal is: everyone should pay their fair share (this says nothing, of course, about what a fair share is). The question, then, is how? The U.S. model—which is, by global standards, successful, since despite Americans' vehement anti-tax rhetoric they actually evade taxes far less than Europeans do—suggests that while law and regulation have a key role to play in encouraging taxpaying, they work only when there is an underlying willingness to contribute to the public good. Widespread taxpaying amounts to a verdict that the system, in at least a vague sense, works. That kind of verdict can only be reached over time, as people—who perhaps first started paying taxes out of fear of prosecution—recognize the mutual benefits of taxpaying and institute it as a norm.

Another way of putting this is to say that successful taxpaying breeds successful taxpaying. And that positive-feedback loop is at work, I'd argue, in most successful cooperative endeavors. The mystery of cooperation, after all, is that Olson was right: it is rational to free ride. And yet cooperation, on both a small and a large scale, permeates any healthy society. It's not simply the obvious examples, like contributing to charities or voting or marching on picket lines, all of which are examples of collective action that people participate in. It's also the subtler examples, like those workers who, by all rights, could shirk their responsibilities without being punished (because the costs of monitoring them are too high) and yet do not, or those customers who leave tips for waitresses in restaurants in distant cities. We can anatomize these acts and explain what gives rise to them. But there is something irreducible at their heart, and it marks the difference between society on the one hand and just a bunch of people living together on the other.

PART II

7

TRAFFIC: WHAT WE HAVE HERE IS

A FAILURE TO COORDINATE

I

In 2002, central London was, to all intents and purposes, a perpetual traffic jam. On a typical day, a quarter of a million vehicles would drive into the eight square miles of central London, ready to do battle with a million commuters who used public transportation. In place of long, wide boulevards, London has tightly packed, narrow, winding streets, which kept the average speed of traffic below ten miles an hour. On a bad day, it was more like three miles an hour. You can walk faster than that and not even break a sweat.

Traffic was so bad, in fact, that it turned the mayor of London, Ken Livingstone, from an avowed socialist into the advocate of a plan that warmed the hearts of capitalist economists everywhere. In February of 2003, London started charging people to drive into the centre. If you wanted to enter central London between 7 AM and 6:30 PM, you now had to pay £5. If you neglected to pay, and one of the 230 cameras the city had installed recorded your license plate, you got stuck with an £80 fine. In theory, the plan was supposed to raise £180 million a year for the city to invest in public transportation, and to cut traffic congestion by 20 percent.

The principle behind the London plan was a simple one: when someone drives into the city and makes traffic worse, he inflicts costs on everyone else that he never pays for. When you're that driver and you're sitting in bumper-to-bumper traffic while toddlers speed by you on the sidewalk, it feels like you've paid more than enough. But the mathematics of congestion suggest that you haven't. The toll is an attempt to collect the bill.

"Congestion pricing" has been around as an idea since the 1920s, but its most important advocate was the Nobel Prize-winning economist William Vickrey. For Vickrey, road space was like any other scarce resource: if you wanted to allocate it wisely, you needed some way to make the costs and benefits of people's decisions obvious to them. Because, say, the main road into the city is free, everyone chooses to drive on that road during rush hour even when it would be better for just about everybody if some of them drove earlier or later, some took public transportation instead, and some worked from home. If that same road had a toll on it, different people would make different choices, because they would have different answers to the question, "How much is this trip really worth to me?" And so, instead of everyone ending up on the same road at 6:30 PM, they'd leave work earlier or later, or take the train, or telecommute.

It's a nice idea in theory, but putting it into practice has always required a very hard sell. Livingstone had to fight off massive lobbying efforts in opposition to his plan for London. In the United States, meanwhile, congestion pricing has always been a nonstarter. Americans don't like paying highway and bridge tolls, but they hate the idea of having to pay more money to drive during rush hour. Most people feel as if they have no choice about when or how they commute, and the thought of the wealthy paying to zip along empty roads while everyone else takes the long way around grates. As a result, we'd rather suffer in traffic than allow some to pay for freedom. The authors of a study of a failed attempt to introduce congestion pricing on San Francisco's Bay Bridge, for instance, concluded that both voters and politicians need to be convinced there are literally no other alternatives before they'll accept a Vickrey scheme. There are a few exceptions to this rule, most notably

New York City, where it costs more to use certain bridges and tunnels during rush hour. But there are only a few.

Oddly, we've happily adjusted to something like congestion pricing in other parts of our life. Long-distance calls are more expensive during the day, drinks are cheaper during happy hour, and it costs more to go to Las Vegas on the weekend than during the week. (And don't forget the early-bird special, either.) All these are cases of price responding to demand—when demand is high, the price goes up, and when it's low, the price goes down. But when it comes to driving, Americans seem to prefer it when there's no price—at least in money terms—at all.

It's not surprising, then, that the one place in the world that's made an art out of congestion pricing is the antithesis of America in cultural terms, namely Singapore. Blessed with not having to worry about angry drivers' groups or disgruntled voters, Singapore's government put congestion pricing in place for the first time in 1975. The initial version of the plan looked a lot like London's more recent scheme: you had to pay a toll if you wanted to get into the country's central business district (CBD) during rush hour. As time went on, the plan expanded, until you had to pay if you wanted to get into the CBD at any time during the day. But the most important changes have been technological. Once upon a time, the system was enforced by meter maids who recorded the license plate numbers of rule breakers. Today, every car in Singapore has an electronic smart card attached to the dashboard, and as soon as you cross into a pay zone, you see the money disappear from your card. This has two advantages: it makes cheating impossible, and it makes the cost of your decision to drive immediately obvious to you. Singapore has also made its pricing rules more sophisticated. While there was once one price to drive during the morning rush hour, now there is "peak-within-peak" pricing (it's half as expensive to drive between 7:30 and 8 AM as it is to drive between 8 and 9 AM), and evening pricing. Singapore even offers weekend-only cars (on which drivers get a tax break and price rebates). Not surprisingly, traffic in Singapore is much better than it is in London or New York, even though the country has more cars per mile of road than any Western country. (Of course, it is a very small country.)

The interesting thing about Singapore's success is that for all of the country's authoritarian ways, it has left the actual decision about whether or not to drive in the hands of the individual. One way to cure congestion, after all, would simply be to ban certain people from driving on certain days. And this, in fact, is exactly what Mexico did, albeit in an attempt to curb air pollution. If you live in Mexico City and your license plate ends with a 5 or 6, you can't drive on Monday. (A 7 or 8 means you're out of luck on Tuesday, 3 or 4 on Wednesday, and so on. Everyone gets to drive on Saturday and Sunday.) But this hasn't done much to reduce traffic, because drivers have no incentive to find alternatives to driving on the six days a week when they can drive, and because many Mexicans just bought second cars that they could use on their supposed off days. Singapore's plan, by contrast, tells the drivers how much it'll cost to use their cars, and then trusts that the sum of all those individual decisions about whether or not to drive will be smart.

Figuring out how much driving *should* cost, though, is a tough problem, and economists have spilled a lot of ink trying to solve it. One obvious challenge is that the wealthier you are, the easier it is to trade money for time and convenience (you'll pay to drive into London because it's easier than taking the tube). Poorer people can avoid the toll by not driving, but that doesn't make them any better off than they were before. So any fair congestion-pricing plan has not only to charge tolls but also redistribute the revenue they raise. Singapore did that by building a hyper-modern mass rapid transit system, and Livingstone's plan for London similarly involves spending hundreds of millions on public transportation. Another alternative, proposed by the traffic engineer Carlos Daganzo, is to allow people to drive for free on some days and charge them on others.

That keeps the right incentives in place, but also keeps the money-for-time crowd from dominating the highways.

An ideal pricing system would be considerably more sophisticated than London's £5 all-day system. Vickrey, for instance, imagined a world in which traffic was governed by "responsive pricing," so that how much you had to pay to use a road might vary depending on how heavy the traffic on that road was right then, or on the weather, or on the type of vehicle you were driving. If I-5 between Sacramento and San Francisco suddenly became clogged with traffic because of a broken-down tractor trailer, it would cost you more to use it. That, presumably, would divert people to other routes, and keep the congestion from getting out of control. Today a system like this is actually technologically feasible. It is, of course, a political pipe dream, and hyper-responsive pricing may in any case be more trouble than it's worth. (Is it a good idea to have people carrying out complex price calculations while traveling at seventy miles an hour?) But the possibilities created by things like highways wired with traffic-detecting sensors and cars equipped with global positioning systems are endless.

Still, crude as it is, the London plan has been far more successful than most noneconomists thought it would be. Traffic has fallen by almost 20 percent, congestion has been significantly reduced, and, according to at least one study, cars are able to go 40 percent faster. (That still means they're only going eleven miles an hour, but you take what you can get.) The biggest concern people have now is that the plan may have been too successful in curtailing driving. After all, the point of congestion pricing isn't to stop people from driving, since from an economic perspective (and setting aside the environmental one), a highway that's empty is hardly better than one that's too full. The point of congestion pricing is to get people to coordinate their activities better by balancing the benefits they get from driving against the costs they inflict on everyone else. In the London case, the concerns about the traffic decline have been overblown. The roads are still full of cars.

They're just moving more easily. More important, the flow of traffic is now a better reflection of the real value people place on driving. At least for the moment, London traffic is wiser.

11

The idea that you can wipe out traffic jams if you just get the road tolls exactly right is undoubtedly a comforting thought, especially when you're trapped on the Cross Bronx Expressway for a couple of hours. And in fact, many traffic jams really are the result of having too many cars on the road. As drivers, we're supposed to leave two seconds between cars. That means a single highway lane can accommodate 1,800 cars an hour. Now most of us aren't quite as cautious behind the wheel as we should be, and on a fast-moving California freeway a lane can hold as many as 2,400 cars an hour. But whether it's 1,800 or 2,400, if Vickrey pricing can get the number of cars on the road below that point, it will help eliminate the traffic jams that result from pure congestion.

Unfortunately, road tolls can't do anything about the myriad other problems that can wreak havoc on a daily commute. Some of these are obvious—accidents, construction, on-ramps, off-ramps— and others are more subtle, like small dips in the road, mild curves, inclines, a plodding truck in the right lane. Some scientists even argue that occasionally traffic jams happen for no reason at all. Start to look too closely at the way traffic works, in fact, and it comes to seem miraculous that any of us ever get home on time.

Cars on a crowded highway are like pedestrians on the street or birds in a flock. They're decentralized individuals following simple rules—don't hit the car ahead, shift lanes when you can, drive as fast as you can safely drive—and trying to coordinate their activities with each other. In traffic, each driver wants to get ahead of everyone else, but he also wants traffic as a whole to move as fast as possible. In other situations, we've seen people in similar circumstances coordinate their actions quite nicely. But more often than not, the decisions of those decentralized drivers on a crowded highway end up producing a snarled mess. So what goes wrong?

The basic physics of traffic are fairly simple. When there aren't too many cars on the road, vehicles are able to move freely from lane to lane and speed up or slow down without causing trouble. Each car can keep a safe distance from its neighbors and still travel as fast as it wants. This is what scientists call "free flow." Gradually, though, as more cars enter the highway—or as cars slow down in order to exit the highway—everyone needs to brake to maintain the same safe distance. As they hit their brakes, everyone behind them does the same, and a wave of braking passes through the packed cars. In faster lanes, the wave moves faster because drivers have to react more quickly to keep their distance. That means the fast lane actually gets slower faster (if that makes sense). And as cars trying to move faster change lanes, the lane speeds become evened out as all the available gaps are filled. Instead of free flow, the cars fall into an unstable pattern where they're all traveling at similar speeds but more slowly than they were before. From there, it takes very little to send the whole pack into classic stop-and-go traffic. And the brutal thing about traffic jams is that once in them, it's hard to get out. Cars leaving the front of a traffic jam, it turns out, move more slowly than those entering the back of it. That's why as you watch a traffic jam on television, it moves backward up the highway. And it's why jams are not easily dispelled. As Kai Nagel, a pioneer in traffic research, put it, "Traffic jams, once created, are fairly stable and can move without major changes in their form for several hours against the flow of traffic."

As for where traffic jams come from in the first place, that is the subject of a raging debate. On one side of this debate, roughly speaking, are physicists, who look at the motion of cars on a high-

way as fundamentally similar to the motion of water down a river
or grains of sand falling down a glass tube. We know that grains of
sand can suddenly jam up and stop flowing smoothly, and in computer simulations of traffic flow the same thing happens, so the
physicists argue that what they call "spontaneous jams" probably
happen in the real world as well. On the other side of the debate
are traffic engineers, who insist that every jam is caused by some
kind of obstacle or bottleneck. As an academic matter, the debate
is fascinating, but it's not clear what its practical implications are,
since even the traffic engineers acknowledge that the "inhomo-
geneities" they believe are responsible for every traffic jam can be
exceedingly small, like a car simply moving too slowly.

On the morning of June 14, 2000, Carlos Daganzo and Juan
Munoz, engineers from the Institute of Transportation Studies at
Berkeley, demonstrated this by sending a test vehicle onto the
Richmond–San Rafael Bridge near San Francisco, with instructions
to travel significantly slower than the flow of traffic, which was moving along at a healthy clip (a little faster than sixty miles an hour) for
late rush hour. The bridge is five and half miles long, two lanes in
each direction, and has no entrance or exit ramps. The effects were
obvious right away. There was far more movement between lanes,
and farther back up the highway—traffic people call it "up-
stream"—congestion started to build. Even though the bottleneck
was moving, it made a significant dent in the flow of traffic.

One of the reasons bottlenecks cause so much trouble is that
on multiple-lane highways they create a situation in which different lanes are moving at different speeds. (You may think that the
lane speeds even out in the end, and that you will eventually catch
those cars going by on the left. But you won't.) In any case, when
different lanes are moving at different speeds, drivers are more
likely to change lanes. That, in turn, makes drivers more cautious.
They lengthen the distance between themselves and other cars,
which paradoxically ends up making lane changes more likely

(since there's more space between cars). Each lane on the highway ends up carrying 10 percent fewer vehicles than it would if it were a single-lane road.

Once a road becomes sufficiently crowded, then it becomes harder for drivers to coordinate with each other. Each driver has to anticipate what other drivers will do, and because information is only transmitted between cars via brake lights and turn signals, which are crude devices at best, anticipation often becomes over-reaction. A single driver who's too ready to hit the brakes can slow down an entire highway. And because drivers have no bigger pic-ture of what traffic looks like, their decisions—whether to get off at this exit or trudge onward, whether to move out of this lane or stay in it—are haphazard at best. Instead of the elegant, patterned movements of a flock of birds, the drivers produce the stop-and-go disorganization of a traffic jam.

III

One reason coordination on the highway is so difficult is the diver-sity of the drivers. As we've seen, diversity is essential to much good decision making. But diversity can also make solving coordination problems harder. Mitch Resnick demonstrated this many years ago in a traffic simulation he devised with his computer program Star-Logo, which represented one of the first forays into modeling the way individual interactions produce unanticipated results. In the simulation, Resnick writes in his book *Turtles, Termites, and Traffic Jams,* as long as cars went off at evenly spaced intervals and trav-eled at equal speeds, the traffic flowed smoothly. But as soon as speed became variable and cars were forced to react to each other by braking or speeding up, the traffic jams started. All it took was a bit of randomness programmed into each car's position and speed for the trouble to start. Similarly, the appearance of a radar trap, which forced drivers to decelerate quickly and made speeds highly variable, could create a jam. All of which raises an obvious question: If driver diversity is the problem, could driver homogeneity be the solution?

In August of 1997, a group of researchers from California's PATH program took over a seven-and-a-half-mile stretch of I-15 near San Diego to try to answer that question. The researchers brought with them eight Buick LeSabres, which they had automated by equipping them with a couple of hundred thousand dollars of equipment, including steering and gas-pedal controls, motion sensors, radar, and a radio communication system that could transmit information about the car's speed and acceleration fifty times a second. The point of the automation was twofold: first, to allow the cars to drive themselves, and second, to allow a platoon of vehicles to travel together down the road, synchronizing their speeds via radio communication. And it worked. The LeSabres went off in a convoy, separated from each other by a mere twenty-one feet. The cars' movements were perfectly synchronized, because the delay caused by driver reaction was absent. As soon as one car changed speed, all the others immediately adjusted. Over the course of four days, the cars traveled at sixty-five miles an hour for hundreds of miles, carrying real passengers, with nary an accident. It was an ideal vision of a perfectly organized highway.

How would it work in the real world? Essentially, you'd create dedicated highways, by burying magnetic markers four feet apart along the road. (The cars use the markers to read the road and ensure that they're in the right lane.) Once you were on the highway, your car would be lined up in a platoon with others, and you'd travel down the road together until your exit. (Presumably each platoon could be pegged to a particular off-ramp.) Equipping the highways wouldn't be cheap. It would cost at least $10,000 a mile, and you'd have to pay to equip cars, too. But a smoothly running automatic highway could double or even triple capacity, while also eliminating traffic jams. That would mean that fewer new highways would be built, and that people would spend less time in gridlock. So it's possible that automatic highways would actually save us money.

And although the plan makes a kind of intuitive sense—if drivers are the problem, then take the steering wheel out of their hands—it's hard to imagine it being implemented anytime soon. Part of that is simply because drivers are uncomfortable giving up control, and even more uncomfortable handing their lives over to a computer. Of course, planes are now flown on autopilot all the time, but few of us have ever flown planes. Just about all of us have driven. And part of what makes the plan dead on arrival is that it seems like a top-down solution at a time when people are much more fond of bottom-up answers. Are we really ready to let the government orchestrate our movement down the highway? Maybe it's better to take our chances with traffic jams.

Actually, it may be better to take our chances with a different approach, this one pioneered by the German physicist Dirk Helbing. Helbing is fascinated by anything that moves: his work includes studies of pedestrians, cars, crowds, and supply chains. And when it comes to traffic, he's devised what may be the first believable and realistic way of solving traffic problems. Helbing's solution has its roots in studies he did a few years ago with Bernardo Huberman, a Hewlett-Packard scientist. Essentially, Helbing and Huberman identified a traffic state that they called "coherent flow." In coherent flow, the cars are traveling as one—what they called a "solid block"—and even though each car is going slower than it would like to go, traffic as a whole is moving at an optimal pace, meaning that the maximum number of cars is passing by a particular point every minute.

The peculiar thing about coherent flow is that it can't arise if there are too few cars on the road. With too few cars, you have lane changing, sudden accelerations, and braking, all of which disrupt the steady flow of traffic. Individual cars may make better headway, but the crowd as a whole moves more slowly than it otherwise would. To achieve coherent flow, you need two things: a way to keep drivers from constantly slowing down and speeding up, and a way to smooth out the flow of cars entering the highway. What's important, it turns out, is not just how many cars are getting onto the highway but also when they are.

More recently, Helbing and another colleague, Martin Treiber, showed that two innovations could make a huge difference in the way traffic moves. The first is what's called a "driver-assistance system," which is a miniaturized radar and sensor system that would help keep cars evenly spaced and would warn drivers of impending hazards, as well as alert them to dangers from behind that they may be missing because of blind spots. The driver-assistance systems would, the idea goes, smooth out rides and make it easier for drivers to avoid slamming on the brakes. Automakers are already working on incorporating the technology in future models. And not everyone would need to use the systems, either. Helbing and Treiber show that even if only 10 or 20 percent of the cars on the road were equipped with the sensors, it would eliminate much stop-and-go traffic.

The second innovation is much closer to becoming reality, and it simply involves a more sophisticated use of the on-ramp stoplights that already dot highways across Europe and the United States. In the United States, the stoplights are generally on a simple timed cycle, so that every thirty seconds or so another car is allowed onto the highway. What Helbing and Huberman's work suggests, though, is that spacing out cars randomly isn't the answer. What you want to do is ensure that the cars get on the highway when there's room for them and when their presence will fill a gap, thereby encouraging the traffic to fall into a coherent flow. (This would mean, of course, installing a system that could track oncoming traffic and time the lights accordingly.) Sometimes this would mean holding traffic at an on-ramp for a few minutes, which would probably be pretty aggravating at first. But by doing so, Helbing argues, you actually end up shortening the total travel time for everyone. If an intelligent crowd cannot save itself from traffic jams, perhaps intelligent highways can.

8.

SCIENCE: COLLABORATION, COMPETITION,

AND REPUTATION

In early February of 2003, the Ministry of Health of the People's Republic of China notified the World Health Organization that since November of 2002, 305 people in Guangdong Province had been stricken with a severe respiratory disease, which had killed five of them. Although the disease's symptoms resembled the flu, laboratory tests had come back negative for influenza viruses. A couple of weeks after the WHO got this news, a man returning from a trip to China and Hong Kong fell ill with a severe respiratory disease in Hanoi and was hospitalized, even as a number of workers at a Hong Kong hospital came down with similar symptoms. Reports of new outbreaks continued to arrive, and by early March, it seemed clear that SARS—as the illness had been dubbed—was not a new kind of flu but an entirely new disease. In response, the WHO issued a global warning about SARS, cautioning travelers about journeying to southern Asia and activating a global surveillance system that was meant to alert the organization to any new outbreaks of the disease.

While tracking the disease was important—since it was already clear that SARS was transmitted from person to person, and that therefore quarantining might be an important strategy in fighting the disease—it was just as important to discover the cause of the disease, which would open the door for testing and, perhaps, an eventual vaccine. And so even as it issued its global alert, the WHO set in motion a global effort to uncover the source of SARS. On March 15 and 16, the organization contacted eleven research laboratories from countries around the world—including France, Germany, the Netherlands, Japan, the United States, Hong Kong, Singapore, Canada, the United Kingdom, and China—and asked them to work together to find and analyze the SARS virus. All of them agreed, and on March 17 embarked on what the WHO called a "collaborative multicenter research project." Every day the labs took part in daily teleconferences, where they shared their work, discussed avenues for future investigation, and debated current results. On a WHO Web site, the labs posted electron-microscope photographs of viruses isolated from SARS victims (any one of which might have been the cause of the disease), virus analyses, and test results. The labs regularly traded virus samples, allowing them to both check on and learn from each other's work.

Because of the way the collaboration functioned, different labs were able to work at the same time on the same samples, multiplying their speed and effectiveness. In the first few days of the effort, the labs considered and then dismissed a host of possible causes of the disease, including a series of viruses that were found in samples from some SARS patients but not others. By March 21, scientists at Hong Kong University had already isolated a virus that seemed like a likely candidate. That same day, scientists at the Centers for Disease Control in the United States separately isolated a virus that, under the electron microscope, looked like what's called a coronavirus. This was something of a surprise. Coronaviruses make animals very sick, but in humans their effects tend to be rather mild. But over the next week, labs in the network detected the coronavirus in a wide variety of samples from people who had been diagnosed with SARS. Labs in Germany, the Netherlands, and Hong Kong began sequencing the virus. In early April, monkeys in the Netherlands laboratory who had been infected with the coronavirus came down with full-blown cases of

SARS. By April 16, a mere month after their collaboration had begun, the labs were confident enough to announce that the coronavirus did, in fact, cause SARS.

The discovery of the SARS virus was, by any measure, a remarkable feat. And when we're faced with a remarkable feat, our natural inclination is to ask: Who did it? Who actually discovered the cause of SARS? But the truth is, that's an impossible question to answer. We know the name of the person who first spotted the coronavirus. She was an electron microscopist named Cynthia Goldsmith, who worked in the Centers for Disease Control and Prevention lab in Atlanta. But you can't say she discovered what caused SARS, since it took weeks of work by labs all over the world to prove that the coronavirus actually made people sick. For that matter, all the work that proved that other viruses didn't cause SARS was instrumental as well, since it narrowed the field of possible candidates. Ultimately, no one person discovered the cause of SARS. Instead, as the WHO's own account of the search for the virus argues, it was the group of labs that "collectively . . . discovered" the coronavirus. Working on their own, any one of those labs may very well have taken months or years to isolate the virus. Together it took them just a matter of weeks.

The intriguing thing about the success of the laboratories' collaboration is that no one, strictly speaking, was in charge of it. Although the WHO orchestrated the creation of the network of labs, there was no one at the top dictating what different labs would do, what viruses or samples they would work on, or how information would be exchanged. The labs agreed that they would share all the relevant data they had, and they agreed to talk every morning, but other than that it was really up to them to make the collaboration work. The guiding assumption of the search for SARS was that on their own, the labs would figure out the most efficient way to divide up the work. Part of this, of course, was simple necessity: the WHO has no real authority to make academic or government laboratories do anything. But in this case, necessity became virtue. In the absence of top-down direction, the laboratories did a remarkably good job of organizing themselves. The collaborative nature of the project gave each lab the freedom to focus on what it believed to be the most promising lines of investigation, and to play to its particular analytical strengths, while also allowing the labs to reap the benefits—in real time—of each other's data and analyses. And the result was that this cobbled-together multinational alliance found an answer to its problem as quickly and efficiently as any top-down organization could have.

THE SCOPE AND SPEED of the SARS research effort made it unique. But in one sense the successful collaboration between the labs was simply an exemplary case of the way much modern science gets done. Although in the popular imagination science remains the province of the solitary genius working alone in his lab, in fact it is, in more ways than one, a profoundly collective enterprise. Before World War I, collaboration was relatively rare for scientists. But that began to change in the decades before World War II, and in the postwar years teamwork and group projects proliferated rapidly. Researchers, particularly experimental researchers, routinely work in large groups, and it's no longer strange to see scientific papers that are co-authored by ten or twenty people. (This is in sharp contrast to the humanities, where single authorship remains the norm.) A classic example of this phenomenon was the discovery, in 1994, of the quantum particle called the "top quark." When the discovery was announced, it was credited to 450 different physicists.

Why do scientists collaborate? Part of it is a result of what's often called the "division of cognitive labor." As science has become ever-more specialized and as the number of subfields within each discipline has proliferated, it's become difficult for a single person to know everything he needs to know. This is especially true in experimental science, where sophisticated machinery demands unique skills. Collaboration allows scientists to incorporate many different kinds of knowledge, and to do so in an active way (rather than simply learning the information from a book). Collaboration also makes it easier for scientists to work on interdisciplinary problems—which happen to be among today's most important and interesting scientific problems. Small groups do face tremendous challenges in solving problems and making decisions, and they can waste a great deal of time dividing up the labor, discussing results, and debating conclusions. But those potential costs are clearly, for most scientists, outweighed by the benefits.

Collaboration also works because, when it works well, it guarantees a diversity of perspectives. In the case of the search for the SARS virus, for instance, the fact that different labs had different initial ideas about the possible origin of the virus meant that a wide range of possibilities would be considered. And the fact that different laboratories were doing parallel work on the same samples, while it ran the risk of producing too much duplicated effort, also produced rich results in the form of unique data.

Ultimately, for a collaboration to be successful it has to make each individual scientist more productive. A wide array of studies have found that, more often than not, collaboration seems to do just that. Economist Paula Stephan has argued, "Scientists who collaborate with each other are more productive, often times producing 'better' science, than are individual investigators." And social scientist Etienne Wenger adds: "Today's complex problem solving requires multiple perspectives. The days of Leonardo da Vinci are over."

Saying that the days of Leonardo da Vinci are over, though, is not the same as saying that collaboration waters down or squelches individual creativity. In fact, one of the more intriguing aspects of scientific collaboration is that the more productive and better known a scientist is, the more frequently he or she works with others. This has been the case for decades. In a 1966 study of 592 scientists' publications and collaborative activities, for instance, D. J. de Solla Price and Donald B. Beaver found that "the most prolific man is also by far the most collaborating, and three of the four next most prolific are also among the next most frequently collaborating." A similar study by Harriet Zuckerman, which compared forty-one Nobel laureates with a sample of similarly placed scientists, found that the laureates collaborated more often than regular scientists. Of course, it's easier for well-known scientists to collaborate because everyone wants to work with them. But the fact that they are committed to working with others, when you might expect them to assume that they have nothing to gain from it, testifies to the centrality of cooperative efforts to modern science.

Still, the kind of global collaboration that we witnessed in the search for the SARS virus remains unusual. Although the scientific community clearly is global in nature, most collaboration takes place, even today, with people in a scientist's immediate vicinity. Barry Bozeman, for instance, found that academic researchers spend only a third of their time working with people who are not in their immediate work group, and only a quarter of their time working with people who are outside their university. That's not too surprising. For all the talk of the "death of distance," people still prefer to work in close physical proximity to their colleagues. But as the SARS example suggests, this may be changing. Technology is now making global collaboration not just possible but easy and productive. And the value of working across not only universities but nations is clearly immense, while limiting yourself to the skill set found in your immediate department or working group seems self-defeating. It's perhaps not surprising, then, that researchers who spend a lot of time working with researchers in other nations are significantly more productive than researchers who don't. Again, it's possible that the correlation here runs in the opposite direction: that it's easier for more productive—which generally means better known—scholars to collaborate internationally. But regardless of why it's true, what's telling is that it is.

EXPLICIT COLLABORATION ON ACADEMIC papers and research projects is not the only thing that makes science a collective enterprise. Science is collective because it depends on and has tried to institutionalize the free and open exchange of information. When scientists make an important new discovery or experimentally prove some hypothesis, they do not, in general, keep that information to themselves so that they alone can ponder its meaning and derive additional theories from it. Instead, they publish their results and make their data available for inspection. This makes it possible for other scientists to reconsider their data and possibly refute their conclusions. More important, though, it makes it possible for other scientists to use that data to construct new hypotheses and perform new experiments. The assumption is that society as a whole will end up knowing more if information is diffused as widely as possible, rather than being limited to a few people. In a strict sense, every scientist depends on the work of other scientists.

Newton pointed to something like this when he spoke of "standing on the shoulders of giants." But Newton, who did most of his theoretical work alone and who was obsessed with being sui generis, was suggesting only that his insights depended on the work of those who had come before him. He was making the point that scientific knowledge is, in some sense, cumulative. (Of course, Newton used the phrase in a letter to his rival Robert Hooke, who happened to be a dwarf, so it's possible that the phrase was intended only as a cruel joke.) But that knowledge is more than cumulative. It's collective. Scientists depend not just on the work of their predecessors, but also on the work of their contemporaries, who are in turn dependent on them. Even scientists whose hypotheses fail are helping their peers, by letting them know where they do not need to go.

Although the effect of the work of individual scientists is to accumulate scientific knowledge for the community as a whole, that's not really the point of scientific endeavor. Scientists want to solve particular problems. And they want to be recognized, to earn the attention of their contemporaries, to transform the way other scientists think. The coin of the realm, for most scientists, is not cash but rather recognition. Even so, scientists are undoubtedly as self-seeking and as self-interested as the rest of us. The genius of the way science is organized, though, makes their self-interested behavior redound to the benefit of all of us. In the process of winning notoriety for themselves, they make the group—that is, the scientific community and then, indirectly, the rest of us—smarter.

What's striking about the organization of modern science is that—like the SARS network of labs—no one is in charge. Obviously, there have been massive and important top-down research projects—think of the Manhattan Project or the Atlas missile project—in which scientists worked under explicit direction to solve particular problems, and these projects, most of them government sponsored, have often been successful. At the same time, since the late nineteenth century, a good deal of scientific work has taken place in corporate research labs, where there has often—though not always—been a more systematized, command-and-control approach to research. But in the history of science and technology, top-down organization has always been more of an anomaly than the ordinary way of doing business. For the most part, scientists (at least established ones) have been left to their own devices to choose what they were interested in, how they would work on it, and what they would do with their results.

That's not to say that the choices that scientists make are innocent. A scientist does not enter his lab as a blank slate, waiting to hear what the data will tell him. Instead he enters it as someone whose understanding of what problems are interesting, what problems can be solved, and what problems should be solved has been shaped by the interests (in both senses of the word) of his community. And since a hefty chunk of scientific research has been and is still today funded by the government, with grants handed out by peer review boards, the interests of a scientist's peers often have a direct and concrete impact on the kind of work he chooses to do. Even so, the important point is that there is no Science Czar telling researchers what they should do. We trust that allowing individuals to pursue their own self-interest will produce collectively better results than dictating orders.

Pursuing their own self-interest is more complicated for scientists than it might sound. While scientists are fundamentally competing for recognition and attention, that recognition and attention can only be afforded them by the very people they're competing against. So science presents us with the curious paradox of an enterprise that is simultaneously intensely competitive and intensely cooperative. The quest for recognition ensures a steady infusion of diverse thought, since no one becomes famous for restating what's already known. (This makes it less important that scientists tend to be interested in what other scientists are interested in, since the quest for originality forces researchers to think past convention.) And the competition also works to provide an inherent check on flawed ideas, since, as the philosopher David Hull has argued, showing the flaws in other people's work is one way to make a name for yourself. But all that competition depends on a given level of cooperation, because it's the rare scientist who can flourish in isolation from the work of his peers.

What allows this strange blend of collaboration and competition to flourish is the scientific ethos that demands open access to information. This ethos dates back to the origins of the scientific revolution in the seventeenth century. In 1665, the Royal Society—one of the first institutions, and certainly the most important, formed to foster the growth of scientific knowledge—published the first issue of its *Philosophical Transactions*. It was a seminal moment in the history of science, because of the journal's fierce commitment to the idea that all new discoveries should be disseminated as widely and freely as possible. Henry Oldenburg, the first secretary of the Royal Society and the editor of the *Transactions*, pioneered the idea that secrecy was inimical to scientific progress, and convinced scientists that they should give up their sole ownership of their ideas in exchange for recognition they would receive as the creator or discoverer of those ideas. What Oldenburg grasped was the peculiar character of knowledge, which does not, unlike other commodities, get used up as it is consumed and which can be therefore spread widely without losing its value. If anything, in fact, the more a piece of knowledge becomes available, the more valuable it potentially becomes, because the wider the array of possible uses for it. As a result, the historian Joel Mokyr writes, the scientific revolution became the period "in which 'open science' emerged, when knowledge about the natural world became increasingly nonproprietary and scientific advances and discoveries were freely shared with the public at large. Thus scientific knowledge became a public good, communicated freely rather than confined to a secretive exclusive few as had been the custom in medieval Europe."

This tradition of open publication and communication of insights was, of course, central to the success of Western science. It's open science that made the self-interested behavior of scientists collectively beneficial. Scientists were willing to publish their insights because that was the route to public recognition and influence. If one wanted to think about this process in market terms—as some have tried to do—you could say that scientists were paid by other people's attention. As the sociologist of science Robert K. Merton famously put it, "In science, one's private property is established by giving its substance away."

The challenge the scientific community faces today is whether the success of Western science can survive the growing commercialization of scientific endeavors. Science and commerce have, of course, been intertwined for centuries. But as an increasing share of scientific research and development is funded by corporations, which see themselves as having an economic interest in protecting information rather than in disseminating it widely, the nature of scientific exchange may change. The sociologist Warren Hagstrom talked about science as a "gift economy" rather than an exchange economy. And the idea of science as made up of "invisible colleges" of researchers bound by their common interest in expanding knowledge, if perhaps naïve, still has a powerful hold not just on laypeople but on scientists themselves. Corporations, on the other hand, are generally not gift givers nor do they thrive on collegiality. The fact that public funding is still instrumental to science, and particularly to basic research, insulates scientists to some extent from commercial pressures. And although the patent system limits what others can do with a given invention, it also—by requiring the inventor to publish the details of his invention in order to get a patent—plays a role in continuing to fuel the free flow of information. But the conflict between science and business is not imaginary. The spectacle of companies funding studies and then demanding that they be suppressed when the results do not come back to their satisfaction is not something that would have pleased Henry Oldenburg.

TALKING ABOUT SCIENTIFIC ENDEAVOR in terms of the quest for recognition may make it sound as if scientists were simply fame hounds (which, of course, some of them are). But recognition is not, at least in theory, about celebrity or fashion. Recognition is instead the proper reward for genuinely new and interesting discoveries. Scientists want to be recognized because it's nice to be recognized. But they also want to be recognized because recognition is what allows new ideas to be incorporated into the general body of scientific knowledge. What's intriguing about science from the perspective of collective problem solving is that it is the community as a whole that bestows the recognition, which is to say that it's the community as a whole that decides whether or not a scientific hypothesis is true and whether it's original. This doesn't mean that scientific truth is in the eye of the beholder. The coronavirus caused SARS before the WHO announced that the coronavirus caused SARS. But in scientific terms, the coronavirus only became the cause of SARS once other scientists had scrutinized the work of the labs and accepted it as proving what they said it proved. Academic labs and corporate research labs across the world are now busy working on possible tests and vaccines for SARS, all predicated on the idea that the SARS virus is a coronavirus. They are doing so only because the scientific community has reached—in an indirect way—a consensus on the issue. As Robert K. Merton wrote, "There is no such thing as a scientific truth believed by one person and disbelieved by the rest of the scientific community; an idea becomes a truth only when a vast majority of scientists accept it without question. That is, after all, what we mean by the expression 'scientific contribution': an offering that is accepted, however provisionally, into the common fund of knowledge."

This seems so obvious to us that it's easy to miss how much faith this places in the good judgment of the scientific community as a whole. Instead of relying on an elite group of scientists to pronounce on the validity of new ideas, scientists simply toss their ideas out into the world, trusting that the ones that survive are the ones that deserve to. The process is dramatically different from the way markets or democracies work. There are no literal votes taken, and ideas do not carry a price tag. But at the core of the process of accepting new ideas into the common fund of knowledge is a kind of unexpressed faith in the collective wisdom of scientists.

It's true, of course, that since scientific results should be replicable, you don't in theory have to trust anyone's judgment. If an experiment works, it will work whether or not the vast majority of scientists say it does or not. But the picture is more complicated than this. Most scientists are never going to replicate other experiments. They're going to trust that the data is correct and that the experiments worked as the scientist who performed them said they did. A successful hypothesis is a hypothesis that most scientists find credible, not a hypothesis that most scientists have tested for themselves and found to be true. In fact, once a theory has been accepted, simply failing to replicate the data on which it's based isn't enough. As the Hungarian scientist and philosopher Michael Polanyi argued, if you tried to reproduce a well-known experiment and failed, your initial response wouldn't be to doubt the experiment. You would doubt, and rightly so, your own lack of skill. This is best for science, since if researchers were constantly testing each other's results, they'd spend all their time retracing old ground instead of breaking new ground. And in any case, even to test another scientist's data requires you to rely on a host of other things that you almost certainly haven't tested yourself. Of an experiment in which he extracted DNA from an animal, the historian of science Steve Shapin wrote, "My extraction of DNA took on trust the identity of the animal tissue supplied, the speed of the centrifuge, the reliability of thermometric readings, the qualitative and quantitative makeup of various solvents, the rules of arithmetic."

Of course, experiments can be, and are, replicated. And scientific fraud is revealed. So the point is not that all truths are relative. Instead, the fact that what scientists know depends on the communications of others has two important consequences. First, good science requires a degree of trust among scientists that even as they compete, they will also cooperate by playing fair with their data. Second, and more important, science depends not only on an ever-replenishing pool of common knowledge, but also on an implicit faith in the collective wisdom of the scientific community to distinguish between those hypotheses that are trustworthy and those that are not.

UNFORTUNATELY, THERE IS SOMETHING of a flaw in this idealized picture of the way the scientific community discovers truth. And the flaw is that most scientific work never gets noticed. Study after study has shown that most scientific papers are read by almost no one, while a small number of papers are read by many people. Famous scientists find their work cited vastly more often than scientists who are less well known. When famous scientists collaborate with others they're given a disproportionate share of the credit for the work. And when two scientists—or two teams of scientists— independently make the same discovery, it's the famous scientists who end up getting the credit for that, as well. Merton dubbed this "the Matthew effect," after the Gospel lines "From unto every one that hath shall be given, and he shall have abundance: but from him that hath not shall be taken away even that which he hath." The rich get richer and the poor get poorer.

The Matthew effect can be seen in part as a kind of heuristic device, a way for other scientists to filter the torrent of information that they are confronted with every day. And since there is a great deal of redundancy in scientific effort—that is, scientists often come up with the same hypotheses or run the same experiments— the Matthew effect does have the virtue of ensuring that some attention gets paid to work that otherwise might just disappear. Even so, the power of name recognition is startling. The geneticist Richard Lewontin, for instance, tells a story of publishing two papers, which he had co-authored with the biochemist John Hubby, back-to-back in the same issue of a scientific journal in 1966. The two papers, Lewontin writes, "were a genuinely collaborative effort in conception, execution, and writing and clearly form an indivisible pair." For the first paper, the biochemist Hubby's name was listed first. For the second, the geneticist Lewontin's name was listed first. There seemed to be no obvious reason why people should be more interested in one paper than the other. Yet the paper that listed Lewontin's name first was cited 50 percent more than the other. The only answer, Lewontin suggested, was that he was at that point fairly well known as a geneticist while Hubby was still relatively unknown. When his name came first, scientists assumed the paper was more of his work and that it was, therefore, more valuable.

The problem, of course, is that the reverence for the well known tends to be accompanied by a disdain for the not so well known. The physicist Luis Alvarez summed up this point of view decades ago when he said: "There is no democracy in physics. We can't say that some second-rate guy has as much right to opinion as Fermi." While this approach makes sense in terms of economizing on your attention—you can't listen to or read everyone, so you only listen to the best—it has a number of dubious assumptions built into it, including the idea that we automatically know who the second-rate are, even before hearing them, as well as the idea that everything Fermi had to say was inherently valuable. The obvious peril is that important work will be ignored because the person who produced it does not have the right brand name. Perhaps the classic example of this is Gregor Mendel, who found his work on heredity ignored, at least in part, because he was an unknown monk and who, as a result, simply stopped publishing his results.

The point is not that reputation should be irrelevant. A proven record of achievement does—and should—confer credibility on a person's ideas. The point instead is that reputation should not become the basis of a scientific hierarchy. The genius of the scientific ethos, at least in theory, is its resolute commitment to meritocracy. As Merton wrote in a famous essay on scientific norms, "The acceptance or rejection of claims entering the lists of science is not to depend on the personal or social attributes of the protagonist; his race, nationality, religion, class, and personal qualities are irrelevant." Ideas are meant to triumph not because of who is (or who is not) advocating them but because of their inherent value, because they seem to explain the data better than any of the others. This is perhaps just an illusion. But it's a valuable one.

9

COMMITTEES, JURIES, AND TEAMS:
THE *COLUMBIA* DISASTER AND HOW SMALL
GROUPS CAN BE MADE TO WORK

On the morning of January 21, 2003, the Mission Management Team (MMT) for NASA mission STS-107—the twenty-eighth flight of the space shuttle *Columbia*—held a teleconference, its second since the *Columbia*'s launch on January 16. An hour before the meeting, Don McCormack had been briefed by members of the Debris Assessment Team (DAT), a group of engineers from NASA, Boeing, and Lockheed Martin, who had spent much of the previous five days evaluating the possible consequences of a large-debris strike on the *Columbia*. During the shuttle's ascent into the atmosphere, a large piece of foam had broken off the left bipod area of the shuttle's external fuel tank and had smashed into the ship's left wing. None of the cameras that were tracking the shut-tle's launch had provided a clear picture of the impact, so it was difficult to tell how much damage the foam might have caused. And although by January 21 a request had been made for on-orbit pic-tures of the *Columbia*, they had not been approved. So the DAT had done what it could with the information it had, first estimating the size of the foam and the speed at which it had struck the *Co-lumbia*, and then using an algorithm called Crater to predict how deep a piece of debris that size and traveling at that speed would penetrate into the thermal-protection tiles that covered the shuttle's wings.

The DAT had reached no conclusions, but they made it clear to McCormack that there was reason to be concerned. McCormack did not transmit that sense of concern to the MMT during its teleconference. The foam strike was not mentioned until two-thirds of the way through the meeting, and was brought up only after discussions of, among other things, a jammed camera, the scientific experiments on the shuttle, and a leaky water separator. Then Linda Ham, who was the MMT leader, asked McCormack for an update. He simply said that people were investigating the possible damage and what could potentially be done to fix it, and added that when the *Columbia* had been hit by a similar strike during mission STS-87, five years earlier, it had suffered "fairly significant damage." This is how Ham answered: "And I really don't think there is much we can do so it's not really a factor during the flight because there is not much we can do about it."

Ham, in other words, had already decided that the foam strike was inconsequential. More important, she decided for everyone else in the meeting that it was inconsequential, too. This was the first time the MMT had heard any details about the foam strike. It would have been logical for McCormack to outline the possible consequences and talk about what the evidence from past shuttles that had been struck with debris showed. But instead the meeting moved on.

Hindsight is, of course, twenty-twenty, and just as with the critiques of the U.S. intelligence community after September 11, it's perhaps too easy to fault the MMT at NASA for its failure to see what would happen to the *Columbia* when it reentered the Earth's atmosphere on February 1. Even those who have been exceptionally critical of NASA have suggested that focusing on this one team is a mistake because it obscures the deep institutional and cultural problems that plague the agency (which happen to be many of the same problems that plagued the agency in 1986, when the *Challenger* exploded). But while NASA clearly is an object lesson in organizational dysfunction, that doesn't fully explain just why the MMT handled the *Columbia* crisis so badly. Sifting through the evidence collected by the Columbia Accident Investigation Board (CAIB), there is no way to evade the conclusion that the team had an opportunity to make different choices that could have dramatically improved the chances of the crew surviving. The team members were urged on many different occasions to collect the information they needed to make a reasonable estimate of the shuttle's safety. They were advised that the foam might, in fact, have inflicted enough damage to cause "burn-through"—heat burning through the protective tiles and into the shuttle's fuselage—when the shuttle reentered the Earth's atmosphere. The team's leaders themselves raised the possibility that the debris damage might have been severe. And yet the MMT as a whole never came close to making the right decision on what to do about the *Columbia*.

IN FACT, THE PERFORMANCE of the MMT is an object lesson in how not to run a small group, and a powerful demonstration of the way in which, instead of making people wiser, being in a group can actually make them dumber. This is important for two reasons. First, small groups are ubiquitous in American life, and their decisions are consequential. Juries decide whether or not people will go to prison. Boards of directors shape, at least in theory, corporate strategy. And more and more of our work lives are spent on teams or, at the very least, in meetings. Whether small groups can do a good job of solving complex problems is hardly an academic question.

Second, small groups are different in important ways from groups such as markets or betting pools or television audiences. Those groups are as much statistical realities as experiential ones. Bettors do get feedback from each other in the form of the point spread, and investors get feedback from each other in the stock market, but the nature of the relationship between people in a small group is qualitatively different. Investors do not think of themselves as members of the market. People on the MMT thought of themselves as members of that team. And the collective wisdom that something like the Iowa Electronic Markets produces is, at least when it's working well, the result of many different independent judgments, rather than something that the group as a whole has consciously come up with. In a small group, by contrast, the group—even if it is an ad hoc group formed for the sake of a single project or experiment—has an identity of its own. And the influence of the people in the group on each other's judgment is inescapable.

What we'll see is that this has two consequences. On the one hand, it means small groups can make very bad decisions, because influence is more direct and immediate and small-group judgments tend to be more volatile and extreme. On the other hand, it also means that small groups have the opportunity to be more than just the sum of their parts. A successful face-to-face group is more than just collectively intelligent. It makes everyone work harder, think smarter, and reach better conclusions than they would have on their own. In his 1985 book about Olympic rowing, *The Amateurs,* David Halberstam writes: "When most oarsmen talked about their perfect moments in a boat, they referred not so much to winning a race but to the feel of the boat, all eight oars in the water together, the synchronization almost perfect. In moments like that, the boat seemed to lift right out of the water. Oarsmen called that the moment of *swing.*" When a boat has swing, its motion seems almost effortless. Although there are eight oarsmen in the boat, it's as if there's only one person—with perfect timing and perfect strength—rowing. So you might say that a small group which works well has intellectual swing.

Swing, though, is hard to come by. In fact, few organizations have figured out how to make groups work consistently well. For all the lip service paid, particularly in corporate America, to the importance of teams and the need to make meetings more productive, it's still unusual for a small group to be more than just the sum of its parts. Much of the time, far from adding value to their members, groups seem to subtract it. Too often, it's easy to agree with Ralph Cordiner, the former chairman of General Electric, who once said, "If you can name for me one great discovery or decision that was made by a committee, I will find you the one man in that committee who had the lonely insight—while he was shaving or on his way to work, or maybe while the rest of the committee was chattering away—the lonely insight that solved the problem and was the basis for the decision." On this account, groups are nothing but obstacles, cluttering the way of people whose time would be better spent alone.

The performance of the MMT helps explain why. First, the team started not with an open mind but from the assumption that the question of whether a foam strike could seriously damage the shuttle had already been answered. This was, to be fair, partly a matter of bad luck, since one of the team's technical advisers was convinced from the beginning that foam simply could do no serious damage, and kept saying so to anyone who would listen. But there was plenty of evidence to suggest otherwise. Rather than begin with the evidence and work toward a conclusion, the team members worked in the opposite direction. More egregiously, their skepticism about the possibility that something might really be wrong made them dismiss the need to gather more information, especially in the form of pictures, leading to the DAT's requests for on-orbit images being rejected. Even when MMT members dealt with the possibility that there might be a real problem with *Columbia*, their conviction that nothing was wrong limited discussion and made them discount evidence to the contrary. In that sense, the team succumbed to what psychologists call "confirmation bias," which causes decision makers to unconsciously seek those bits of information that confirm their underlying intuitions.

These problems were also exacerbated by the team's belief that it knew more than it did. For instance, when the shuttle managers turned down the request for pictures, one of the justifications they offered was that the resolution of the images would not be good enough to detect the small area where the foam struck. In fact, as the CAIB noted, none of the managers had the necessary security clearances to know how good the resolution of the photos would be, nor did any of them ask the Department of Defense—which would have taken the pictures—about picture quality. In other words, they were "making critical decisions about imagery capabilities based on little or no knowledge," and doing so with an air of complete assurance.

Social scientists who study juries often differentiate between two approaches juries take. Evidence-based juries usually don't even take a vote until after they've spent some time talking over the case, sifting through the evidence, and explicitly contemplating alternative explanations. Verdict-based juries, by contrast, see their mission as reaching a decision as quickly and decisively as possible. They take a vote before any discussion, and the debate after that tends to concentrate on getting those who don't agree to agree. The MMT's approach was practically, though not intentionally, verdict-based. You can see this especially clearly in the way Linda Ham asked questions. On January 22, for instance, the day after the meeting where the foam was first mentioned, Ham e-mailed two members of the team about whether the foam strike might, in fact, pose a threat to the shuttle's safety. "Can we say that for any ET [external tank] foam lost," she wrote, "no 'safety of flight' damage can occur to the Orbiter because of the density?" The answer that Ham wanted was built into the question. It was a way of deflecting genuine inquiry even while seeming to pursue it. As it happens, one of the members of the team did not give Ham the answer she was looking for. Lambert Austin answered her question by writing, "NO," in capital letters, and then went on to explain that there was no way at that point to "PRECLUDE" the possibility that the foam might have seriously damaged the tiles. Yet Austin's cautionary note garnered little attention.

One reason for the team's lack of follow-through may have been its implicit assumption that if something was wrong, there was no possibility of fixing it. At that January 21 meeting, you'll remember, Ham said, "And I really don't think there is much we can do so it's not really a factor during the flight because there is not much we can do about it." Two days later, Calvin Schomburg, the technical expert who insisted throughout that the foam could not seriously damage the tiles, met with Rodney Rocha, a NASA engineer who had become the unofficial representative of the DAT. By this point, the DAT was increasingly concerned that the damage inflicted by the foam could potentially lead to burn-through on reentry, and Rocha and Schomburg argued over the question. At the end of the discussion, Schomburg said that if the tiles had been severely damaged, "Nothing could be done."

The idea that nothing could have been done if the damage to the tiles had been uncovered in time was wrong. In fact, as part of the CAIB investigation, NASA engineers came up with two different strategies that might have brought the *Columbia* crew back to earth safely (though the shuttle itself was doomed from the moment the foam struck). There was no reason for the MMT to know what those strategies were, of course. But here again, the team had made a decision before looking at the evidence. And that decision—which roughly amounted to saying, "If there is a problem, we won't be able to find a solution"—undoubtedly shaped the team's approach to figuring out whether there was a problem at all. In fact, the CAIB report includes personal notes from an unnamed NASA source that say that when Ham canceled the DAT's request for pictures of the *Columbia*'s wing, "[she] said it was no longer being pursued since even if we saw something, we couldn't do anything about it." This was not exactly the ethos that brought *Apollo 13* safely back to earth.

One of the real dangers that small groups face is emphasizing consensus over dissent. The extreme version of this, as we've already seen, is the kind of groupthink that Irving Janis described in his account of the planning of the Bay of Pigs, where the members of the group become so identified with the group that the possibility of dissent seems practically unthinkable. But in a more subtle way small groups can exacerbate our tendency to prefer the illusion of certainty to the reality of doubt. On January 24, the DAT engineers met again with Don McCormack, who had become their unofficial liaison to the MMT, to present the findings of their foam-strike study. The briefing room where the presentation took place was so crowded that engineers ended up out in the hallway, which said a lot about how worried people were. In any case, the DAT offered five different scenarios of what might have happened. The team's conclusion was that it was likely that the shuttle was safe. But they qualified their conclusion by saying that their analysis was profoundly limited by their tools and their lack of good information. Because the MMT had refused to authorize on-orbit images, the engineers did not know where exactly the foam had struck. And the Crater algorithm they were using had been designed to measure the impact of pieces of debris hundreds of times smaller than the one that hit *Columbia,* so there was no way to be sure that its results were accurate. The engineers stressed, in other words, how uncertain their analysis was. But NASA management focused instead on their conclusion.

An hour after the briefing, the MMT met, and McCormack summarized what the DAT had said. "They do show obviously there's potential for significant damage here, but thermal analysis does not indicate that there is potential for a burn-through," he said. "Obviously there is a lot of uncertainty in all this in terms of the size of the debris and where it hit and the angle of incidence and it's difficult." This was a relatively obscure way of explaining that the engineers' analysis was built on a lot of untested assumptions, but it was at least an attempt at caution. Ham responded by again asking a question that answered itself: "No burn-through, means no catastrophic damage and the localized heating damage would mean a tile replacement?" McCormack said, "We do not see any kind of safety of flight issue here yet in anything that we've looked at." Ham came back with another nothing-is-wrong question: "No safety of flight and no issue for this mission nothing that we're going to do different, there may be a turnaround?" Then, after a short interchange between Ham and McCormack and Calvin Schomburg, one of the other team members on the conference call said that they hadn't been able to hear what McCormack had said. Ham summarized neatly: "He was just reiterating with Calvin that he doesn't believe that there is any burn-through so no safety of flight kind of issue, it's more of a turnaround issue similar to what we've had on other flights. That's it? Alright, any questions on that?" For all intents and purposes, when that meeting ended, the *Columbia*'s fate had been sealed.

What's most striking about that January 24 meeting is the utter absence of debate and minority opinions. As the CAIB noted, when McCormack summarized the DAT's findings, he included none of its supporting analysis nor any discussion of whether there was a division of opinion on the team about its conclusions. More strikingly, not one member of the MMT asked a question. Not one member expressed any interest in seeing the DAT study. One would have thought that when McCormack mentioned the uncertainties in the analysis, someone would have asked him to explain and perhaps even quantify those uncertainties. But no one did. In part, that may have been because Ham was so obviously anxious for the problem to be resolved, and so convinced that there was nothing to talk about. Her attempts to briskly summarize McCormack's conclusions—"No burn-through, means no catastrophic damage"—effectively shut off discussion. And anyone who's ever been in a business meeting knows that "Alright, any questions on that?" really means "There are no questions on that, right?"

The MMT failed to make the right decision in part because of problems that are specific to the culture of NASA. Although we think of NASA as a fundamentally meritocratic, bottom-up culture, it is in fact deeply hierarchical. This meant that even though the DAT engineers had serious qualms from the beginning about the foam strike, their concerns—and, in particular, their insistence that they needed images of the Orbiter's wing before they could make a truly informed analysis—never received a serious hearing from the MMT. At the same time, the MMT violated nearly every rule of good group decision making. To begin with, the team's discussions were simultaneously too structured and not structured enough. They were too structured because most of the discussions—not just about the debris strike, but about everything—consisted of Ham asking a question and someone else answering it. They were not structured enough because no effort was made to ask other team members to comment on particular questions. This is almost always a mistake, because it means that decisions are made based on a very limited supply of analysis and information. One of the consistent findings from decades of small-group research is that group deliberations are more successful when they have a clear agenda and when leaders take an active role in making sure that everyone gets a chance to speak.

The team also, as I've mentioned, started with its conclusion. As a result, every new piece of information that came in was reinterpreted to fit that conclusion. This is a recurring problem with small groups that have a hard time incorporating new information. Social psychologist Garold Stasser, for instance, ran an experiment in which a group of eight people was asked to rate the performance of thirty-two psychology students. Each member of the group was given two relevant pieces of information about the students (say, their grades and their test scores), while two members of the group were given two extra pieces of information (say, their performance in class, etc.), and one member of the group received another two. Although the group as a whole therefore had six pieces of useful information, their ratings were based almost entirely on the two pieces of information that they all shared. The new information was discounted as either unimportant or unreliable. Stasser has also shown that in unstructured, free-flowing discussions, the information that tends to be talked about the most is, paradoxically, the information that everyone already knows. More curiously, information can be presented and listened to and still make little difference, because its contents are misinterpreted. New messages are often modified so that they fit old messages, which is especially dangerous since unusual messages often add the most value. (If people are just saying what you expect them to say, they're hardly likely to change your thinking.) Or they are modified to suit a pre-existing picture of the situation.

What was missing most from the MMT, of course, was diversity, by which I mean not sociological diversity but rather cognitive diversity. James Oberg, a former Mission Control operator and now NBC News correspondent, has made the counterintuitive point that the NASA teams that presided over the *Apollo* missions were actually more diverse than the MMT. This seems hard to believe, since every engineer at Mission Control in the late 1960s had the same crew cut and wore the same short-sleeved white shirt. But as Oberg points out, most of those men had worked outside of NASA in many different industries before coming to the agency. NASA employees today are far more likely to have come to the agency directly out of graduate school, which means they are also far less likely to have divergent opinions. That matters because, in small groups, diversity of opinion is the single best guarantee that the group will reap benefits from face-to-face discussion. Berkeley political scientist Chandra Nemeth has shown in a host of studies of mock juries that the presence of a minority viewpoint, all by itself, makes a group's decisions more nuanced and its decision-making process more rigorous. This is true even when the minority viewpoint turns out to be ill conceived. The confrontation with a dissenting view, logically enough, forces the majority to interrogate its own positions more seriously. This doesn't mean that the ideal jury will follow the plot of *Twelve Angry Men,* where a single holdout convinces eleven men who are ready to convict that they're all wrong. But it does mean that having even a single different opinion can make a group wiser. One suspects that, had there been a single devil's advocate pushing the idea that the foam strike might have seriously damaged the wing, the MMT's conclusion would have been very different.

Without the devil's advocate, though, it's likely that the group's meetings actually made their judgment about the possible problem worse. That's because of a phenomenon called "group polarization." Usually, when we think of deliberation, we imagine that it's a kind of recipe for rationality and moderation, and assume that the more people talk about an issue, the less likely they will be to adopt extreme positions. But evidence from juries and three decades of experimental studies suggests that much of the time, the opposite is true.

Group polarization is still a phenomenon that is not well understood, and there are clearly cases where it has little or no effect. But since the 1960s, sociologists have documented how, under certain circumstances, deliberation does not moderate but rather radicalizes people's point of view. The first studies of the phenomenon tried to elicit people's attitudes toward risk, by asking them what they would do in specific situations. For instance, they were asked, "If a man with a severe heart illness is told that he must either change his way of life completely or have an operation that will either cure him or kill him, what should he do?" Or, "If an electrical engineer who has a safe job at a small salary is given the chance to take a new job that pays much better but is also less secure, should he move?" Individuals answered these questions privately at first, then gathered into groups to reach collective decisions. At first, researchers thought that group discussions made people more likely to advocate risky positions, and they termed this the "risky shift." But as time went on, it became clear that the shift could be in either direction. If a group was made up of people who were generally risk averse, discussion would make the group even more cautious, while groups of risk takers found themselves advocating riskier positions. Other studies showed that people who had a pessimistic view of the future became even more pessimistic after deliberations. Similarly, civil juries that are inclined to give large awards to plaintiffs generally give even larger awards after talking it over.

More recently, University of Chicago law professor Cass Sunstein has devoted a great deal of attention to polarization, and in his book *Why Societies Need Dissent,* he shows both that the phenomenon is more ubiquitous than was once thought and that it can have major consequences. As a general rule, discussions tend to move both the group as a whole and the individuals within it toward more extreme positions than the ones they entered the discussion with.

Why does polarization occur? One reason is because of people's reliance on "social comparison." This means more than that people are constantly comparing themselves to everyone else (which, of course, they are). It means that people are constantly comparing themselves to everyone else with an eye toward maintaining their relative position within the group. In other words, if you start out in the middle of the group and you believe the group has moved, as it were, to the right, you're inclined to shift your position to the right as well, so that relative to everyone else you're standing still. Of course, by moving to the right you're moving the group to the right, making social comparison something of a self-fulfilling prophecy. What's assumed to be real eventually becomes real.

It's important to see, though, that polarization isn't just the result of people trying to stay in tune with the group. It also results, strangely, from people doing their best to figure out what the right answer is. As we saw in our discussion of social proof—remember the passersby who ended up staring into an empty sky—people who are uncertain about what they believe will look to other members of the group for help. That's the point of deliberating, after all. But if a majority of the group already supports one position, then most of the arguments that will be made will be in support of that position. So the uncertain people are likely to be swayed in that direction, in part simply because that's more of what they'll hear. Similarly, people who have more extreme positions are more likely to have strong, coherent arguments in favor of their positions and are also more likely to voice them.

This matters because all the evidence suggests that the order in which people speak has a profound effect on the course of a discussion. Earlier comments are more influential, and they tend to provide a framework within which the discussion occurs. As in an information cascade, once that framework is in place, it's difficult for a dissenter to break it down. This wouldn't be a problem if the people who spoke earliest were also more likely to know what they were talking about. But the truth is that, especially when it comes to problems where there is no obvious right answer, there's no guarantee that the most-informed speaker will also be the most influential. On juries, for instance, two-thirds of all foremen—who lead and structure deliberations—are men, and during deliberations men talk far more than women do, even though no one has ever suggested that men as a gender have better insight into questions of guilt and innocence. In groups where the members know each other, status tends to shape speaking patterns, with higher-status people talking more and more often than lower-status people. Again, this wouldn't matter as much if the authority of higher-status people was derived from their greater knowledge. But oftentimes it doesn't. Even when higher-status people don't really know what they're talking about, they're more likely to speak. A series of experiments with military fliers who were asked to solve a logic problem, for instance, found that pilots were far more likely to speak convincingly in defense of their solution than navigators were, even when the pilots were wrong and the navigators were right. The navigators deferred to the pilots—even when they had never met the pilots before—because they assumed that their rank meant they were more likely to be right.

That kind of deference is important, because in small groups ideas often do not succeed simply on their own merits. Even when its virtues might seem self-evident, an idea needs a champion in order to be adopted by the group as a whole. That's another reason why a popular position tends to become more popular in the course of deliberations: it has more potential champions to begin with. In a market or even a democracy, champions are far less important because of the sheer number of potential decision makers. But in a small group, having a strong advocate for an idea, no matter how good it is, is essential. And when advocates are chosen, as it were, on the basis of status or talkativeness, rather than perceptiveness or keenness of insight, then the group's chance of making a smart decision shrinks.

Talkativeness may seem like a curious thing to worry about, but in fact talkativeness has a major impact on the kinds of decisions small groups reach. If you talk a lot in a group, people will tend to think of you as influential almost by default. Talkative people are not necessarily well liked by other members of the group, but they are listened to. And talkativeness feeds on itself. Studies of group dynamics almost always show that the more someone talks, the more he is talked to by others in the group. So people at the center of the group tend to become more important over the course of a discussion.

This might be okay if people only spoke when they had expertise in a particular matter. And in many cases, if someone's talking a lot, it's a good sign that they have something valuable to add. But the truth is that there is no clear correlation between talkativeness and expertise. In fact, as the military-flier studies suggest, people who imagine themselves as leaders will often overestimate their own knowledge and project an air of confidence and expertise that is unjustified. And since, as political scientists Brock Blomberg and Joseph Harrington suggest, extremists tend to be more rigid and more convinced of their own rightness than moderates, discussion tends to pull groups away from the middle. Of course, sometimes truth lies at the extreme. And if the people who spoke first and most often were consistently the people with the best information or the keenest analysis, then polarization might not be much of a problem. But it is.

THE OBVIOUS TEMPTATION IS to do away with or at least minimize the role that small groups play in shaping policy or making decisions. Better to entrust one reliable person—who at least we know will not become more extreme in his views—with responsibility than trust a group of ten or twelve people who at any moment, it seems, may suddenly decide to run off a cliff. It would be a mistake to succumb to that temptation. First of all, groups can be, as it were, depolarized. In a study that divided people into groups of six while making sure that each group comprised two smaller groups of three who had strongly opposed views, it was found that discussion moved the groups from the extremes and toward each other. That same study found that as groups became less polarized, they also became more accurate when they were tested on matters of fact.

More important, as solid as the evidence demonstrating group polarization is, so too is the evidence demonstrating that nonpolarized groups consistently make better decisions and come up with better answers than most of their members, and surprisingly often the group outperforms even its best member. What makes this surprising is that one would think that in a small group, one or two confused people could skew the group's collective verdict in the wrong direction. (The small group can't, in that sense, rely on errors canceling themselves out.) But there's little evidence of that happening.

One of the more impressive studies of small-group performance was done in 2000 by Princeton economists Alan S. Blinder and John Morgan. Blinder had been vice chairman of the Federal Reserve Board during the mid-1990s, and the experience had made him deeply skeptical of decision making by committee. (Interest-rate changes are set by the Federal Open Market Committee, which consists of twelve members, including the seven members of the Federal Reserve Board and five presidents of regional Federal Reserve banks.) So he and Morgan designed a study that was meant to find out if groups could make intelligent decisions and if they make decisions as a group quickly, since one of the familiar complaints about committees is that they are inefficient.

The study consisted of two experiments that were meant to mimic, crudely, the challenges faced by the Fed. In the first experiment, students were given urns that held equal numbers of blue balls and red balls. They started to draw the balls from the urns, having been told that sometime after the first ten draws, the proportions in the urn would shift, so that 70 percent of the balls would be red and 30 percent blue (or vice versa). The goal was to identify, as soon as possible, which color had become more prevalent. This was roughly analogous to the Fed's job of recognizing when economic conditions have changed and whether a shift in monetary policy is needed. To place a premium on making the right decision quickly, students were penalized for every draw they made after the changeover had happened. The students played the game by themselves first, then played together as a group with free discussion, played as individuals again, and finally once more as a group. (This was to control for the effect of learning.) The group's decisions were both faster and more accurate (the group got the direction right 89 percent of the time, versus 84 percent for individuals), and outperformed even the best individual.

The second experiment demanded more of the students. Essentially, they were asked to play the role of central bankers, and to set interest rates in response to changes in inflation and unemployment. What the experiment was really asking was whether they could detect when the economy had started to slow or was picking up steam, and whether they would move interest rates in the right direction in response. Once again, the group made better decisions than the individuals, who moved interest rates in the wrong direction far more often, and made them as quickly as the individuals. Most strikingly, there was no correlation between the performance of the smartest person in the group and the performance of the group. In other words, the groups were not just piggybacking on really smart individuals. They genuinely were smarter than the smartest people within them. A Bank of England study modeled on Blinder and Morgan's experiment reached identical conclusions: groups could make intelligent decisions quickly, and could do better than their smartest members.

Given what we've already seen, this is not shocking news. But there are two important things about these studies. The first is that group decisions are not inherently inefficient. This suggests that deliberation can be valuable when done well, even if after a certain point its marginal benefits are outweighed by the costs. The second point is probably obvious, although a surprising number of groups ignore it, and that is that there is no point in making small groups part of a leadership structure if you do not give the group a method of aggregating the opinions of its members. If small groups are included in the decision-making process, then they should be allowed to make decisions. If an organization sets up teams and then uses them for purely advisory purposes, it loses the true advantage that a team has: namely, collective wisdom. One of the more frustrating aspects of the *Columbia* story is the fact that the MMT never voted on anything. The different members of the team would report on different aspects of the mission, but their real opinions were never aggregated. This was a mistake, and it would have been a mistake even had the *Columbia* made it home safely.

THE COMPANY: MEET THE NEW BOSS,

SAME AS THE OLD BOSS?

I

Every Tuesday and Saturday in SoHo, a big truck pulls to the curb on the east side of Broadway to have its cargo unloaded. From out of the truck emerge not fresh New Jersey tomatoes or Long Island sweet corn, but rather stacks of dress shirts in soft colors, slim-cut black skirts, and elegant women's jackets that look—from a distance—like they just came off a Milan runway. All the pieces of clothing have two things in common. They come from a million-square-foot warehouse owned by a company called Zara, in the town of La Coruña in the Spanish province of Galicia. And, in all likelihood, three weeks before they were unloaded, they weren't even a glint in their designers' eyes.

Twice-weekly deliveries may be common in the grocery-store business, but in fashion retailing they're unheard of. The curse of the fashion business is the enormous lag time between the initial sketches of that new A-line skirt and its arrival on store floors. That lag time means that instead of reacting quickly to what customers actually want now, retailers have to try to guess what they *will* want in six or nine months. That kind of market forecasting is hard enough if you're trying to sell televisions or DVD players. It's close to impossible if you're trying to sell something as determinedly

ephemeral as fashionable clothing. And so even the most successful clothing companies often end up with piles of unsold inventory
that has to be marked down or shipped off to the outlet store,
which is great for the assiduous bargain hunter but terrible for the
companies.

What Zara has done is scrap this whole inefficient system in
favor of something new. Instead of delivering products only sea-
sonally, Zara has those twice-weekly deliveries at its six hundred
stores around the world. Instead of producing two or three hundred
different products a year, Zara comes out with more than twenty
thousand. It does not overstock, and unsuccessful designs are often whisked off shelves in the space of a week, so the company
doesn't have to discount or slash prices. All of Zara's store managers
are equipped with handheld devices that are linked directly to the
company's design rooms in Spain, so that the managers can make
daily reports on what customers are buying, what they're scorning,
and what they're asking for but not finding. Most important, it
takes the company just ten to fifteen days to go from designing a
dress—which, to be sure, often means knocking off a hot new
look—to selling it. That means if there's buzz about a product, an
affordable version of it is probably in a Zara store. This is the combination of speed, design, and price that made LVMH fashion director Daniel Piette call Zara "possibly the most innovative and
devastating retailer in the world."

Zara is able to act so quickly because the company was built
from the bottom up to be fast and flexible. Like most fashion retailers, Zara gets 90 percent of its raw fabrics from abroad. But unlike
most fashion retailers, which tend to have their products manufactured by subcontractors in Asia or Latin America, Zara turns most of
those fabrics into products all by itself. The company owns fourteen
highly automated Spanish factories, where robots work twenty-four
hours a day stamping, cutting, and dyeing. That gives Zara tremendous control over what it does and doesn't make. Instead of gambling on ten thousand pairs of those new Capri pants, it can make

products in very small lots, which allows it to see how the first few hundred sell before making more. And if a product does look like a hit, the company can crank up production overnight. As for the final stage of the process, when the cut fabrics are assembled into skirts and dresses and suits, Zara entrusts that to a network of three hundred or so small shops in Galicia and northern Portugal. That allows the company to reap the benefits of independent craftsmanship, while still having control over the final product—since the small shops are more Zara's partners than suppliers.

Flexibility is important to Zara because it allows the company to avoid any retailer's true nemesis: piles of stuff that nobody wants. In a perfect business, you would never have anything in a store that you weren't going to sell that very day. In business jargon, you would carry only one day of inventory. Zara isn't there yet, since it carries about a month's worth of inventory. But by fashion industry standards, that's remarkable. The Gap, for instance, carries more than three months of inventory, which is why, when the Gap guesses wrong about what people want, its stores are full of discounted merchandise. Low inventories also mean low prices, since if you sell more of something you generally don't charge as much for it. In other words, Zara can sell its goods cheaply because it sells them more quickly. And the sheer velocity with which Zara's goods move also means that its customers never get bored.

What all this means is that Zara is doing two different things very well. First of all, it's anticipating and adjusting to its customers' ever-changing demands, trying to make sure that no one ever comes to a Zara store and cannot find what she's looking for (or, alternatively, finds too much of what she's not looking for). Another way of putting it is that Zara is trying to *coordinate* its behavior to match that of customers (present and future), in a way not all that different from the way Brian Arthur's computer agents tried to coordinate their actions with all the other would-be El Farol bargoers, or even the way two pedestrians coordinate their movements as they pass by each other on a narrow sidewalk. The pedestrians want to avoid each other, while Zara wants to bump into its customers (or vice versa), but the challenges are similar.

The second thing Zara is doing well is that it's coordinating the actions and decisions of tens of thousands of its employees, getting them to direct their energies and their attention toward the same goal: making and selling clothes that people want to buy. Every day at 10 AM, the door to that Zara store in SoHo opens. Every Tuesday and Saturday, when the truck arrives, someone is waiting there for it. When Zara's designers come up with a new look, the robot cutters immediately go to work. For the company to thrive, all of these actions need to be in tune with each other, so that there's as little wasted time and effort as possible. Companies that do a better job of coordination flourish. Those that don't, struggle.

But there's something worth noting here. Zara is able to coordinate its behavior with that of its customers even though it has no control over them at all. The coordination between them takes place through the market, thanks to price. If Zara offers good enough products at a reasonable enough price, customers will come through its door. For that matter, Zara is able to coordinate its behavior with that of its fabric suppliers even though it has no control over them either. Again, the coordination takes place through the market (albeit with the protection of a contract behind it). Why, then, does Zara need to coordinate the actions of its employees by managing them? Or, to put it differently, why do its employees need Zara to coordinate them? If coordination is possible through the market, what's the point of having large firms that orchestrate the movements of people and products all over the world? Why do corporations even exist?

The fundamental paradox of any corporation is that even though it competes in the marketplace, it uses nonmarket instruments—plans, commands, controls—to accomplish its goals. As the British economist D. H. Robertson evocatively explained it, corporations are "islands of conscious power in this ocean of unconscious co-operation like lumps of butter coagulating in a pail of buttermilk." When Zara wants to design a new dress, for instance, it doesn't put the project up for bid to different outside teams to find out which one will give it the best price. Instead, one of its managers tells its design team to design a new dress. The company trusts its designers to do a good job for their employer, and the designers trust the company not to make them bargain for a job every time a need arises.

Why does Zara do this, instead of simply outsourcing the job of design? After all, most companies outsource tasks like janitorial services and lawn care. Others outsource the actual production of their goods (Nike, for instance, owns no factories). So why stop there? Why not simply outsource it all? Why not make things the way small movies get made? Independent filmmakers don't have full-time employees. Instead, a group of people comes together: someone writes a script, someone agrees to direct, someone else puts up the money, actors and a production crew get chosen, the film is made, a distributor is found, and then the group disassembles, perhaps never to see each other again. Why not do everything this way?

The oldest—and still the best—answer to that question was offered by British economist Ronald Coase in 1937. The problem with the "outsource everything" model, Coase saw, was that setting up and monitoring all those different deals and contracts takes a lot of time and effort. It takes work to find the right people, and to haggle with them over how much you'll pay them. It takes work to ensure that everyone's doing what they promised they would do. And it takes work to make sure, after everything's done, that everyone gets what's coming to them. These are all what Coase called "transaction costs," which include "search and information costs, bargaining and decision costs, policing and enforcement costs." A well-run company reduces these costs. If your e-mail goes on the fritz, it's easier and faster to call the office tech guy instead of some outside company. And it's often smarter for a company to hire full-time employees who are always available to work than it is to go hunting for talented people every time a new project arises. Certainly planning future projects is much easier if you're running a corporation with thousands of employees than if you have to assemble a new team every time you want to launch a product. And it's hard to imagine anyone but a corporation investing $2 billion to build a semiconductor plant that won't start production for three years.

At the same time, keeping things in-house creates its own problems. Sometimes the advantages of outsourcing the work outweigh the ease of doing it yourself. Take this book. I don't work for Little, Brown. Instead, I signed a contract with Little, Brown to create one of the products that it will sell. Theoretically, Little, Brown could have a staff of full-time writers, whom it could pay to produce books. Then it wouldn't have to bother with bidding for books or negotiating with agents (and it would probably be easier to deal with slow writers, too). But the company thinks its chances of publishing interesting books are better if it leaves the door open to lots of different writers, and so it's willing to endure the hassle of having to sign each book on a case-by-case basis. (It's also a hassle for writers, of course, who have to write and sell books on a case-by-case basis. One way publishers and authors try to reduce the hassle, which is to say, reduce transaction costs, is by signing multibook deals.)

Although companies typically don't think of it in this way, what they're really wrestling with when they think about outsourcing are the costs and benefits of collective action. Doing things in-house means, in some sense, cutting themselves off from a host of diverse alternatives, any of which could help them do business better. It means limiting the amount of information they get, because it means limiting the number of information sources they have access to. In exchange, though, they get the benefits of quicker action and no haggling. The general rule, then, is that companies will do things for themselves when it is cheaper and easier than letting someone else do them. But it's also the case that companies will do things for themselves if they are so important that it's not worth the risk of letting someone else do them. For Zara, speed and control are more important than sheer cost. It might actually be cheaper to let some factory in China cut and dye its fabrics. But that would deprive Zara of its most distinctive attribute: its ability to respond quickly and precisely to what consumers want.

II

One place to look at the promise and perils of different ways of co-ordinating a business is, strangely, Hollywood, and in particular Hollywood gangster films. What all gangster films have in common is that they are about a group of men (it's almost always men) who have organized themselves in order to accomplish a task, the ultimate goal of which is to make money. This is, of course, also a perfectly good description of your average business. More important, gangster movies also often do a surprisingly good job of representing the challenges that are created anytime you try to get a group of self-interested people to work together to achieve a common goal. Roughly speaking, there are three different kinds of organizations gangsters rely on in the movies. The first is exemplified by *The Godfather, Part II*. Here, business is run by a top-down hierarchy, much like a traditional corporation. The Corleone family empire is represented, quite explicitly, as a kind of far-flung conglomerate, with Michael Corleone as the CEO who ceaselessly expands the family's operations into new lines of business, including legitimate ones. The organization has a number of virtues: it allows the man at the top to make decisions quickly and to have them carried out decisively. It allows for long-term investments and planning. Because Michael has lieutenants everywhere, he's able to manage distant operations effectively, without having to be present himself. And because the business generates cash steadily, Michael can make large investments without depending on other people for financing.

The downside of the corporate structure, though, is also obvious. Michael has a difficult time getting the information he needs, because it's often not in his lieutenants' interest to disclose all they know. The fact that these lieutenants and foot soldiers work for the Corleones does not keep them from pursuing their own interests, either by skimming or by talking to the family's competitors. And these problems increase as the business gets bigger, because it becomes harder to stay on top of everything. Most important, the top-down nature of the organization means that Michael becomes more and more isolated from points of view other than his own. In a sense, although Michael has hundreds or thousands of men working for him, the organization doesn't just belong to him. It *is* him, which bodes ill for the family in the long run.

A very different model of group organization can be seen in Michael Mann's film *Heat,* in which Robert De Niro plays the head of a small, tight-knit, and highly professional gang of armed robbers. The gang is, in a peculiar sense, much like a successful small business. It has all the advantages that small, coherent groups have: trust, specialization, and mutual awareness of each member's abilities. Because it's so easy for members to monitor each other, people in small groups are less likely to slack off or free ride than people in large organizations are. And since the rewards for the gang's activity are immediate and directly connected to their efforts, there's a powerful incentive for each member to contribute.

But being a small group also limits the gang's possibilities. The members' ambitions are limited by their resources. Because their rewards depend entirely on their own efforts, there is little room for error in what they do. One person's mistake can end up wrecking the entire group. The gang's downfall, in fact, begins when it admits a new, unfamiliar member who does not follow the agreed-upon script and ends up disrupting the group's well-laid plans.

The third model can be found in movies like *The Asphalt Jungle* and *Reservoir Dogs,* where a group of individuals comes together to pull off a single job and then disperses, very much the way an in-dependent film gets made. This model allows people to be hand-picked for their diverse abilities (planning, safecracking, explosives, etc.), so that the group can have exactly what it needs for the job. And the one-off nature of the project insures that everyone on the team has an incentive to perform well.

The problems with this model, though, are precisely those that Ronald Coase had in mind when he talked about transaction costs. It takes a lot of work to put the group together. It's difficult to ensure that people are working in the group's interest and not their own. And when there's a lack of trust between the members of the group (which isn't surprising given that they don't really know each other), considerable energy is wasted trying to deter-mine each other's bona fides. (Of course, jewel thieves face a hur-dle that normal businessmen don't: they can't rely on contracts to make people commit to their responsibilities.)

What the gangster-film theory of business suggests is that no organizational model offers an ideal solution. Once you leave the market behind and attempt to consciously organize individuals toward a common goal, you face inevitable trade-offs. That's one reason why today companies like Zara are effectively trying to blend the three gangster-film models of business into one. Com-panies want to retain the structure and institutional coherence of the traditional corporation. They want tightly knit groups to do much of the work at the day-to-day level. And they want to be able to have access to workers and thinkers (if not safecrackers) from outside the corporation as well.

III

Let's say that corporations exist because they reduce the cost of getting large numbers of people to act in a coordinated fashion to accomplish particular future goals, and because they make the future (at least a company's small part of it) more predictable. What's interesting about that description, though, is everything it leaves out. It says nothing about the way companies deal with their suppliers and customers (who are essential to accomplishing anything but whom the company can't order around), nothing about *how* companies should get their employees to act in a coordinated fashion, and, most interestingly, nothing about how the company decides which goals it should pursue and in what fashion it should pursue them. In other words, the fact that corporations exist doesn't tell us anything about the way they really work.

For much of the twentieth century, though, we knew how companies worked. In fact, we assumed that corporations all, in some sense, had to work in the same way, at least if they wanted to be successful. First, a corporation was vertically integrated, which meant that it had full control over most of its supply chain. Few companies went to the extremes that Henry Ford did in insisting that Ford Motor Company own the iron ore and the sand that went into its cars, but on the whole the assumption was that what a company could do for itself, it should do for itself. Second, a corporation was hierarchical, with many layers of management, each responsible for the one below it. The people at each level of the hierarchy could handle certain problems on their own, but more difficult or complex or consequential problems got handed up the chain to someone more important (and, supposedly, more skilled). And third, a corporation was centralized. This didn't mean that headquarters controlled everything that a company's divisions did. In fact, the company that set the mold for the twentieth-century corporation, General Motors, prided itself on its decentralized structure, since each division—Buick, Chevrolet, Cadillac—was run on a day-to-day basis much like an independent business. But all of the big decisions that shaped GM's strategy or its internal organization were made at GM headquarters. More to the point, perhaps, in the old-model corporation final decision-making power was concentrated in the hands of a very few people, and often in the hands of one person: the CEO.

Paradoxically, even as American companies became more hierarchical, more centralized, and more rigid, they paid increasing lip service to the idea that top-down organizations were oppressive and damaging. In fact, the idea that worker "empowerment" is a key to a healthy company, which became something of a managerial conceit in the 1990s, has been a perennial favorite of management gurus for almost a hundred years. In the second decade of the twentieth century, for instance, a number of major corporations established profit-sharing plans and gave their workers voting rights in the company. In the 1930s, the so-called "human relations movement," led by the sociologist Elton Mayo, purported to have proved that workers were happier and more productive when they felt that their concerns were being listened to by management. (In retrospect, Mayo's studies now seem to prove that the workers were happier and more productive when they were getting paid more by management.) And in the 1950s, which today is thought of as the heyday of the old-line, bureaucratic corporation, companies were positively obsessed with teamwork and committee meetings. William H. Whyte's classic critique of middle-class conformity, *The Organization Man*, was driven, in no small part, by his frustration with the corporate emphasis on the value of groups. For Whyte, companies were entirely too infatuated with the virtues of the people in the middle of the pyramid and not respectful enough of the men at the top. As he put it, "It is not the leaders of industry that are idealized . . . but the lieutenants."

Although they were rhetorically committed to the virtues of collective decision making, most American corporations were not especially interested in turning rhetoric into reality and did not try to do so. Collective decision making was too often confused with the quest for a consensus. This was, in particular, Whyte's bête noire, and justifiably so. You do not need a consensus in order, for instance, to tap into the wisdom of a crowd, and the search for consensus encourages tepid, lowest-common-denominator solutions which offend no one rather than exciting everyone. Instead of fostering the free exchange of conflicting views, consensus-driven groups—especially when the members are familiar with each other—tend to trade in the familiar and squelch provocative debate. If, as the saying goes, a camel is a horse produced by a committee, it was undoubtedly made by a committee looking for consensus.

This "can't we all get along" approach exacerbated the problems created by the seemingly endless layers of management that most corporations acquired in the years after World War II. Paradoxically, in trying to make the decision-making process as inclusive as possible, companies actually made top executives more—not less—insulated from the real opinions of everyone else. Before any decision could be made, it had to make its way through each layer of the management hierarchy. And since at each level the decision was vetted by a committee, the further you got from the front line, the more watered-down the solution became. At GM, for instance, something as relatively straightforward as the design of a new headlight had to be considered in fifteen different meetings, and, bizarrely, the CEO of the company sat in on the last five of those.

What the fifteen meetings suggest is that even those companies that tried to make the decision-making process more "democratic" thought democracy meant endless discussion rather than a wider distribution of decision-making power. They also epitomize the bureaucratic sclerosis that began to take its toll on American companies in the late 1960s and early 1970s. The endless layers of management made people less willing to take responsibility for their own work. Managers thought they could simply sign off on the advice submitted by their subordinates, and then pass the information on to higher-ups. But since the subordinates knew that their boss was ultimately responsible for what information he passed along, they assumed he would make sure everything was as it should be. And because power was not being delegated so much as the illusion of power, there was little incentive for workers lower down the totem pole to show any initiative.

Whatever its flaws, for most of the twentieth century the American corporation had no serious rivals in its ability to mass-produce goods cheaply and efficiently. But even the ability to coordinate the different parts of their organizations had deserted many American companies by the 1970s. It may seem as if corporations don't have to worry about coordination, because they can coordinate by ordering people around. But although authority works better on the factory floor and in corporate headquarters than it does in everyday life, attempting to run an entire company by command and control is a futile task. It's too costly in terms of time; it requires far too much information—information that top executives should not be bothering with; and it saps the initiative of workers and managers. When coordination takes place inside a company without being dictated by top-down leadership, it has the potential to make the company as a whole lighter and more flexible. But that can't happen when power is concentrated at the top of a company or when there are so many layers of management that people have to order others around because otherwise they would have nothing to do. Both were true of American companies in the 1970s. At Ford, for instance, more than fifteen layers of managers separated the chairman from a factory-floor supervisor. At Toyota, there were just five.

The costs on the factory floor were palpable. Consider this story, from Maryann Keller's book *Rude Awakening*, about a GM plant in Van Nuys, California. A supervisor there saw a pair of assembly-line workers who kept failing to install a bracket that held the car's sunshade in place. If the bracket wasn't installed, at the end of the line the car's carpet had to be torn out and the bracket welded into place. "I took them out and said, 'Look, this is what happens when you miss one of those,' " the supervisor told Keller. "The repair guy showed them how he had to rip out all the carpet, and they were shocked. And the woman said, 'You mean to tell me that bracket holds the sunshade?' She'd been doing this job for two years and nobody had ever told her what part she was welding."

Perhaps the deepest problem with the rigidly hierarchical, multilayered corporation was—and is—that it discouraged the free flow of information, in no small part because there were so many bosses, each one a potential stumbling block or future enemy. In their 1982 book *In Search of Excellence,* Thomas J. Peters and Robert H. Waterman reprinted a remarkable chart from an un-named company that showed how many different paths through the bureaucracy a new product idea would have to traverse before it could be accepted. The number was 223. And with so many lay-ers separating the men in the executive suite from workers in the field, it was hard for top executives to know if the picture they had of their own corporation resembled reality.

The only reason to organize thousands of people to work in a company is that together they can be more productive and more in-telligent than they would be apart. But in order to do that, individ-uals need to work as hard to get and act upon good information as they would if they were a small businessman competing in the mar-ketplace. In too many corporations, though, the incentive system was (and is) skewed against dissent and independent analysis. A 1962 study of young executives, for instance, found that the more anxious they were about moving up the job ladder, "the less accu-rately they communicate[d] problem-related information." They were smart to do so. Another study of fifty-two middle managers found that there was a correlation between upward mobility and not telling the boss about things that had gone wrong. The most successful executives tended not to disclose information about fights, budget problems, and so on.

Finally, there was the fundamental problem of a lack of diversity—cognitive and otherwise—among top managers, which was compounded by the fact that most big American companies faced little or no competition from foreign firms or small companies. This helps explain, for instance, Ford's decision in the late 1950s to invest hundreds of millions of dollars in the Edsel, a car for which there was no consumer market. And it explains why remarkably few management or product innovations were pioneered by American companies during the 1970s and 1980s. That was likely the result, in part, of the almost complete insulation of top managers from competition and from outside perspectives. Locked in their cozy executive suites, they simply lost access to the kind of information they needed to make good forecasts of the future and to produce interesting solutions to organizational problems. In the end, they never even saw trouble coming until it was unmistakable. In the early 1970s, Japanese and West German companies began introducing better products faster, and paying more attention to what consumers really wanted, than American companies. The elaborate managerial hierarchies that had been serviceable in the post-World War II era of captive customers and middling competition were ill suited to encouraging the dramatic organizational and product-line changes that were required to compete with the Japanese. For that matter, U.S. corporations had been free of real competition for so long that it took them a while to remember what it entailed. The quintessential American product of the seventies was the Pinto, which Ford introduced in 1971. It was an ugly car with a feeble four-cylinder engine that occasionally blew up when it was hit from behind. Miraculously, Ford actually sold a million Pintos in the seventies, but it was a last hurrah. Over the course of the decade, American corporate profits, market share, and productivity growth went into free fall. By the end of the seventies, Chrysler and Lockheed had to be bailed out by the government and Ford looked as if it might be next. The myth of American corporate excellence had been replaced by the story of a country "managing its way into economic decline."

I V

There is no doubt that American companies responded well to the implosion of the old corporate model in the wake of the 1970s. In the decades since, U.S. firms have reinvented and reengineered themselves, emerging from the 1980s as leaner and more efficient. But the old corporate model and what happened to it are still worth paying attention to because in some deep way the assumptions that underwrote that model—that integration, hierarchy, and the concentration of power in a few hands lead to success—continue to exert a powerful hold on much of American business. While the success of Silicon Valley companies—which, in general, do have more decentralized structures with less emphasis on top-down decision making—made companies anxious to at least appear to be, as they would say, pushing authority down the hierarchy, reality has only rarely matched appearance, even though dramatic improvements in information technology have made the diffusion of information to large numbers of employees feasible and cost-effective.

At the same time, there's not much evidence that the flow of information up the hierarchy has improved much either. To state the obvious, unless people know what the truth is, it's unlikely they'll make the right decisions. This means being honest about performance. It means being honest about what's not happening. It means being honest about expectations. Unfortunately, there's little evidence that this kind of sharing takes place. Chris Argyris, one of the deans of organizational theory, has been studying the subject for forty years, and he argues that what he calls "inauthentic behavior" is actually the norm within most organizations. One of the things that gets in the way of the exchange of real information, Argyris suggests, is a deep-rooted hostility on the part of bosses to opposition from subordinates. This is the real cost of a top-down approach to decision making: it confers the illusion of perfectibility upon the decision makers and encourages everyone else simply to play along. What makes this especially damaging is that, as Argyris suggests, people in an organization already have a natural inclination to avoid conflict and potential trouble. It's remarkable, in fact, that in an autocratic organization good information ever surfaces.

Compounding this problem is the fact that managerial pay is often based not on how one performs but rather on how one performs relative to expectations. Many bonus systems, for instance, offer executives disproportionate rewards only when they surpass a given target. Companies do this in order to push executives and encourage them to meet goals that seem unattainable. But the real effect of these kinds of targets is to encourage people to be deceptive. Consider the experience of the sociologist Donald Roy, who in the early 1950s took a job as a lathe operator in a machine shop. The lathe operators in the shop were paid according to what's called a piece-rate incentive system. In other words, they started out with a rate per piece. Once they hit a certain target, their rate per piece shot up, and once they got over a second hurdle, their rate per piece went up again, and then was capped. The crucial questions for the workers was how high the hurdles would be set. The problem they faced was that if they worked too hard or too fast, the hurdle would be raised, since the company didn't want to reward them for doing just what was reasonable. Not surprisingly, the workers restricted their output and worked more slowly than they might have. Instead of trying to be as productive as possible, they spent their time figuring out how to manipulate the rate per piece so they could make as much money as possible. Roy called his article on the experience "Goldbricking in a Machine Shop."

The exact same phenomenon is at work in the way budget and performance targets get set in corporations. As Harvard Business School professor Michael C. Jensen points out, tell a manager that he or she will get a bonus when targets are realized and two things are sure to happen. First, managers will attempt to set targets that are easily reachable by lowballing their estimates for the year ahead and poor-mouthing their prospects. Second, once the targets are set, they will do everything they can to meet them, including engaging in the kind of accounting gimmickry that boosts this year's results at the expense of the future. (Just look, for instance, at how CEOs behaved in the late 1990s, when faced with the pressure to meet Wall Street's expectations.) The result, Jensen says, is that companies are "paying people to lie." Companies need good information in order to make plans for the future. But too often corporations are organized in such a way that good information is precisely what they are unlikely to get.

In this context, it's useful to compare the way knowledge and effort are organized by the corporation to the way they're organized by markets. Companies tend to pay people based on whether they do what they're expected to do. In a market, people get paid based simply on what they do. After all, your local deli owner doesn't make any more money if his sales at year end beat his own expectations. He just makes as much money as he makes. Ideally, the same would be true inside a company.

Similarly, top-down corporations give people an incentive to hide information and dissemble. In a market, on the other hand, businesses have an incentive to uncover valuable information and act on it (like, say, information about what kind of sneaker kids will be buying this summer or what kind of stereo is the best bargain). And as soon as they do, the information becomes, in some sense, public. That's an essential part of what markets do: encourage people to find new valuable information and then let everyone else know about it. And this, too, is what corporations should be looking for: ways to provide their employees with the incentive to uncover and act on private information.

One tool that, in the 1990s, firms came to rely on increasingly to solve the problem of aligning the individual's interests with the corporation was, of course, stock options, which theoretically give workers an investment in the company's economic well-being. The benefits of stock-option grants that go to a large number of employees (as opposed to being confined to a small number of top executives) appear to be real. The most important study of such grants, by economists Joseph Blasi and Eric Kruse, found that they boost corporate productivity, profits, and stock-market returns. This is frankly a little perplexing, since for the vast majority of workers, the impact of their labor—no matter how hard they work—on their company's overall performance is negligibly small. But even small option grants seem to instill a sense of ownership, and we know that owners are, in general, more likely to take good care of their property than renters are. Blasi and Kruse stress, though, that only companies which distribute options to most of their workers are likely to see any benefits. Most U.S. corporations still distribute the vast amount of their stock options to a small coterie of executives.

More important than stock options, though, would be the elimination of rigid managerial hierarchies and the wider distribution of real decision-making power. As Blasi and Kruse write, "employee participation alone isn't enough. The tangible rewards of employee ownership or some form of sharing the fruits of ownership must go hand in hand with work practices that give workers greater decision-making." It's telling, after all, that the two most-respected CEOs of the twentieth century—Alfred Sloan of General Motors and Jack Welch of General Electric—were both ardent advocates of a more collective approach to management. While Sloan had a blind spot when it came to assembly-line workers, his decision-making style was resolutely non-autocratic, and he refused to allow the merit of an idea to be determined by the status of the person advocating it. As he put it, "Our decentralized organization and our tradition of selling ideas, rather than simply giving orders, impose the need upon all levels of management to make a good case for what they propose. The manager who would like to operate on a hunch will usually find it hard to sell his ideas to others on this basis. But, in general, whatever sacrifice might be entailed in ruling out a possibly brilliant hunch is compensated for by the better-than-average results which can be expected from a policy that can be strongly defended against well-informed and sympathetic criticism."

Similarly, Welch's most important initiative as CEO of General Electric was his transformation of the company into what he called a "boundaryless corporation." Harking back to the questions raised by Ronald Coase, Welch tried to make the boundaries between GE and outside markets more permeable. He broke down boundaries between GE's different divisions, arguing that a more interdisciplinary approach to problems fostered diversity. He sharply reduced the layers of management separating the people at the top from the rest of the company. And by creating what were known as "Work-Out" sessions, where managers were subjected to often stinging public criticism from those they managed, he tried to make the boundaries between bosses and subordinates less rigid. Welch hardly succeeded in all he tried, and when it came to certain decisions, like whether or not to spend tens of billions of dollars on acquisitions, he seemed to disregard opposing views in favor of his own unwavering convictions. But boundarylessness was one of the things that allowed GE, unlike most old-line American industrial corporations, to flourish.

V

So what would the wider distribution of real decision-making power" look like? To begin with, decisions about local problems should be made, as much as possible, by people close to the problem. Friedrich Hayek, as we've seen, emphasized that tacit knowledge—knowledge that emerged only from experience—was crucial to the efficiency of markets. It is just as important to the efficiency of organizations. Instead of assuming that all problems need to be filtered up the hierarchy and every solution filtered back down again, companies should start with the assumption that, just as in the marketplace, people with local knowledge are often best positioned to come up with a workable and efficient solution. The virtues of specialization and local knowledge often outweigh managerial expertise in decision making.

Although many companies talk a good game when it comes to pushing authority away from the top, the truth is that genuine employee involvement remains an unusual phenomenon. (Blasi and Kruse, for instance, estimate that fewer than 2 percent of American companies make real use of what they call "high performance work systems.") Yet the evidence in favor of decentralization is overwhelming, including not just much of the work I've discussed in this book, but practical evidence from corporations around the world. In their recent comprehensive study of what makes companies work, Nitin Nohria, William Joyce, and Bruce Roberson found that in the best companies, "Employees and managers were empowered to make many more independent decisions, and urged to seek out ways to improve company operations, including their own."

The virtues of decentralization are twofold. On the one hand, the more responsibility people have for their own environments, the more engaged they will be. In one classic study, two groups of people were put in rooms to work on puzzles and do proofreading while loud, random noises recurred in the background. One group was left alone, while the other was given a button they could press to turn off the sound. The second group solved five times as many puzzles and made many fewer proofreading errors. You can probably guess that no member of the group ever pressed the button. Knowing it was there was all that mattered. Similar results from both experimental and empirical studies show that allowing people to make decisions about their own working conditions often makes a material difference in how they perform.

The second thing decentralization makes easier is coordination. Instead of having to make constant resort to orders and threats, companies can rely on workers to find new, more efficient ways of getting things done. That reduces the need for supervision, cuts transaction costs, and allows managers to concentrate on other things. The supreme example of this kind of approach is the Toyota Production System, Toyota's legendarily efficient system for making cars. At the core of TPS is the idea that frontline workers should be trained to have a wide range of skills and that they have to understand how the production process works from the bottom up if they are to take best advantage of it. At the same time, Toyota has eliminated the classic assembly line, in which each worker was isolated from those around him and, often, worked on a single piece of a vehicle, and substituted for it teams of workers who are effectively put in charge of their own production process. The familiar symbol of this is the fact that any worker can pull a cord to stop the production line if he sees something that needs to be fixed. The cord is rarely pulled. As with the button, its mere existence is enough.

One critique of decentralization is that even if workers or frontline managers are given more control over their immediate environments, the real power will continue to reside in the hands of top management. On this account, the fact that workers work harder when they're given some say in their working conditions is not interesting but rather depressing, since it means workers can be duped by a façade. In his recent book, *False Prophets,* for instance, the business theorist James Hoopes suggests that advocates of the more democratic, bottom-up corporation are either fooling themselves or else providing a useful cover story for executives who, when push comes to shove, have the final say. Top-down

power is built into the very DNA of the corporation, Hoopes argues, and there's no point in trying to eliminate it.

Perhaps. Certainly when it comes to questions like who will
be fired, there's very little delegation of decision making. But if we
set that admittedly important decision aside, the conclusion that a
corporation is by nature a hierarchical, top-down animal is simplis-
tic. Any corporation, like any organization, has to solve different
kinds of problems. And coordination and cooperation problems, as
we've seen throughout this book, are surprisingly susceptible to decentralized solutions. More important, perhaps, is that in many
cases the relevant knowledge to deal with a problem is in the heads
of the workers dealing with it, not their boss's. They should have
the authority to solve it.

There is a catch in all this, though. Decentralized markets
work exceptionally well because the people and companies in those
markets are getting constant feedback from customers. Companies
that aren't doing a good job or that are spending too much learn to
adjust or else they go out of business. In a corporation, however,
the feedback from the market is indirect. Different divisions can
see how they're doing, but individual workers are not directly rewarded (or punished) for their performance. And although corporate budgets should theoretically echo the market's verdict on
corporate divisions, in practice the process is often politicized.
Given that, divisions have an incentive to look for more resources
from the corporation than they deserve, even if the company as a
whole is hurt. The classic example of this was Enron, in which
each division was run as a separate island, and each had its own
separate cadre of top executives. Even more strangely, each division
was allowed to build or buy its own information-technology system,
which meant that many of the divisions could not communicate
with each other, and that even when they could, Enron was stuck
paying millions of dollars for redundant technology.

The important thing for employees to keep in mind, then, is
that they are working for the company, not for their division.

Again, Enron took exactly the opposite tack, emphasizing competition between divisions and encouraging people to steal talent, resources, and even equipment from their supposed corporate comrades. This was reminiscent of the bad old days at companies like GM, where the rivalries between different departments were often stronger than those between the companies and their outside competitors. The chairman of GM once described the way his company designed and built new cars this way: "Guys in [design] would draw up a body and send the blueprint over and tell the guy, 'Okay, you build it if you can, you SOB.' And the guy at [assembly] would say, 'Well, Jesus, there's no damn way you can stamp metal like that and there's no way we can weld this stuff together.' "

The beneficial effects of competition are undeniable, but serious internal rivalries defeat the purpose of having a company with a formal organization in the first place, by diminishing economies of scale and actually increasing the costs of monitoring people's behavior. You should be able to trust your fellow workers more than you trust workers at other firms. But at a company like Enron, you couldn't. And because the competition is, in any case, artificial—since people are competing for internal resources, not in a real market—the supposed gains in efficiency are usually an illusion. As is the case with today's American intelligence community, decentralization only works if everyone is playing on the same team.

EVEN IF, IN PRACTICE, many companies are still more like the old Ford Motor Company than they are like Toyota or the steelmaker Nucor (where there are only four layers of management—foremen, department heads, plant managers, and president), most executives at least recognize how decentralizing responsibility and authority can meaningfully change the way companies are run on a day-to-day basis. That's become more true as the kind of work most Americans do has changed. On an old-fashioned assembly line, it's possible that top-down coordination was the best solution (although Toyota's transformation of auto production suggests otherwise). But in service businesses or companies whose value depends on intellectual labor, treating workers as cogs will not work (which isn't to say that companies won't try). The efficiency expert Frederick Winslow Taylor, in the early 1900s, described the good worker as someone whose job was to do "just what he is told to do, and no back talk. When the [foreman] tells you to walk, you walk; when he tells you to sit down, you sit down." This approach would fail today.

Yet even as companies at least acknowledge the potential benefits of decentralization, what's notably missing is any sense that bottom-up methods of the kind we've seen in this book might be useful in transforming the way companies solve cognition problems, too. These are the problems that define corporate strategy and tactics. They include everything from deciding among potential new products to building new factories to forecasting demand to setting prices to contemplating mergers. Today, in most corporations, the answers to these problems are ultimately decided by one man: the CEO. Yet they are the problems that, as this book has suggested, are probably most amenable to collective decision making, even if the collective is a relatively small group.

One of the deep paradoxes of the 1990s, in fact, was that even as companies paid greater attention to the virtues of decentralization and the importance of bottom-up mechanisms, they also treated their CEOs as superheroes. Of course, it wasn't just companies. It was investors, the press, and even the general public. In the 1940s, the average American would not have known who Alfred P. Sloan was. In the 1990s, the average American certainly knew who Jack Welch was. This trend dates back to the 1980s, with the transformation of Chrysler CEO Lee Iacocca into the symbol of resurgent American capitalism. But it accelerated during the 1990s, when even the most ordinary-seeming personalities were suddenly, after a few good years, christened visionaries. As Harvard

Business School professor Rakesh Khurana wrote, companies expected their CEOs to be "corporate saviors."

The problem with this was not just the hype, or the massive salary packages that CEOs of all stripes were able to pull down during the decade. The problem was that people actually believed the hype, taking it for granted that putting the right individual at the top was the key to corporate success. This idea found its expression in the familiar refrain that a successful CEO such as Cisco's John Chambers had created "$300 billion in shareholder value," as if he had single-handedly not just given Cisco its domination of an entire technology sector but also made investors inflate Cisco's stock price. Of course, the latter assumption was not entirely unjustified. One of the more remarkable surveys done in the 1990s, a Burson Marsteller poll, found that 95 percent of investors said that they would buy a stock based on what they thought of the company's CEO.

Oddly, though, even as things had never been better for CEOs, there was also a sense in which things had never been worse. CEO job tenure in the 1990s was shorter than it had ever been, as chief executives who failed to improve corporate bottom lines or to deliver on promises found themselves quickly removed from office. All of them, of course, enjoyed soft landings with their golden parachutes, but the fact that CEOs were treated as both superheroes and abject failures was telling. CEOs were shown the door with undue haste for the same reason that they were lavished with such attention: because they were expected to be miracle workers.

What's perplexing about this faith is how little evidence there is that single individuals can consistently make superior forecasts or strategic decisions in the face of genuine uncertainty. And although there is an ongoing debate about how important CEOs are at all—some academics suggest that they have, at best, a minor impact on corporate performance—even those who argue that CEOs do make a difference are careful to say that the difference can be

either positive or negative. Jeff Skilling certainly had a major impact on Enron, but one would be hard-pressed to find many people who think it was a good decision to hire him.

Evaluating CEO performance is difficult, because it's hard to
look at an executive outside the context of his company, and because the decisions that executives make rarely have clean, mea-
surable outcomes. But the data we do have does not exactly inspire.
Something like 80 percent of all new products introduced in a
given year—products that CEOs presumably have signed off on—
do not survive their first twelve months. Corporate profit margins
did not increase over the course of the 1990s, even as executive
compensation was soaring. And, tellingly, roughly two-thirds of all
mergers end up destroying shareholder value, meaning that the acquiring company would have been better off never making the deal.
Mergers involve a yes/no decision. They are, as a rule, decided on
and initiated by the CEO (and rubber-stamped by the board of directors). They have a relatively clear outcome. And most of the
time, making the deal is the wrong decision. This suggests that,
at the very least, CEOs are not in general extraordinary decision
makers.

At any moment, of course, there are always CEOs with exceptional track records, executives who just seem better able to
outthink their competitors, anticipate their customer market, and
motivate their employees. But the business landscape of the last
decade is littered with CEOs who went from being acclaimed as
geniuses to being dismissed as fools because of strategic mistakes.
Gary Wendt, for instance, was regarded as the smartest non-CEO
in the country when he ran GE Capital under Jack Welch. His
mind was "as focused as a laser beam," one journal wrote of him in
the early 1990s, and he was seen as GE's secret weapon because of
the immense amounts of cash that his division generated. When
Wendt was hired to take over troubled finance company Conseco
in 2000, he was given $45 million upon signing and the chance to
earn a $50 million bonus. Conseco's stock price tripled during his

first year in power as investors waited for him to work his magic. They were still waiting two years later, when Wendt abruptly resigned. Conseco went bankrupt, and the company's stock was trading for pennies. Similar stories could be told about the executives who tried to run Kodak, Xerox, AT&T, Lucent, and a host of others. And that's not to mention the highest-profile flame-outs, like WorldCom's Bernard Ebbers, who turned a small phone company into a global telecommunications giant and then nearly as quickly turned it into a bankrupt firm best known for having a horde of its top executives indicted for cooking the books.

The point is not that these executives were fools. In fact, the point is just the opposite. These people didn't go from being brilliant to being stupid overnight. They were as smart and skilled at the end as they were at the beginning. It's just that they were never skilled enough to get the right answers most of the time, probably because almost no one is. It's natural for us to look at successful people and assume that their success is due to some innate quality they have, rather than to think that it might be the result of circumstance or chance. This is sometimes a reasonable assumption to make. But in the case of corporate performance, it's dangerous. As business professor Sydney Finkelstein, author of a fascinating study of corporate failure, wrote: "CEOs should come with the same disclaimer as mutual funds: *Past success is no guarantee of future success.*"

There are a couple of reasons for this. First, as the economist Armen Alchian pointed out in 1950, in an economy like ours, in which there are an enormous number of people and companies striving to get ahead, success is not necessarily an indicator of skill or foresight, but may be, as he says, "the result of fortuitous circumstances." Or, to put it more bluntly, success may be the result of luck. Alchian offers this metaphor. Imagine that thousands of travelers set out from Chicago, choosing their destinations and routes completely at random. Assume also that only one road has a gas station on it. If you look at that situation, you know that one person will make it out of Chicago. But it would be strange to say that this person knew more than all the other travelers. He just happened to be on the right road. Now, Alchian was not saying that most successful businessmen are lucky, nor was he saying that skill doesn't matter. But he was saying that it is hard to know why a company has ended up doing well.

Alchian was also saying that companies often thrive because they have the right skills for a given situation. Henry Ford, for instance, was unquestionably exceptional at understanding how a factory worked and even at understanding how men worked. But his skills would have been relatively useless fifty years earlier or sixty years later. Ford earned his success, but he was also in the right place at the right time. In fact, by the 1930s, it was no longer his time. After building Ford into the most powerful manufacturing company in the world, he presided over its eclipse by GM. As we saw in the chapter on diversity, the idea that intelligence is fungible—that it is equally effective in every context—is difficult to resist, but it tends to lead us astry. Finkelstein wrote of the debacles he studied that two issues recurred in them: "The remarkable tendency for CEOs and executives of new ventures to believe that they are absolutely right, and the tendency to overestimate the quality of managerial talent by relying on track record, especially in situations that differ markedly from the present new venture."

NO DECISION-MAKING SYSTEM is going to guarantee corporate success. The strategic decisions that corporations have to make are of mind-numbing complexity. But we know that the more power you give a single individual in the face of complexity and uncertainty, the more likely it is that bad decisions will get made. As a result, there are good reasons for companies to try to think past hierarchy as a solution to cognition problems. In practice, what would this mean? The flow of information within the organization shouldn't be dictated by management charts. Specifically, companies can use methods of aggregating collective wisdom—like, most obviously, internal decision markets—when trying to come up with reasonable forecasts of the future and even, potentially, when trying to evaluate the probability of possible strategies. Despite the evidence from experimental economics and places such as the IEM, companies have been strangely hesitant to use internal markets. But the few examples that we have suggest that they could be very useful. In the late 1990s, for instance, Hewlett-Packard experimented with artificial markets—set up by the economists Charles R. Plott and Kay-Yut Chen—to forecast printer sales. (Essentially, Hewlett-Packard employees, who were drawn from different parts of the company to ensure the diversity of the market, bought and sold shares depending on what they thought sales in the next month or the next quarter would be.) The number of people participating was small—between twenty and thirty—and each market ran for only a week, with people trading at lunch and in the evening. But over the course of three years the market's results outperformed the company's 75 percent of the time.

Even more impressive was an experiment performed recently at Innocentive, a spinoff of Eli Lilly, which set up an experimental market to test whether its employees could distinguish between drug candidates that were likely be approved by the FDA and those that were likely to be rejected. Investing in potential drugs is among the most important decisions a pharmaceutical company can make, because its profits depend on maximizing the number of successful drugs and minimizing the number of unsuccessful drugs it develops. A reliable method of predicting in advance which drug candidates were likely to win FDA approval would therefore be tremendously valuable. Innocentive set up the experiment by devising realistic profiles and experimental data for six different drugs, three of which it knew would be approved and three it knew would be rejected. When trading opened on these drugs, the market—made up of a diverse mix of employees—quickly identified the winners, sending their prices soaring, while the losers' prices sank.

Decision markets are well suited to companies because they circumvent the problems that obstruct the flow of information at too many firms: political infighting, sycophancy, and a confusion of status with knowledge. The anonymity of the markets and the fact that they yield a relatively clear solution, while giving individuals an unmistakable incentive to uncover and act on good information, means that their potential value is genuinely hard to overestimate.

Major corporate decisions should be informed by decision markets, not made by them. But when the decisions *are* made, it makes little sense, given everything we know about the virtues of collective decision making and about the importance of diversity, to concentrate power in the hands of one person. In fact, the more important the decision, the more important it is that it not be left in the hands of a single person. In theory, all corporations recognize this, since the final say on major decisions is supposed to belong to the board of directors, not to the CEO. But in practice, boards defer. The assumption that authority ultimately needs to rest in the hands of an individual is a difficult one to overcome. Alph Bingham, the chairman of Innocentive, recently put it this way, "We would think it was very strange to have a system in which the CEOs of Goldman Sachs, Morgan Stanley, and Merrill Lynch got up every morning and decided for everyone what companies' stock prices should be. We assume that the market will do a better job of determining value than a few people, no matter how smart, could. But we don't find it at all strange that every morning drug company CEOs get up and say, 'We'll keep investing in this drug and we'll kill that one.' "

The best CEOs, of course, recognize the limits of their own knowledge and of individual decision making. That's why important decisions at GM, in the days when it was the most successful corporation in the world, were made by what Alfred Sloan called "group management." And it's why legendary business thinker Peter Drucker has said, "The smart CEOs methodically build a management team around them." The lesson of Richard Larrick and

Jack Soll's work applies to business as much as it does to other fields: chasing *the* expert is a mistake. The Federal Reserve's decisions, after all, aren't made by Alan Greenspan. They're made by the board as a whole. In the face of uncertainty, the collective judgment of a group of executives will trump that of even the smartest executive. Think about John Craven's work in finding the *Scorpion*. A relatively small group of diversely informed individuals making guesses about the likelihood of uncertain events produced, when their judgments had been aggregated, an essentially perfect decision. What more could a company want?

11.

MARKETS: BEAUTY CONTESTS,

BOWLING ALLEYS, AND STOCK PRICES

I

In 1995, the finance ministry of Malaysia suggested that a certain group of troublemakers needed to be punished for their sins. Mandatory caning, the ministry said, would be the right punishment. And who were the malefactors who were threatened with the rap of rattan? Not drug dealers or corrupt executives or even chewers of bubblegum. Instead, they were short sellers.

Most investors go *long* on stocks, meaning that they buy a stock hoping that its price will rise. A short seller goes *short*. He borrows a stock and sells it, hoping that its price will fall, so he can buy it back at a lower price and pocket the difference. (If I sell 1,000 shares of GE short at $30 a share, I get $30,000 from the sale. If GE's price falls to $25, I buy the stock back for $25,000, return the shares to their original owner, and clear a $5,000 profit.) This seems innocent enough. But it means that short sellers are betting against companies' stock prices, which in turn means, in the minds of many, that they are trying to profit from the misfortune of others. If you go long as an investor, you're making an optimistic bet. If you go short, you're predicting that bad things will happen. And, as a rule, doomsayers make people uneasy. As a result, short sellers of all kinds (you can sell just about any asset short, ranging from currencies to wheat to gold) have historically been regarded with great suspicion. While the Malaysian minister's suggestion that short sellers should be physically thrashed may have been novel, the hostility that provoked the suggestion was not. In fact, short sellers have been the target of investor and government anger since at least the seventeenth century. Napoleon deemed the short seller "an enemy of the state." Short selling was illegal in New York State in the early 1800s, while England banned it outright in 1733 and did not make it legal again until the middle of the nineteenth century (though all indications are that the ban was quietly circumvented).

The noisiest backlash against short selling came, perhaps predictably, in the wake of the Great Crash of 1929, when short sellers were made national scapegoats for the country's economic woes. Shorting was denounced on the Senate floor as one of "the great commercial evils of the day" and "a major cause of prolonging the depression." A year after the crash, the New York Stock Exchange was discouraging investors from lending their shares (if the shorts can't borrow, they can't sell short) and the "anti-shorting climate was hysterical," according to a paper by economists Charles M. Jones and Owen A. Lamont. President Hoover voiced concern about the possible damage done by the short sellers. Even J. Edgar Hoover got in the act, saying he would take a look at whether they were conspiring to hold down prices.

Congress, too, weighed in, holding hearings into short sellers' alleged nefarious activities. But the congressmen came away empty-handed, since it became clear that most of the real villains of the crash had been on the long side, inflating stock prices with hyped-up rumors and stock-buying pools and then getting out before the bubble burst. Nonetheless, the skepticism about short selling did not abate, and soon after, federal regulations were put in place that made short selling more difficult, including a rule that banned mutual funds from selling stocks short (a rule that stayed in place until 1997). In the decades that followed, many things about investing in America changed, but the hatred of short sellers was not one of them. In the popular imagination even today, short sellers are conniving sharpies, spreading false rumors and victimizing innocent companies with what Dennis Hastert, before he became Speaker of the House, called "blatant thuggery." Although short sellers have to abide by the exact same SEC regulations about touting stocks or deceiving investors that other money managers do, people remain convinced that short sellers have the ability to manipulate stock prices at will.

Listening to the short sellers' critics, one imagines a cabal of sinister geniuses spread out across the world, controlling huge pools of capital that they use to demolish companies when the whim strikes them. But in fact you can count on two hands the number of full-time short sellers in America, and combined they control less than $20 billion in capital, which is a drop in the ocean in a stock market worth $14 trillion. (Hedge funds, which control much more capital, also sell stocks short, but they don't do so exclusively or systematically.) The stock market, on the whole, is a market made up of people who think stock prices are going to go up.

That isn't just because of the regulations on short selling. Even without the regulations, most investors—and this includes most professional money managers—find shorting stocks unappealing. In part that's because shorting stocks is riskier than buying them, since on average the stock market has risen steadily over time. Also, when you short a stock, your potential losses are unlimited, because the stock could just keep going up. And then there's the emotional dimension.

"I used to think that it should be as easy to go short as it is to go long," Jim Chanos, head of the short fund Kynikos, said. Chanos was among the first to see that Enron was a house of cards. "After all, the two things seem to require the same skill set. In both cases, you're doing the same thing: evaluating whether a company's stock price reflects its fundamental value. But now I think that they aren't the same at all. Very few human beings perform consistently well in an environment of negative reinforcement, and if you're a short, negative reinforcement is what you get all the time. When we come in every day, we know that Wall Street and the news and ten thousand public-relations departments are going to be telling us that we're idiots, and we know that we're going to see the market acting as if black is white. You don't have that steady drum beat of support behind you that you have if you're buying stocks. You have a steady drum beat on your head." Given this, it's not surprising that in a typical year, a mere 2 percent of the shares on the New York Stock Exchange are shorted. Between the SEC rules, the added risk, the challenge of bucking an entire industry devoted to making stocks go up, and the added fillip of being labeled un-American, it's almost surprising that anyone shorts at all.

This may not seem so terrible, since rising stock prices seem, intuitively, like a good thing. But of course rising stock prices are *not*, in and of themselves, a good thing. If Enron's stock price had never gone up in the late 1990s—allowing it to raise huge amounts of capital that got poured down sinkholes and allowing its executives to walk away with hundreds of millions of dollars that investors could have used to, say, pay for their kids' college educations—just about everyone would have been better off. The measure of the stock market's success is not whether stock prices are rising. It's whether stock prices are right. And it's harder for the market to get prices right when there is so little money on the short side.

That's not because short sellers are exceptionally brilliant investors, or because their skepticism about companies' prospects is always justified. It's true that short sellers like Chanos have an impressive record of uncovering corporate malfeasance and corruption, and of recognizing when stock prices reflect fantasy rather than substance. But we don't want the market to get only the prices of corrupt companies right. We want it to get all the prices right. And so the real value of short selling is simpler. We know that the crowds that make the best collective judgments are crowds where there's a wide range of opinions and diverse sources of information, where people's biases can cancel themselves out, rather than reinforcing each other. If a company's stock price, as we've seen, represents a weighted average of investors' judgments, it's more likely to be accurate if those investors aren't all cut from the same cloth. Earlier, I wrote that markets, because of their size and depth, are prima facie diverse. But the unwillingness of the vast majority of investors to sell stocks short means that, in the stock market at least, this is not quite true. (In markets for many other kinds of financial assets, short selling is, while not loved, understood to be necessary and valuable.)

The dearth of short sellers doesn't mean that the market's judgment is always flawed. For instance, if the point spread for an NFL game was set by allowing people to bet on just one of the two teams, the spread wouldn't necessarily be wrong. Bettors would still only make money if their forecasts were accurate. But the chances that the spread was wrong would be greater than if people were allowed to bet on both teams, because there'd be a greater chance that those who were betting would have similar biases, and therefore would make similar mistakes. And when bettors *were* wrong, they would be really wrong. The same is true of the stock market. Limiting short selling increases the chance that prices will be off, but what it really increases is the chance that if the price of a stock gets out of whack, it will get really out of whack. Internet stocks, for instance, were almost impossible to short, and that may have something to do with why their prices went into orbit. Short selling isn't one of the "great commercial evils of the day." The lack of short selling is.

I I

Chanos's assertion that one reason why there isn't more short selling is that most people are not psychologically built to endure constant scorn struck me, when I first heard it, as correct. And most people would probably find the idea unexceptionable that emotion or psychology might affect the way individuals invest. But to economists it is very exceptionable, and over the years some of the most important thinkers in the field have taken exception to it. Traditionally economists worked from the assumption that people were fundamentally rational in their economic lives. To be sure, most economists knew that consumers did not conform perfectly to an ideal picture of rationality. But they assumed that, on the whole, people acted *as if* they were rational. And, in any case, without a clear sense of just how people deviated from rationality, it was difficult to say anything rigorous or distinctive about the way markets worked. Of late, this has all changed. Economists have begun to devote enormous amounts of attention and energy to understanding the psychology and the behavior of investors and consumers, and have uncovered a number of ways in which significant groups of people deviate quite unmistakably from rationality.

For instance, investors sometimes herd, preferring the safety of the company of others to make independent decisions. They give too much credence to recent and high-profile news while underestimating the importance of longer-lasting trends or less dramatic events, in the same way that people worry about being killed in a plane crash while not paying attention to their high cholesterol. Investors get fooled by randomness, believing that money managers who have had a few good quarters have figured out the trick of beating the market. They find losses more painful—by some accounts, twice as painful—as they find gains pleasurable, and so they hold on to losing stocks longer than they should, believing that as long as they haven't sold the stock, then they haven't suffered any losses. And, above all, investors are overconfident, which, among other things, means that individuals trade more than they should and end up costing themselves money as a result. One classic study by Brad M. Barber and Terrance Odean looked at all the stocks that sixty-six thousand individual investors bought and sold between 1991 and 1996. The average investor turned over 75 percent of his portfolio every year, which is far more than most economists would recommend, but the most aggressive traders turned over an incredible 250 percent of their portfolios every year. These traders paid the price for their conviction that they could beat the market. Between 1991 and 1996, the market gave investors an annual return of 17.9 percent. The active investors earned just 11.4 percent, and even the average investor lost money by trading (the average return was 16.4 percent). In general, people would have done better had they just sat on their hands.

Of course, what's true of your average joe may not be true of someone who manages money for a living, and one argument often made against behavioral finance is that the more experienced or professional an investor is, the more rational his behavior will be. Yet, there's plenty of evidence that professional investors suffer from many of the same flaws as the rest of us. They herd, they're overconfident, they underestimate the impact of randomness, and they explain good results as the product of skill and bad results as the product of bad luck. And since the vast majority of money managers do worse than the market as a whole, it's a little hard to see them as paragons of rationality.

What does it mean that the average investor is not the rational man of economics textbooks? For many behavioral economists, it means that the market is deeply flawed in its judgments, which we should assume are always out of whack in one way or another. But that conclusion doesn't follow from the evidence. If investors, as individuals, are irrational, it's still possible that when you aggregate all their choices, the collective outcome will be rational and smart. As we've seen throughout this book, what's true of the individual is not necessarily true of the group.

Take overconfidence. There's no doubt it explains why there's so much trading, and no doubt that it hurts individual traders. But what we want to know is whether it systematically skews the market (or the price of particular stocks) in one direction. There's no reason to believe that it does, because the fact that investors are overconfident tells us nothing about *what* opinion they're overconfident about. I can be overconfident that the stock I just bought is going to go up, or I can be overconfident that the stock I just sold short is going to go down. But my feeling of certainty will not have a systematic effect on market prices because there's no reason to think that overconfidence is somehow correlated with a particular attitude toward stocks. If it was—if, say, overconfident people all hated technology stocks—then its effect on prices would be severe. But the evidence for such a connection is still missing. The same is true of our overvaluation of recent news. Even if investors overvalue recent news about a company, there's no reason to think they will all overvalue it in the same way, because any piece of information will mean different things to different investors.

The point is that only those behavioral quirks that create systematic biases in opinion—that is, in the way investors value particular stocks, or the way they evaluate investing as a whole—do real damage to the market. Vernon Smith's work, after all, shows that investors do not need to be rational, and markets do not need to be perfect, for markets still to be excellent at problem solving. Or, to put it differently, individual irrationality can add up to collective rationality. The economists Karim Jamal and Shyam Sunder have run an experiment with robot traders that demonstrates this. One of the tendencies that behavioral economists have uncovered is the way people rely on "anchors" when they make decisions. Anchors are essentially arbitrary numbers—like, say, the current price of a stock—that people nonetheless seize on and allow to affect the way they make choices. For instance, instead of simply studying a company and deciding what the appropriate price for the company's stock should be given its future prospects, investors are likely to be unduly influenced, to one degree or another, by the stock's current price. To test the impact of this influence, Sunder and Jamal equipped one group of their robot investors with what they call a straight anchor-and-adjust strategy. In other words, the investors start in a particular place and instead of simply considering each new piece of information on its own, they always refer it back to where the stock was when they bought it. They adjust in response to new information, but never completely freely, the way economic theory predicts they should. But, in the end, it doesn't make a difference. The buying and selling of the robot traders eventually converges to very near the optimal price. These traders are actively irrational and the market still gets things right.

Can we say, then, that behavioral quirks are just anomalies, and that they're irrelevant to the way markets work? Hardly. There are stretches of time, as we'll see shortly, when markets are indisputably ruled by emotion and prices are systematically wrong. And the bias against short selling, which appears to have an emotional dimension, clearly matters. As long as the deviances from "rationality" are random, the errors will cancel themselves out and the group will still produce the right answer. When the errors are not random but systematic, then markets do a much poorer job of finding a good solution. One example of this is Americans' tendency to undersave. Economic theory suggests that people's consumption should be relatively stable over the course of their adult lives. After all, each moment you're alive is presumably as valuable as any other, so why should you enjoy yourself less (by spending less) when you're older? In order to do this, though, people need to save significant portions of their income when they're working. They need to restrain their present consumption in the interest of their future consumption.

Most Americans don't. In fact, consumption drops dramatically when people retire, and senior citizens get by on considerably less than they did when they were working. Oddly, this isn't because people don't want to save. In fact, if you ask people about what they ought to do they'll express a preference for saving. But when it comes to actually doing it, Americans are college students (and writers) at heart: they procrastinate. In economic terms, they value the present so much more than the future that saving seems to make little sense.

The paradox is that although Americans aren't willing to make sacrifices in the present to improve their future, they say they're willing to make sacrifices in the future to improve their long-run prospects. In other words, although they're not willing to save any part of their income today, they're willing to save significant parts of their income tomorrow. The problem is that people turn out not to be that good at estimating what their preferences in the future will be. This may not be that surprising: we change, circumstances change, why should we imagine that we know what we will want. But one consequence of that is that the plans we make today in anticipation of how we will act tomorrow may not work. Specifically, if we say we will not worry about saving today because tomorrow we will finally get around to saving, it will not be surprising if when tomorrow rolls around we find ourselves still spending.

In this case, individual irrationality provokes collective irrationality—if we can assume that it's irrational to have a bunch of people who will not have enough money to live comfortably in retirement. All is not lost, however. People do want to save. And the evidence suggests that they do not need a massive push in order to do so. What they do need, you might say, is a way to make saving easier and spending harder. One way of doing this is to make enrollment in retirement plans automatic, rather than asking people to sign up for them. It turns out that if people have to take action to opt *out* of a retirement plan rather than having to take action to opt *in*, they are significantly more likely to stay in the plan and therefore significantly more likely to save. Inertia is a powerful tool. Similarly, if people are offered the chance to set aside part of their future income, they're far more likely to do so than they are to set aside current income. So, the economists Richard H. Thaler and Shlomo Benartzi set up a retirement plan at a company where workers could adopt different savings rates for present and future income. Not surprisingly, the workers adopted much higher rates for income that was months in the future, and within a short time, they had doubled their average savings rate.

What makes these solutions so powerful is that instead of imposing top-down requirements or mandates, they try to harness people's preferences in a productive way by offering them more options and by shifting the frames through which people see their own financial lives. By creating the right market structures, they allow collectively more rational behavior to emerge. New structures, as we've seen, are not always necessary. Some individual irrationalities matter more than others. The task that remains for behavioral economics is figuring out which is which.

III

At the heart of the argument over whether investors are rational or irrational, of course, is a more basic question: Can the stock market do a good job of predicting the future? The question is rarely phrased that bluntly, and people will sometimes try to evade it by arguing that the real measure of the stock market's performance is how quickly it reacts to information. But fundamentally, what we want to know about the market's performance is how well individual companies' stock prices predict how much cash those companies will make in the future. If Pfizer's stock price today makes it worth $280 billion, then for the market to be right, Pfizer will have to generate $280 billion in hard cash over the next two decades.

Figuring out whether Pfizer will do this, though, is an absurdly difficult task. Think of all the different things that are going to affect Pfizer's business over the next twenty years: the drugs that it will or won't invent and that its competitors will or won't invent; the changes in FDA regulations and Medicare and health insurance; the changes in people's lifestyles and attitudes toward drugs; the evolution of the global economy; and so on. Then think about Pfizer the company, and whether current management will still be around five years from now, and how deep its current drug pipeline is, and whether brilliant scientists will want to keep working for big pharmaceutical companies or will prefer biotech firms instead, and whether the CEO is putting enough money into research and development, and so on. Then take all the hard numbers from Pfizer's financial reports, decide how your evaluation of those future factors will affect the numbers, project the results for fifteen or twenty years, and you'll have a number that'll be measuring the same thing Pfizer's stock price does. If twenty years from now we could look back at that number and say it was accurate, I think we'd count that as miraculous.

The point isn't that the task of predicting how a company will do for the next decade and a half is impossible. But it's damn hard. So when we evaluate how good a job the stock market is doing—how "efficient" it is—we need to remind ourselves what the job entails before deciding what would count as a good answer. The economist Fischer Black once said that he thought the market would count as efficient if companies' stock prices were between 50 percent and 200 percent of their true value. (So if a company's true value was $10 billion, Black would say the market was efficient if it never valued the company at less than $5 billion or more than $20 billion.) At first glance, that seems ridiculous. How many jobs are there in which you can miss the mark by 100 percent and still be considered accurate? But what if you're trying to predict twenty years of an uncertain future? Is being off by 100 percent really inaccurate?

The important question about the accuracy of the market's forecast is, of course, "Inaccurate compared to what?" Missing the mark by 100 percent—and the truth is that, in general, stock prices are probably not off by that much—is not good, but it's certainly better than missing it by 300 percent. The idea of the wisdom of crowds is not that a group will always give you the right answer but that on average it will consistently come up with a better answer than any individual could provide. That's why the fact that only a tiny fraction of investors consistently do better than the market remains the most powerful piece of evidence that the market is efficient. That's especially true when you consider that most investors are trying to evaluate only a small number of stocks, while the market has to come up with prices for more than five thousand of them. The fact that the market is, even under those conditions, smarter than almost all investors is telling.

Even so, financial markets are decidedly imperfect at tapping into the collective wisdom, especially relative to other methods of doing so. The economist Robert Shiller, for instance, has shown convincingly that stock prices jump around a lot more than is justified by changes in the true values of companies. That's very different from the NFL betting market or the IEM or even racetrack betting, where the swings in opinion are significantly milder and the crowd only rarely pulls a U-turn. Part of the reason for this is, again, that predicting twenty years of a company's future is infinitely harder, and far more uncertain, than predicting who's going to win on Sunday or even who'll be elected in November. But there's something else, too. With football games, elections, *Millionaire* questions, and Google searches, there is a definitive answer, which at some point is settled once and for all. If you bet on a horse race, when the race is over, you know whether you won or lost. There's no way to pretend that your prediction will be accurate tomorrow. Similarly, when you have Google do a search, it knows—or could, if it was able to talk to you—whether it found the right page or not. Many financial markets are like this, too. If you buy November wheat futures, then when November rolls around, you'll know whether you paid too much or whether you got a bargain.

The virtue of having this kind of definite outcome is that it keeps the crowd tethered to reality. One problem markets have, as we'll see, is that they're fertile ground for speculation. Speculators aren't trying to figure out whether Pfizer's future corporate performance will justify its current stock price. They don't buy stocks because they think their prices are inaccurate. They buy them because they think they'll be able to sell them to someone else for more. All markets have speculators. But it's harder to speculate if everyone knows that, within a couple of weeks, the market will be over, and people will be rewarded or not depending on the accuracy of their forecasts. The problem with the stock market is that there never *is* a point at which you can say that it's over, never a point at which you will definitively be proved right or wrong. This is one reason why a company's stock price can easily soar far past any reasonable valuation, because people can always convince themselves that something in the future will happen to make the company worth it. And it's the same reason why you can make money in the stock market even when you're wrong: even if the market does eventually get the price right, it can be wrong for a long time, because there is no objective means to demonstrate it's wrong. Twenty years from now, we'll know whether Pfizer's stock price on January 1, 2004, was accurate. But that doesn't change anything in the meantime. This is what John Maynard Keynes meant when he said that markets can stay wrong longer than you can stay solvent.

In the summer of 1998, a small group of experts forgot this lesson and in the process brought the world to the brink of financial catastrophe. The experts worked for Long-Term Capital Management (LTCM), a hedge fund that was started in 1994 by John Meriwether, a former bond trader whose trading skills had made him a legend on Wall Street. From the outside, LTCM looked a little like the Manhattan Project of investing. Meriwether had hired a host of Wall Street whiz kids who were experts in using computer models to figure out how to make money. And he'd brought on board some of the founding fathers of modern finance. Myron Scholes and Robert Merton had invented the model that investors everywhere use to figure out how much options were worth, and now they were working for LTCM. It was hard to see how such a dream team could go wrong. Even though investors had to put up a minimum of $10 million to get into the fund, and 25 percent of each year's profits went to the fund's managers, people still clamored to get in, especially after LTCM turned in impressive returns four years in a row.

But in August of 1998, that all changed when Russia defaulted on its debt. The collapse of Asian economies months earlier had already left investors skittish, and the Russian default provoked what economists like to call a massive "flight to quality." Suddenly, no one wanted to own anything that seemed less than 100 percent reliable, and everyone was anxious to sell any asset that smacked of risk. LTCM suddenly found itself stuck with billions of dollars in assets that no one wanted to buy, the price of which was plummeting daily. In the space of just a couple of months, it lost $4.5 billion, and as it tried to sell off everything it could in a desperate attempt to stay afloat, it sent prices down even further, inflicting hundreds of millions in losses on Wall Street banks. In September, a consortium of thirteen Wall Street banks stepped up and bailed out the fund, giving it enough money to stay in business until conditions returned to normal.

So why did it all go wrong? There were two important things about LTCM's business. First, it used an enormous amount of what economists call "leverage," which simply means that most of its bets were placed with borrowed money. In 1998, LTCM had about $5 billion in equity (that is, real cash it could invest). But it had borrowed more than $125 billion from banks and securities firms. If LTCM wanted to invest $100 million in Danish bonds, for instance, it might put up only $5 million of the purchase price. The bank would guarantee the rest.

The virtue of leverage is that if things go well you can earn a very hefty return on your investment. If the price of those Danish bonds rose 10 percent, LTCM would clear $10 million, which would mean that it had doubled its money (since it only put up $5 million of its own). The problem with leverage is that if things go wrong, you can easily get wiped out. But LTCM claimed that it wasn't taking big gambles. It wasn't investing in markets where prices swung wildly from day to day. So, the fund insisted, all that leverage wasn't really all that risky. Either way, what LTCM's reliance on borrowed money did was make the fund far more important—because it controlled so many more dollars—than it would otherwise have been. Although $5 billion is minuscule relative to the size of the global financial markets, the way LTCM used that $5 billion turned it into a huge player.

This mattered because of the second important thing about LTCM, which was that it was investing in illiquid markets, which means markets where there were not many buyers and sellers. The financial wizards behind LTCM assumed (rightly) that it was too hard to make money in big, deep markets—like the U.S. stock market—where there were lots of people perpetually hunting for some kind of edge. So they preferred smaller markets and more esoteric assets, like Danish mortgage bonds. They employed a variety of strategies, but their core approach was relatively simple in concept. They looked for pairs of assets whose values historically moved in tandem with each other, and waited until those values, for whatever reason, temporarily diverged, with one asset becoming more expensive than the other. When that happened, LTCM bought the cheap asset while selling the expensive one short. As soon as the values converged again, LTCM got out. Each trade, then, was a small score. One LTCM founder described it as "vacuuming up nickels." But since the fund was using so much leverage, it was a very big vacuum.

This was a good idea, in theory. But there were a couple of problems with it. The first was that LTCM assumed that prices would always return to their true values in a reasonable period of time and would never get too far out of whack. The second was that LTCM's fondness for small markets and esoteric trading strategies meant that much of the time there were very few people it could do business with. If you want to buy stock in Cisco, there are lots of people out there who will sell it at a reasonable price. But if you want to, say, sell equity volatility, as LTCM did, there are only a few firms in the entire world that you can deal with, which means, practically speaking, that there are only a few *people* in the entire world that you can deal with. And all of these people know each other.

Now, these people were undoubtedly smart. But there were not many of them, and they were very much alike in the way they thought about things like risk and reward. And they became even more alike after the mid-1990s, when firms began imitating LTCM after it enjoyed tremendous success in its first few years. What that meant was that once things started to go wrong in the summer of 1998, no one was willing to step up and take a chance that other people wouldn't take. LTCM had built its entire business around the idea that the prices of things like Danish mortgage bonds will always return to their real value. But for that strategy to work, someone has to be interested in buying Danish bonds when their price plummets. And in the summer of 1998, none of the people who might have thought those bonds were a bargain were interested in buying them. In fact, since all of those people knew how LTCM did business, the fact that LTCM was interested in selling the bonds was reason enough *not* to buy them. What LTCM needed were investors with a different attitude toward risk. But in that summer of 1998, it was as if all investors—at least all those it might have dealt with—were the same. The most striking measure of this is that the prices of the different assets that LTCM owned became very tightly correlated with each other—that is, they started moving practically in tandem—even though there was no real-world reason for them to do so. Roughly speaking, in that last month, the simple fact that LTCM owned an asset meant it was going down.

Given more time, of course, LTCM might very well have survived. Many (though not all) of the positions it had taken were good ones, and the Wall Street firms that bought out LTCM ended up clearing a profit. But the fact is that LTCM was right in the long run. If everyone had known that at the end of September Danish bonds would be worth their value, their price would not have fallen as it did, and buyers would have materialized. Instead, no one knew how low prices could go or how long the crisis would last. And because LTCM was using so much leverage, it had less room for error, because every mistake it made was geometrically costly.

It's a familiar truism that at any one moment, financial markets are dominated by either fear or greed. But the healthiest markets are those that are animated by both fear and greed at the same time. To state the obvious, any time you sell a stock, the person who's buying it thinks differently about the future prospects of that stock. You think it's going down, he thinks it's going up. One of you will be right, but the important thing is that it's only through the interaction of those differing attitudes that the market is able to do a good job of allocating capital. What happened to LTCM is that there were no differing attitudes. Everyone thought the same because the group of people who were making decisions was too small and too prone to imitate each other. It didn't matter how individually intelligent the experts were. By the end, they were too much alike to be smart.

IV

The biggest stock-market bubble of the 1950s was born in, of all places, a rundown turkey coop in the small town of Pearl River, New York. The coop belonged to Gottfried Schmidt, an engineer and pattern maker who also happened to be an avid bowler. In 1936, Schmidt became frustrated by the fact that if he wanted to bowl a few frames after work, there was no one around to set pins for him. At the time, bowling pins had to be set by hand. But a machine, Schmidt imagined, could set pins quickly and efficiently. So he assembled a small team, including a couple of car mechanics and another engineer, and set about building the first automatic pinsetter in the turkey coop behind his house. This was the middle of the Great Depression, so the erstwhile inventors had to rely on scrap metal, bicycle chains, and used auto parts. Within the year, Schmidt had a fairly good working model and a patent. What he didn't have was any way of mass-producing his invention.

Enter Morehead Patterson. An amateur inventor himself, Patterson was also a vice president at American Machine and Foundry (AMF). The company specialized in making machines for the bakery and tobacco industries, but it was interested in diversifying, and Patterson recognized that with the right marketing, Schmidt's invention could revolutionize the bowling industry. Since bowling alleys had to rely on pin boys to set pins, they were limited in the number of lanes they could run at any one time. And, as Andrew Hurley explains in his book *Diners, Bowling Alleys, and Trailer*

Parks, the relationship between pin boys and their customers was contentious at best. Social reformers attacked bowling alleys as dens of vice. Bowling alleys were like pool halls, only noisier. An automatic pinsetter would bring rationality and mechanical efficiency to the alleys, allowing them to expand and upgrade. So Patterson headed to Pearl River, found Schmidt in his turkey coop, and offered him a job. Schmidt became an AMF employee, and AMF got control of the patent.

Had World War II not intervened, the automatic pinsetter might have made its debut at the beginning of the 1940s. As it was, AMF's factories spent the first half of the decade churning out war *matériel.* And though the pinsetter made its first official appearance in 1946, there were still kinks that hadn't been worked out. But in 1951, more than a decade after Schmidt built his first working model, a bowling alley in Mount Clemens, Michigan, introduced the first automatic pinsetter.

The impact was as dramatic as Patterson could have hoped. Alleys turned from dingy holes into glorious palaces. As promised, the machines were quicker and more reliable than the pin boys, so bowling became faster and more pleasurable. The booming middle class took to bowling, as alleys trumpeted the sport as ideal for the whole family. The bowling alley became known as "the people's country club." By the late 1950s, more than 10 million people bowled at least once a week.

One unlikely consequence of this boom was that bowling stocks became the darlings of Wall Street. Between 1957 and 1958, the stocks of AMF and Brunswick—another bowling-equipment manufacturer—doubled. Smaller bowling companies went public, and investors poured money into the industry. If you had a bowling-related idea, people were happy to give you money. Alleys were built across America. By 1960, there were 12,000 alleys, with a total of 110,000 lanes. All told, investors put $2 billion in capital into the bowling business during the bowling bubble. And this was when $2 billion was real money.

Wall Street did its best to foment the frenzy. Analysts, projecting that the popularity of the sport would grow as fast in the future as it did during the fifties, argued that soon every American would be bowling two hours a week. As Charles Schwab, who was then just beginning his career on Wall Street, said: "Compute it out—180 million people times two hours per week, for 52 weeks. That's a lot of bowling." The hype propelled bowling stocks even higher. After a while, the frenzy for bowling-related anything took on a life of its own.

Took on a life of its own, that is, until it died. By 1963, bowling stocks had fallen 80 percent from their all-time highs, and it would take nearly a decade for them to reclaim the lost ground. Bowling got less popular as time passed, and would never again be as popular as it was during the Eisenhower years. Today, there are about half as many bowling alleys nationally as there were forty years ago, even though there are about 100 million more Americans around.

Wall Street's short-lived infatuation with bowling stocks was, of course, an example of a stock-market bubble. Small bubbles, like the bowling one, are common in asset markets, particularly stock markets. A few years before the bowling bubble, for instance, Wall Street, hypnotized by the promise of the Atomic Age, had become infatuated with uranium stocks. In the mid-1960s, it was the conglomerates that investors couldn't get enough of. Then there was that mini-bubble in RV stocks. (Shares of a company called Skyline Homes rose twentyfold in 1969.) Personal-computer companies, biotechs, real estate, biotechs again: all have been the object of investor mania in the past twenty years. But these bubbles were confined to discrete sectors of the market, and most investors were not swept up in them. Far more devastating are those rare historical moments when seemingly all investors are caught up in the frenzy and everyone appears to have succumbed to what Charles Mackay called "the madness of crowds"—like the South Sea Bubble in England of the 1720s, the Japanese real estate market of the

1980s (when one piece of land in Tokyo was supposedly worth more than all of California), and, of course, the tech-stock bubble of the late 1990s. During a true bubble, price and value lose all connection. Prices rise because people expect them to keep rising. At least they do until the moment when they don't. Then comes the stampede for the exit.

Bubbles and crashes are textbook examples of collective decision making gone wrong. In a bubble, all of the conditions that make groups intelligent—independence, diversity, private judgment—disappear. And although bubbles take place in financial markets, they have a huge impact on the "real" economy. The stock market, after all, is really just a giant mechanism that allows investors to decide, indirectly, how much capital different companies should get. If a company's stock price is high, it can raise more money, either by selling stock or issuing bonds, than it would otherwise be able to do. So by bidding up the price of a company's stock, investors are effectively channeling capital to that company and away from other firms. When the market is smart, the companies that have high stock prices use the money they raise productively and efficiently, which is a good thing not only for the companies themselves but for the economy as a whole, too.

When it came to bowling stocks, though, the market was not smart. On the contrary, investors did a very bad job of getting money to the right companies. They invested far more money in bowling stocks than they should have, and bowling companies did not use the money they raised wisely. They overbuilt and overinvested in anticipation of a future that never materialized. The bowling bubble, in other words, was not exactly a glowing testimonial to the wisdom of the crowd. And though major bubbles and crashes are unusual, rather than ubiquitous, understanding how and why they happen sheds an interesting light on what can go wrong when groups make decisions.

IN STARTING TO THINK about bubbles and crashes, one thing comes to mind right away: you don't see bubbles in the real economy, which is to say the economy where you buy and sell television sets and apples and haircuts. In other words, the price of televisions doesn't suddenly double overnight, only to crash a few months later. Prices change—manufacturers raise prices on scarce goods, retailers mark down merchandise that isn't moving—but they don't swing wildly. And you never end up with a situation where the fact that prices are rising makes people more interested in buying (which is what happens in a bubble). Generally, the more expensive a television set gets, the less interested people are in buying it.

Bubbles are really characteristic of what we think of as financial markets. Why? Well, think about what you're buying when you buy a share of stock. What you're buying, literally, is a fraction of that company's future earnings. (If I own one share of a company, and that company earns $2 a share, I pocket $2.) But you're also buying something else. You're buying the right to resell that share of stock to someone else—ideally someone who has a more optimistic view of the company's future than you do, and will therefore pay you more for the stock than you originally spent.

It's true, of course, that any time you buy any physical product you're also buying the right to resell it. But in the real economy, when you buy a product—even a car—you're generally not too worried about reselling it. The value of a personal computer, for instance, depends not on what you'll be able to sell it for somewhere down the road, but rather on the use you'll get out of it while you own it. In part, that's because physical products, with very few exceptions, *lose* value over time. If you do resell them, it's for less than you paid initially.

In financial markets, though, things often become more valuable over time. Prices rise. (The same is true of the antiques market or the art market.) That makes the ability to resell my share of stock or my piece of real estate very important. And—this is the key part—it makes the market's opinion of the value of my share of stock important, too. In theory, if I'm buying a share of stock, what should I care about? I should care about how much that company is going to earn in the future. If the company's going to earn $60 a share (in discounted free cash flow) over the next twenty years, I should be willing to pay $60 for a share. In practice, though, I'm likely to be worried about not just what the company's going to earn. I'm also worried about what everyone else thinks the company's going to earn, because that will determine whether or not I'll be able to sell my stock for more than I bought it.

To see how different this is from the everyday economy, imagine yourself walking into your local grocery to buy an apple. As you do so, you probably have in your head some idea of what a fair price for an apple would be. That doesn't mean if it costs 90 cents and you think 75 cents would be reasonable, you'll storm out in disgust. But it does mean that you know when you're being ripped off and when you're getting a bargain—because you have some sense (even if it's not explicit) of how much that apple is worth to you, which is to say how much value you'll get from it.

What's interesting about that fair price in your head is that you came up with it without worrying too much about what other people think about apples. To be sure, you know what the grocer thinks apples should cost—the price he's charging. And you have a history, presumably, of shopping for apples, which you rely on to figure out what's a reasonable price. But essentially your decision boils down to a pretty simple calculus: How much do you like apples, and how good is this particular apple you're considering buying?

Your decision to buy the apple or not is, relatively speaking, independent. At any moment, in fact, would-be apple buyers are figuring out, on their own, how much apples are worth to them, while on the other side apple producers are calculating how much it costs to grow and ship apples. And the price of apples at any moment therefore reflects all the millions of independent decisions that these buyers and sellers are making.

By contrast, the price of a stock often reflects a series of *dependent* decisions, because when many people calculate what a stock is worth, their evaluation depends, at least in part, on what everyone else believes the stock to be worth. The economist John Maynard Keynes famously described this process as the beauty contest model: "Professional investment may be likened to those newspaper competitions in which the competitors have to pick out the six prettiest faces from a hundred photographs, the prize being awarded to the competitor whose choice most nearly corresponds to the average preferences of the competitors as a whole; so that each competitor has to pick, not those faces which he himself finds prettiest, but those which he thinks likeliest to catch the fancy of other competitors, all of whom are looking at the problem from the same point of view."

That passage is a bit dense. But what's most important about it is the last line. What Keynes recognized is that what makes the stock market especially strange is that often investors are concerned not just with what the average investor thinks but with what the average investor thinks the average investor thinks. And the truth is: Why stop there? Maybe what you need to think about is what the average person thinks the average person thinks the average person's view should be.

Once you start playing this game, obviously, it's very hard to get out. But the truth, Keynes notwithstanding, is that not everyone in the stock market is playing this game. Some people—think of Warren Buffett—are acting independently, simply picking the prettiest girl (that is, the stocks of the best companies), believing that eventually the market will, as it were, pick the prettiest girls, too. Others are picking girls they think are pretty but that other investors seem likely to find fetching as well. And some investors are doing only what Keynes recommended. Most of the time, then, the stock market is an ever-changing but relatively stable mix of independent and dependent decision making.

Bubbles and crashes occur when the mix shifts too far in the direction of dependence. In the case of the bowling bubble, for instance, investors interpreted the rising prices of AMF and Brunswick as evidence that everyone thought bowling was truly the next big thing. Because everyone seemed to love the bowling stocks, investors wanted to own them, which in turn only made the stocks seem all the more attractive. Buying AMF seemed like a no-lose proposition, because there would always be someone else who'd be willing to take the shares off your hands. And as the stocks kept going up, the incentive to do some independent analysis—the kind that would have led people to be skeptical of the whole bowling boom—diminished. As a result, the kind of diversity of opinion that a healthy market depends on was replaced by a sort of single-mindedness. Everyone was saying that bowling was it, so everyone believed that bowling was it.

A crash is simply the inverse of a bubble, although it's typically more sudden and vicious. In a crash, investors are similarly uninterested in the "real" value of a stock, and similarly obsessed with reselling it. The difference, obviously, is that if in a bubble investors are sure that prices will keep going up, in a crash investors become convinced that prices will just keep going down. The real mystery is why crashes occur when they do, since most major crashes in financial history have seemed out of proportion to their immediate causes. Perhaps the best analogy is that offered by the biologist Per Bak, who compares a market crash to the collapse of a sandpile. As you add grains of sand to a pile, it will keep its shape as it grows bigger. But at some point, one grain of sand too many will send the pile tumbling.

INVESTORS TODAY ARE CERTAINLY better informed than any investors in history. They know that bubbles exist, and that they rarely—if ever—end well. So why are bubbles so hard to eliminate?

For an answer, it helps to look at an experiment done at the Experimental Economics Laboratory at Caltech, where economists have demonstrated just how bubbles work. In the experiment, students were given the chance to trade shares in some imaginary company for fifteen five-minute periods. Everyone was given two shares to start, and some money to buy more shares if they wanted. The trick was that each share paid a dividend of 24 cents at the end of each period. If you owned one share at the end of the first period, you'd be given 24 cents. If you owned one share for the entire experiment, you'd get $3.60 (0.24 × 15). So before the game started, if someone asked you how much you'd pay for a share, the correct answer would be "No more than $3.60." After the first period ended, you'd be willing to pay no more than $3.36 ($3.60 − 0.24). After the second, you'd pay $3.12. And so on.

The point of all this is that there was no uncertainty about how much each share was worth (as there is in a real stock market). If you paid more for a share than the amount you were going to collect in dividends, you overpaid. Yet when the experiment was run, the price of the shares jumped immediately to $3.50 and stayed there almost until the very end. When the shares were worth less than $3, people were still exchanging them for $3.50. As the value of the shares dipped below $2, the price did not drop. And even when the shares were worth less than $1, there were still people shelling out $3.50 to pick them up.

What were the students thinking? Economist Colin F. Camerer, who designed the experiment, asked them why they bought at prices they had to know were crazy: "They'd say, 'Sure I knew that prices were way too high, but I saw other people buying and selling at high prices. I figured I could buy, collect a dividend or two, and then sell at the same price to some other idiot.'" In other words, everyone was convinced the greater fool was out there.

The Caltech experiment is interesting because it's so extreme. The students had all the information they needed to make the right decision—that is, not to overpay for the shares. They knew when the experiment would end, which meant there was a limited time for them to dump their shares. And they were not communicating with each other except via their buy and sell orders. (So people weren't egging each other on.) And still a bubble formed. That suggests something about the perils of dependent decision making.

Having said that, real bubbles are more complicated and more interesting than the Caltech experiment suggests. In the first place, it's not always obvious to the people inside a bubble that that's where they are. Camerer's students openly said that they were just looking for the greater fool. But in the midst of a real bubble, people—not all people, but certainly some people—start to believe the hype. People who bought shares of Cisco when the stock was the most expensive in the world undoubtedly did so because they believed that Cisco's stock was just going to keep going up. But hidden inside that belief was the kernel of the idea that Cisco might really be worth $500 billion.

The insidiousness of a bubble, in that sense, is that the longer it goes on, the less bubblelike it seems. Part of that is the fact that no one knows when it's going to end (just as no one, even in retrospect, can really know when it started). There were any number of pundits predicting doom for the Nasdaq in 1998. But if you'd gotten out of the stock market then, you'd have missed a 40 percent gain. If you'd left before 1999, you'd have missed an 85 percent gain. How many years does the market have to keep going up before it starts to seem simply like the way things are?

It's easy to dismiss bubbles as fits of collective hysteria. But the process is more complicated than that. After all, as we saw in the chapter on imitation and information cascades, some piggybacking on the wisdom of others is inevitable and often quite beneficial. If groups on the whole are relatively intelligent (as we know they are), then there's a good chance that a stock price is actually right. The problem is that once *everyone* starts piggybacking on the wisdom of the group, then no one is doing anything to add to the wisdom of the group. Keynes notwithstanding, the beauty contest only has a hope of picking the prettiest girl—which is, after all, what it's there for—if some of the people in it really are thinking about which girl is prettiest.

Just as we don't have a good account of why crashes occur, we don't really have a good sense yet of why bubbles start. What we do know is that they cannot be created out of whole cloth. Bowling was one of the most popular pastimes in America in the 1950s. Biotech companies did revolutionize the pharmaceutical industry. And the Internet was a transformative technology. The problem is that if bubbles begin as logical attempts to cash in on powerful business trends, they soon become something else. The temptation to trade stocks on the basis of what other people are doing is nearly irresistible. Other people's expectations are constantly impinging on your own. And as investors start mirroring each other, the wisdom of the group as a whole declines.

INFORMATION IS USUALLY CONSIDERED a good thing. In fact, as a rule, the more information the better. And one of the real challenges of any economy is to ensure that investors know enough about the companies they're investing in. Yet the experience of bubbles and crashes suggests that, in certain circumstances, certain kinds of information actually seem to make things worse. Not all information, it turns out, is created equal. And the way information is delivered can have a profound effect on the way it's received.

The stock-market bubble of the 1990s coincided with an explosion in financial news. Relative even just to a decade ago, investors now have access to vast troves of information about companies and the markets, thanks to the Internet and cable television. The most influential source of financial news in the late nineties was unquestionably CNBC. *Fortune* columnist Andy Serwer wrote in 1999, "I think CNBC is the TV network of our time . . . The bull market we've been basking in year after year has made investing the national pastime. The more stocks go up, the more of us get into the market, the more we watch CNBC to keep abreast of the action." (Notice that Serwer's description—"the more stocks go up, the more of us get into the market"—perfectly captures the logic of a stock-market bubble.) Seven million people a week watched CNBC at the market's peak, and if you were at all interested in the stock market, it was inescapable. Serwer again: "CNBC is everywhere: trading floors and brokerages, yes, but also health clubs and restaurants, flower shops and oil rigs, factories and frat houses, judges' chambers and prisons."

CNBC provided nonstop coverage of what the market was doing, with a stock ticker running ceaselessly at the bottom of the screen and updates arriving from the various stock exchanges on a regular basis. The network was in one sense just a messenger, letting the market, you might say, talk to itself. But as CNBC's popularity grew, so did its influence. Instead of simply commenting on the markets, it began—unintentionally—to move them. It wasn't so much *what* was being said on CNBC that prompted investors to buy and sell, so much as it was the fact that it was being said on CNBC.

Economists Jeffrey Busse and T. Clifton Green, for instance, did a study of how the market reacted when CNBC ran a positive report on a stock on its *Midday Call* segment. Busse and Green showed that prices reacted almost instantly to the news, moving higher in the first fifteen seconds after the segment appeared. More strikingly, the number of stock trades sextupled in the first minute after the segment. The speed of the reaction testifies, on the one hand, to the market's efficiency at incorporating new "information." But what the study also shows is that investors were not reacting to the content of the report. Fifteen seconds is hardly enough time to decide whether what CNBC is saying makes sense or not. All the investors—or speculators—cared about was that because CNBC said it, somebody would be trading on it. Once you know that other people are going to react to the news, the only question becomes who can move fast enough. (In fact, if you're too late, you'll end up losing money.) Day trader Ken Wolff told *Business Week,* "CNBC is a hot momentum-trading tool. We play it often." And columnist and former hedge-fund manager James J. Cramer wrote of CNBC's morning show *Squawk Box*: "You take stock when you hear somebody is on *Squawk*."

CNBC magnified the *dependent* nature of the stock market because it bombarded investors with news about what other investors were thinking. In the days before CNBC, most of what traders knew about what everyone else was thinking had to be inferred from the ticker. So even if you were trying to decipher everyone else's motives, there was a space between you and the market. In the new world of financial news, inference is no longer necessary (perhaps no longer possible). Instead, you're constantly being told what "traders" are saying and how "the market" is feeling. To return to Keynes's metaphor, it's as if CNBC is screaming all day long about what everyone else is saying about who the prettiest girls are. That makes it harder than it already is for each individual investor to make an independent decision about who's prettiest. Obviously, this becomes most important during those times when investors are already herding together. On a day when the market is plummeting, for instance, and CNBC has emblazoned MANIC MONDAY on the screen, every decision an investor makes is inflected by the panic he can see on the screen in front of him. The herd mentality becomes endemic because it's hard to think about anything except what everyone else is doing.

Even if you set the problem of herding aside, it's not clear that a barrage of news is necessarily conducive to good decision making. In the late 1980s, for instance, psychologist Paul Andreassen did a series of experiments with business students at MIT that showed that more news does not always translate into better information. Andreassen divided students into two groups. Each group selected a portfolio of stocks, and knew enough about each stock to come up with what seemed like a fair price for it. Then Andreassen allowed one group to see only the changes in the prices of their stocks. They could buy and sell if they wanted, but all they knew was whether the price of a stock had gone up or down. The second group was allowed to see the changes in price, but was also given a constant stream of financial news that supposedly explained what was happening. Surprisingly, the less well-informed group did far better than the group that was given all the news.

The reason, Andreassen suggested, was that news reports tend, by their nature, to overplay the importance of any particular piece of information. When a stock fell, for instance, its fall was typically portrayed as a sign that further trouble lay in wait, while a stock that was on the rise seemed to promise nothing but blue skies ahead. As a result, the students who had access to the news overreacted. They bought and sold far more frequently than the people who were just looking at the price, because they took each piece of information as excessively meaningful. The students who could look only at the stock's price had no choice but to concentrate on the fundamentals that they had used to pick their stocks to begin with.

The problem of putting too much weight on a single piece of information is compounded when everyone in the market is getting that information. Consider an experiment that the financial analyst Jack Treynor did. First Treynor had the students in his finance class guess the number of jelly beans in a jar. Not surprisingly, the average guess was within 3 percent of the number of beans in the jar (there were 850 beans in the jar, and the mean guess was 871), and only one person in the class did better than the group as a whole. Up to this point, Treynor was demonstrating what Francis Galton's experiment with the ox had also shown.

Then Treynor had the students guess at the number of jelly beans again. This time, though, they were cautioned to think about the fact that there was air space at the top of the jar and that the jar was made of plastic, not glass, meaning that it could hold more beans than might have been expected. The group's average guess was off by 15 percent, and was considerably worse than the guesses of a number of the people in the class.

The point is that the information skewed the perspectives of the students in a shared way. What the students were told was true. But because it was a truth that seemed to point in one direction— there were probably more beans in the jar than they believed—it destroyed their collective wisdom. And the way the information was disclosed mattered. In a sense, instead of saying here are some jelly beans in a plastic jar, Treynor went out of his way to explain why he thought the plastic was important. In doing so, he subtracted information from the students. The more they were told, the less they actually knew about how many beans were in the jar.

Obviously, economies and societies depend on, and thrive on, the disclosure of public information. What Andreassen's and Treynor's experiments suggest, though, is that the best way to disclose public information is without hype or even commentary from people in positions of power. In this light, the way the Federal Reserve announces its interest-rate hikes—with just a terse summary of its decision—seems wise.

Groups are only smart when there is a balance between the information that everyone in the group shares and the information that each of the members of the group holds privately. It's the combination of all those pieces of independent information, some of them right, some of them wrong, that keeps the group wise. In the stock market, as we've seen, other people's expectations affect your own definition of value. Much of the time, that matters only a little, because the expectations themselves are competing. But what happens in a bubble—or what happens when the bubble bursts— is that the expectations converge. And the media does play a role in that process. During boom times, it's rare to hear a discordant voice suggesting that disaster is nigh, while when things are going bad, it's hard to find someone who suggests that panic is a mistake. In this way, the media often exacerbates—though it doesn't cause— the feedback loop that gets going during a bubble. It's already hard enough, as we've seen, for investors to be independent of each other. During a bubble, it becomes practically impossible. A market, in other words, turns into a mob.

The temptation, of course, is to say that investors in a bubble have just lost their minds, that they're acting irrationally, and that they'll have a huge hangover when they wake up after the crash. And they have. But what they're really doing is simply taking their cues from the crowd. This is not an unusual phenomenon.

Consider, for instance, the Seattle crowd that baited a twenty-six-year-old woman into jumping off the Seattle Memorial Bridge in August of 2001. The woman had stopped her car in traffic and climbed over the railing. Behind her stranded car, traffic quickly began to pile up, and rubberneckers on the other side of the highway slowed traffic there to a crawl as well. Police were called to the scene and began trying to talk the woman off the ledge. As they did so, annoyed drivers, pedestrians, and passengers on a stalled MetroBus began screaming at the woman to jump. "Get it over with!" they cried. "Just jump, bitch! Just do it!" The cops tried to keep the woman calm. But their efforts were futile. As the crowd continued to shout, the woman leaped and fell sixteen stories to the river below. (Incredibly, she lived.)

The Seattle incident was unusual because it took place during the morning, but the presence of what sociologist Leon Mann calls the "baiting crowd" was not a complete surprise. In half of the cases of suicide by jumping that Mann studied, crowds gathered to egg on the would-be jumper. Mann found that crowds were most likely to act this way at night, when it was easier not just to go unidentified but also to imagine oneself as part of a bigger group. And the larger the crowd, the more likely it was to scream at the jumper. The bigger the crowd, the easier it was to feel anonymous, to be sure. But it also seems likely that the more people who were yelling, the more people wanted to yell.

Baiting crowds are, of course, relatively rare. But the dynamic that drives them seems very similar to the behavior of rioting mobs. And the process by which a violent mob actually comes together seems curiously similar to the way a stock-market bubble works. A mob in the middle of a riot appears to be a single organism, acting with one mind. And obviously the mob's behavior has a collective dimension that a group of random people just milling about does not have. But sociologist Mark Granovetter argued that the collective nature of a mob was the product of a complicated process, rather than a sudden descent into madness. In any crowd of people, Granovetter showed, there are some people who will never riot, and some people who are ready to riot at almost any time—these are the "instigators." But most people are somewhere in the middle. Their willingness to riot *depends* on what other people in the crowd are doing. Specifically, it depends on how many other people in the crowd are rioting. As more people riot, more people decide that they are willing to riot, too. (Think of what Andy Serwer wrote about the stock-market boom: "the more stocks go up, the more of us get into the market.")

That makes it sound as if once one person starts a ruckus, a riot will inevitably result. But according to Granovetter, that's not the case. What matters is what combination of people are in the crowd. If there are a few instigators and lots of people who will act only if a sizable percentage of the crowd acts, it's likely nothing will happen. For a crowd to explode, you need instigators, "radicals"— people with low thresholds for violence—and a mass of people who can be swayed. The result is that although it's not necessarily easy to start a riot, once a crowd crosses the threshold into violence, its behavior is shaped by its most violent members. If the image of collective wisdom that informs much of this book is the average judgment of the group as a whole, a mob is not wise. Its judgment is extreme.

Of course, markets are not bubbles all, or even most, of the time. And there is, in Granovetter's work, a hint as to what markets need to avoid endless bouts with irrational exuberance or irrational despair. In Granovetter's world, if there are enough people in the crowd who will not riot under any conditions—that is, whose actions are independent of the crowd's behavior as a whole—then a riot will be far less likely, because the more people who do not riot, the more people there will be who don't want to riot. The analogy to a stock-market bubble is obvious: the more investors who refuse to buy stocks just because other people are buying them, the less likely it will be that a bubble will become inflated. The fewer investors there are who treat the market as if it were Keynes's beauty contest, the more robust and intelligent the market's decisions will be.

DEMOCRACY: DREAMS OF

THE COMMON GOOD

I

In January of 2003, 343 people, carefully chosen so that they represented an almost perfect cross-section of the American population, gathered in Philadelphia for a weekend of political debate. The topic was American foreign policy, with the issues ranging from the impending conflict with Iraq to nuclear proliferation to the global AIDS epidemic. Before the weekend, the participants were polled to get a sense of their positions on the issues. They were then sent a set of briefing materials that, in a deliberately evenhanded fashion, tried to lay out relevant facts and provide some sense of the ongoing debate about the issues. Once they arrived, they were divided up into small groups led by trained moderators, and went on to spend the weekend deliberating. Along the way, they were given the chance to interrogate panels of competing experts and political figures. At the end of the weekend, the participants were polled again, to see what difference their deliberations had made.

The entire event, which bore the unwieldy name of the National Issues Convention Deliberative Poll, was the brainchild of a political scientist at the University of Texas named James Fishkin.

Fishkin invented the deliberative poll out of frustration with the limitations of traditional polling data and out of a sense that Americans were not being given either the information or the opportunity to make intelligent political choices. The idea behind deliberative polls—which have now been run in hundreds of cities across the world—is that political debate should not be, and doesn't need to be, confined to experts and policy elites. Given enough information and the chance to talk things over with peers, ordinary people are more than capable of understanding complex issues and making meaningful choices about them. In that sense, Fishkin's project is a profoundly optimistic one, predicated on a kind of deep faith in both the virtue of informed debate and the ability of ordinary people to govern themselves.

Fishkin would like deliberative polling to become a regular, nationwide process, if not one that could replace traditional polls, at least one that could supplement them. Since deliberative polls are better reflections of what American voters really think about the issues, he argues, it makes more sense for American politicians to heed them instead of your average Gallup survey. This is a quixotic project, to be sure, in no small part because deliberative polling is so time-consuming and expensive that it's hard to imagine them becoming a regular part of the American political landscape. (And it's not exactly clear, in any case, that incumbent politicians really want voters to be informed.) But it's nowhere near as quixotic as another of Fishkin's ideas, namely Deliberation Day. Deliberation Day, which Fishkin and Yale law professor Bruce Ackerman proposed, would be a new national holiday on which, two weeks before major national elections, registered voters would gather in their neighborhoods, in small groups of fifteen and large groups of five hundred, to discuss the major issues at stake in the campaign. Citizens who participated and then voted the following week would be paid $150.

Now, Ackerman and Fishkin know how utopian—or, to some, dystopian—these ideas sound. But they argue that something dramatic needs to be done to stop the hollowing out of American democracy. As they see it, Americans are increasingly isolated from each other and alienated from the political system, public debate is becoming coarser and less informative, and the idea of the public good is being eclipsed by our worship of private interest. What's needed are ways to reengage Americans with civic life, to give them the chance both to voice their opinions in a meaningful forum and to learn about the issues. These deliberative gatherings are one means of doing that.

This idea of "deliberative democracy" makes an easy target for criticism. It seems to rest on an unrealistic conception of people's civic-mindedness. It endows deliberation with almost magical powers. And it has a schoolmarmish, eat-your-spinach air about it. Even if you accept that people are, in fact, sophisticated enough to follow complex political arguments, it's not clear that they have the patience or the energy to do so, or that they want to be told to take a holiday because it's time to talk about politics. Judge Richard Posner, for instance, scorns the idea that deliberation will make us over into exemplars of reason and virtue. "The United States is a tenaciously philistine society," he writes in *Law, Pragmatism, and Democracy*. "Its citizens have little appetite for abstractions and little time and less inclination to devote substantial time to training themselves to become informed and public-spirited voters." And in any case, we should not expect people to be capable of coming up with a workable definition of the common good. "It is far more difficult to form an informed opinion about what is good for society as a whole than it is to determine where one's self-interest lies," Posner writes. "Not that one cannot be deceived on the latter score as well; but reasoning about the most effective means to a given end—instrumental reasoning, the type involved in self-interested action—is a good deal more straightforward than reasoning about ends, the type of reasoning required for determining what is best for society as a whole."

What Posner and the deliberative democrats disagree about is not the nitty-gritty of policies and legislation (though they probably would disagree about that, too). What they disagree about is what democracy is *for* and what we can expect it to accomplish. Do we have it because it gives people a sense of involvement and control over their lives, and therefore contributes to political stability? Do we have it because individuals have the right to rule themselves, even if they use that right in ridiculous ways? Or do we have it because democracy is actually an excellent vehicle for making intelligent decisions and uncovering the truth?

I I

Let's start by asking that question a different way, namely: What do *voters* think democracy is for? In the early 1960s, a group of economists invaded political science to offer their answer to that question. These economists wanted to apply the same kind of reasoning they used in studying how markets work to studying how politics work. The implicit starting point for most analysis on markets is, of course, the pursuit of self-interest. Markets work, at least in part, by harnessing people's individual pursuit of self-interest to collectively beneficial ends. So it was natural for these new students of politics to begin with the premise that all political actors—voters, politicians, regulators—are driven ultimately by self-interest. Voters want to elect candidates who will look after their particular interests, not candidates who are concerned about the well-being of the country as a whole (except insofar as the well-being of the country affects a voter's individual well-being). Politicians want, above all, to be reelected, and therefore vote not in the way that they think is best for the nation but in the way that they think has the best chance of winning over the voters, which often translates into playing pork-barrel politics and paying special attention to the interests of powerful lobbies. Regulators want to keep their jobs and to command more resources, so they are consistently driven to exaggerate the importance of what they do and to look for ways to expand the scope of their mission. Unlike in the market, in politics all this self-interested behavior doesn't necessarily translate into collectively good ends. Instead, these economists—loosely called "public-choice theorists"—saw a government that simply kept getting bigger (since everyone had an individual interest in getting a little more from the state, and no one was looking out for the collective interest), that entered into cozy arrangements with the businesses it was regulating, and that allowed economic policy to be run in the interests of powerful groups instead of the interests of the public as a whole.

Public-choice theory is one of those sets of ideas that seem at the same time remarkably perceptive and remarkably obtuse. In its description of interest-group politics, its recognition of the degree to which long-term problems get deferred in favor of short-term political considerations, and in particular its picture of the way many regulations actually serve the interests of regulated companies, the theory explains why so many Americans are frustrated with government. On the other hand, in its assumptions that principle and the public interest have no place at all in politics, that voters think only of their particular conditions and not at all of bigger social and political questions when casting a ballot, and that interest groups wield almost complete control over the legislative process, it clearly missed something important. To public-choice theorists it was obvious that, as James Buchanan and Gordon Tullock wrote, "The average individual acts on the basis of the same overall value scale when he participates in market activity and in political activity." But this was just a simple assertion of fact rather than something that was proved. It seemed equally plausible that different activities bring out different values in people. After all, do we really treat our family members the way we treat our customers?

The point is not that self-interest is irrelevant to voters. To state only the obvious, even if someone is trying to choose the candidate that he thinks will be best for the country as a whole, self-interest obviously is going to have an influence on the factors he thinks make a candidate strong or weak. The goal of attaining a perspectiveless, completely disinterested view of politics is obviously a futile one. But that doesn't mean that self-interest determines voters' decisions. The simple fact that someone has bothered to vote shows that he is not being guided purely by self-interest. Lamentations about low voter turnout may be de rigueur in American political circles. But from an economist's point of view, the perplexing thing is that *anyone* bothers to vote. After all, your vote has effectively zero chance of changing the outcome of an election, and for most people, the impact any one politician—even the president—will have on their everyday lives is relatively small. If your vote doesn't matter and the choice of the winner doesn't make much of a difference either, why vote?

Public-choice theorists have done their best to explain away people's propensity to vote. William Riker, for instance, argued that by voting, people were "affirming a partisan preference" and "affirming [their] efficacy in the political system," rather than trying to affect the outcome of an election. But the more parsimonious explanation seems more likely to be true. People vote because they think they should—Riker's own data on elections from the 1950s suggested that people's "sense of duty" was the single best predictor of whether they voted or not—and because they want to have a say, however minuscule, in how their government is run. And in any case, if voters' votes are "expressive," as some would have it—expressing their views publicly instead of actually trying to affect the course of an election—it seems possible that this would produce better results for society than having people vote their self-interest.

Now, even if people choose to vote out of something other than self-interested behavior, that doesn't mean their actual votes reflect anything other than self-interest. But here again, there are limits to the self-interest argument. To begin with, there is no clear correlation between self-interest, at least as narrowly conceived, and voting behavior. Most American voters are not wealthy and never will be wealthy. Yet, at least since 1980, they have shown little or no interest in raising taxes on the rich and using the income for their own purposes. More concretely, in a series of studies in the 1980s, Donald R. Kinder and D. Roderick Kiewiet surveyed voters and found that there was no connection between how voters said they were doing personally and their votes, while there was a substantial correlation between how the voters said the economy as a whole was doing and their votes. Even more tellingly, the studies of political scientist David Sears has shown that ideology does a much better job of predicting attitudes on issues than self-interest does. For example, conservatives without health insurance still opposed national health insurance, while liberals who had health insurance favored it.

None of this should be taken to mean that the average American voter is out there doing deep research on the issues and thinking big thoughts before she casts her vote. Far from it. Obviously people will rely primarily on local knowledge in making their decision—much as people do in a market. But there is no contradiction between saying that people's view of the issues and of candidates is shaped by local circumstance and self-interest and saying that voters may still be interested in picking the best man for the job, not just the best man for themselves.

III

According to a University of Maryland poll taken in 2002, Americans think the United States should spend $1 on foreign aid for every $3 it spends on defense. (I can't quite believe that, but that's what the poll says.) In reality, the United States—which has one of the lowest foreign-aid budgets of any developed country—spends $1 on foreign aid for every $19 it spends on defense. Yet when you ask Americans if we're spending too much money on foreign aid, the answer has traditionally been "yes." One reason may be that, as another University of Maryland poll shows, Americans think the United States spends 24 percent of its annual budget on foreign aid. The reality is that it spends less than 1 percent.

That poll was not an isolated example. It is hardly a difficult task to come up with evidence of how little American voters know. For instance, a 2003 poll found that half of those surveyed did not know there had been a tax cut in the previous two years. Thirty percent of Americans thought Social Security and Medicare taxes were part of the income-tax system, and another quarter didn't know if they were or not. At the height of the cold war, half of all Americans thought the Soviet Union was a member of NATO. Given all this, is it really plausible that American voters will really make sensible policy choices?

Well, perhaps not. But the truth is that that's not the real question when it comes to representative democracy. In a representative democracy, the real question is: Are Americans likely to pick the candidate who will make the right decision? On those terms, it seems more than plausible that they are. The fact that people don't know how much the United States spends on foreign aid is no sign of their lack of intelligence. It's a sign of their lack of information, which itself is an indication of their lack of interest in political details. But the point of a representative democracy is that it allows the same kind of cognitive division of labor that operates in the rest of society. Politicians can specialize and acquire the knowledge they need to make informed decisions, and citizens can monitor them to see how those decisions turn out. It's true that some of those decisions will never be noticed, and others will be misinterpreted. But decisions that actually have a concrete impact on people's lives, which is to say the decisions that matter most, will not be ignored. In this sense, one essential ingredient of a healthy democracy is competition. Competition makes it more likely that politicians will make good decisions by making it more likely that they will be punished when they don't.

One knee-jerk reaction to the evidence of democracy's failings is to insist that we would be better off ruled by a technocratic elite, which could make decisions with dispassion and attention to the public interest. To some extent, of course, we already are ruled by a technocratic elite, what with our republican form of government and the importance of unelected officials—for instance, Donald Rumsfeld or Colin Powell—in political life. But one would be hard-pressed to argue that most elites are able to see past their ideological blinders and uncover the imaginary public interest. And trusting an insulated, unelected elite to make the right decisions is a foolish strategy, given all we now know about small-group dynamics, groupthink, and the failure of diversity.

In any case, the idea that the right answer to complex problems is simply "ask the experts" assumes that experts agree on the answers. But they don't, and if they did, it's hard to believe that the public would simply ignore their advice. Elites are just as partisan and no more devoted to the public interest than the average voter. More important, as you shrink the size of a decision-making body, you also shrink the likelihood that the final answer is right. Finally, most political decisions are not simply decisions about how to do something. They are decisions about what to do, decisions that involve values, trade-offs, and choices about what kind of society people should live in. There is no reason to think that experts are better at making those decisions than the average voter. Thomas Jefferson, for one, thought it likely that they might be worse. "State a moral case to a ploughman and a professor," he wrote. "The former will decide it as well and often better than the latter because he has not been led astray by artificial rules."

It's also the case that democracy allows for the persistent injection into the system of what I called earlier "local knowledge." Politics is ultimately about the impact of government on the everyday lives of citizens. It seems strange, then, to think that the way to do politics well is to distance yourself as much as possible from citizens' everyday lives. In the same way that a healthy market needs the constant flow of localized information that it gets from prices, a healthy democracy needs the constant flow of information it gets from people's votes. That is information that experts cannot get because it is not part of the world they live in. And that keeps the system more diverse than it would otherwise be. As Richard Posner puts it: "Experts constitute a distinct class in society, with values and perspectives that differ systematically from those of 'ordinary' people. Without supposing that the man in the street has any penetrating insights denied the expert, or is immune from demagoguery, we may nevertheless think it reassuring that political power is shared between experts and nonexperts rather than being a monopoly of the former."

I V

The preamble of the U.S. Constitution defines the goal of the document as being, in part, to "establish justice" and "promote the general welfare." James Madison, in *Federalist* 51, wrote explicitly that there were two requirements for good government: "first, fidelity to the object of government, which is the happiness of the people; secondly, a knowledge of the means by which that object can be attained." His fear of "factions," meanwhile, was predicated on the idea that they made it harder for government to seek the "public good." That fear survives today in the familiar critique of the power of interest groups and lobbyists, which encourages government to favor private special interests over the broader public interest. And politicians' (often disingenuous) laments about the evils of partisanship in Washington only resonate with voters because of people's sense that party politics get in the way of what's right for the country as a whole. In fact, as we saw in our discussion of self-interested voters, it's the rare politician who doesn't, however vaguely, portray himself as serving the common good. Even as we know that the reality of Washington is dominated by special interests and pork-barrel politics, we remain enthralled by the idea that government should be able to transcend parochial concerns.

The problem, though, is that we have no standard that allows us to judge a political decision to be "right" or "wrong." This is in stark contrast to the workings of markets, where we will be able to evaluate (someday in the future) whether a company's stock price reflected its true present value, or whether a futures price on the Iowa Electronic Market predicted the eventual outcome of an election. It's in contrast also, I would argue, to the case of the corporation, where there is a simple and coherent definition of what's in "the corporate interest"—namely, legally increasing the discounted value of the company's future free cash flows. Now, this doesn't mean that everyone who works for a company is going to care about the corporate interest, and often people—like CEOs blessed with overly friendly boards of directors who pay them hundreds of millions of dollars—do things that are directly opposed to it. But the point is that we have a standard—admittedly not a very high or morally elevated standard—which allows us to say, to a good approximation, whether a particular strategy was good or bad, a success or a failure.

When it comes to democracy, such a standard seems much harder to come by, not so much because people are selfish and may act in ways that are contrary to the public interest (that's true in a corporation as well, and it's even true in a market, where many company executives would prefer it if stocks never approached their true value), but because, as economic theorist Joseph Schumpeter put it, "to different individuals and groups the common good is bound to mean different things." So two politicians may both say, and *mean*, that they are acting in the public interest and then advocate radically different policies. We may agree with one and disagree with the other. But it's not obvious that we can say that one of them has acted against *the* common good.

The reason this question matters is that if we could say that certain policies were against the common good in an objective sense, then it's likely that democracy's reliance on some version of the collective wisdom—as refracted through votes—would make it an excellent decision-making system, and would make any democracy's chances of adopting good policies high. Even the fact that most voters are not especially well-informed or sophisticated wouldn't necessarily be a problem. After all, throughout this book we've seen groups that were hodgepodges of ability, engagement, and information produce superior collective judgments. There's no reason to believe that crowds would be wise in most situations but suddenly become doltish in the political arena.

Unfortunately, there's no reason to think that, if no objective answer to a problem can be found, the crowd will be wise in the way that Francis Galton's fairgoers and Robert Walker's customers and Google's Web-page voters were and are. Choosing candidates and policies in a democracy are not, in that sense, cognition problems and so we should not expect them to yield themselves to the wisdom of the crowd. On the other hand, there's no reason to think that any other political system (dictatorship, aristocracy, rule by elites) will be any better at making policy, and the risks built into those systems—most notably the risk of the exercise of unchecked and unaccountable power—are much greater than those in a democracy.

We could just leave it there, with the thought that having a system that is "least-bad" in the Churchillian sense is better than having one that's bad. But there is something else to be said. At the beginning of this book, I suggested that there were *three* kinds of problems (cognition, coordination, and cooperation) that groups of people were faced with and that collective intelligence, manifesting itself in very different ways in the face of these different kinds of problems, could help solve. As we've seen, the collective solutions to coordination and cooperation problems are not like the solutions to cognition problems. They are fuzzier and less definitive—recall Brian Arthur's solution to the El Farol problem or the way most players in the ultimatum and public-goods games enforce ill-defined but nonetheless real norms of fairness and mutual responsibility. These solutions tend to emerge over time, rather than being the product of a single collective decision—think of the way trading systems in which people trusted only those in their family or clan evolved, over time, into a world in which strangers trade contentedly with each other. And these solutions are often fragile or vulnerable to exploitation by others, such as tax evaders and free riders.

For all that, though, the solutions to cooperation and coordination problems are real in the sense that they work. They are not imposed from above, but emerge from the crowd. And, on the whole, they are better solutions than any group of Platonic guardians could come up with. And this is how we might think of democracy, too. It is not a way of solving cognition problems or a mechanism for revealing the public interest. But it is a way of dealing with (if not solving once and for all) the most fundamental problems of cooperation and coordination: How do we live together? How can living together work to our mutual benefit? Democracy helps people answer those questions because the democratic experience is an experience of not getting everything you want. It's an experience of seeing your opponents win and get what you hoped to have, and of accepting it, because you believe that they will not destroy the things you value and because you know you will have another chance to get what you want. In that sense, a healthy democracy inculcates the virtues of compromise—which is, after all, the foundation of the social contract—and change. The decisions that democracies make may not demonstrate the wisdom of the crowd. The decision to make them democratically does.

ACKNOWLEDGMENTS

This book began, in some sense, with a column I wrote for *The New Yorker* not long after I started there, in the spring of 2000. And much of what the book became was influenced by columns I've written for the magazine since. In more ways than one, if David Remnick hadn't taken a chance on hiring me, and on publishing a business column in *The New Yorker*, this book would not exist. I owe him a lot. Thanks, David.

Henry Finder of *The New Yorker* edited the first pieces I wrote for the magazine, shepherded me through my first year as a columnist, and has remained a constant source of intellectual inspiration. Henry has the rare gift of making a writer feel as if what he does is important—not to the world, necessarily, but just in itself. This is a good thing for anyone to feel about what they do.

I want to thank Nick Paumgarten, who edits my columns, for putting so much time and energy into my work. Nick's made me a better writer and, I think, this book a better book than it otherwise would have been.

Michael Mauboussin, chief investment strategist at Credit Suisse First Boston, first got me thinking about the ideas that animate this book with his remarkable writings on the stock market and complex systems. Michael's work remains a touchstone for me, and my conversations with him over the last year have made me think more and more deeply about the questions in this book. Thanks, Michael.

I want to thank the fact-checkers at *The New Yorker* who work with me on my column. They keep me safe and make my stories better.

Lee Smith was one of the first people I met when I moved to New York City, and my experience of living here is inextricable from our friendship. This book is partly about the difference between a society and just a bunch of people living next to each other. That's something that I learned from Lee in talking about the value of city life.

My editor, Bill Thomas, was the first person to think that there was a book hidden inside my inchoate thoughts about collective decisions. I'm sure there have been times that he regretted ever mentioning the idea of the book, but I'm grateful he did. Bill is a dazzling combination of brilliant editor and old-school bookman, and throughout this process he has been unstinting in his support. He's also shown the patience of Job. I want to thank him for all of it.

My brothers, David and Tim—because they're my brothers and they look out for me.

The thought that I would get to talk to Meghan O'Rourke sometime during the day, and get to hear what she had to say about the world, kept me going while I was writing this book. And her suggestions made it better. I can't imagine what it would have been like without her.

Chris Calhoun is one of my best friends. He's also the best agent any writer could have, and he made this book happen. One of the things I missed most while I was writing this book was talking regularly to Chris. I hope we can start doing that again.

This is for my mom and dad.

NOTES

Introduction

Pages xi–xiii: Francis Galton's original account of his visit to the Plymouth fair can be found in: Francis Galton, "Vox Populi," *Nature* 75 (March 7, 1907): 450–51. He continued his discussion in the letters page of the journal: Francis Galton, "The Ballot-Box," *Nature* 75 (March 28, 1907): 509–10. And he wrote about the ox-weighing contest in his memoir as well: Francis Galton, *Memories of My Life* (London: Methuen, 1908): 280–81. His account of the International Exhibition of 1884 is from *Memories*: 246.

Page xiv: The concept of bounded rationality is well explained in, among other texts, Herbert Simon, "A Behavioral Model of Rational Choice," *Quarterly Journal of Economics* 69 (1955): 99–118; and Herbert Simon, "Theories of Bounded Rationality," in *Decision and Organization: A Volume in Honor of Jacob Marschak*, edited by C. B. McGuire and Roy Radner (Amsterdam: North-Holland Publishing Company, 1972): 161–76.

Page xv: The phrase "chase the expert" comes from Richard Larrick and Jack Soll, "Combining Opinions: Why Don't People Average?," a paper delivered at the 2002 Behavioral Decision Research in Management biennial meeting. A similar analysis can be found in Richard Larrick and Jack Soll, "Intuitions About Combining Opinions: Misappreciation of the Averaging Principle," INSEAD working paper 2003/09/TM (2003), http://ged.insead.edu/fichiersti/inseadwp2003/2003-09.pdf.

Page xv: Charles Mackay, *Extraordinary Popular Delusions and the Madness of Crowds* (New York: Harmony Books, 1980): xx. The quote is from Mackay's Preface to the 1852 edition of his book.

Pages xv–xvi: The Baruch, Thoreau, and Carlyle quotes can be found in Robert Menschel, *Markets, Mobs, and Mayhem* (New York: Wiley, 2002): 37, 51, 136. The Nietszche quote is from Friedrich Nietzsche, *Beyond Good and Evil*, translated by Walter Kaufmann (New York: Random House, 1966): 90.

Pages xvi–xvii: Gustave Le Bon, *The Crowd: A Study of the Popular Mind*, translated anonymously (Marietta, GA: Larlin, 1982 reprint). The text of *The Crowd* is available online at a number of sites, including http://encyclopediaindex.com/b/tcrwd10.htm.

Pages xvii: There have been many very good books that deal with collective decision making, collective action, and the way in which seemingly small pieces can add up to bigger (although not always better) wholes. Two that I found especially useful are Kenneth J. Arrow, *The Limits of Organization* (New York: Norton, 1974); and Thomas C. Schelling, *Micromotives and Macrobehavior* (New York: Norton, 1978). More recent, sophisticated takes on self-organization and the emergence of bottom-up order are Steven Johnson, *Emergence* (New York: Scribner, 2001); and Howard Rheingold, *Smart Mobs* (Boston: Perseus, 2002).

Pages xx–xxi: The account of John Craven's success is taken from Sherry Sontag and Christopher Drew, *Blind Man's Bluff* (New York: Public Affairs, 1998): 146–50. Drew and Sontag also detail Craven's success in using the same search method to find an H-bomb that had been lost in the ocean off Spain (58–60).

PART I
1. The Wisdom of Crowds

Pages 3–4: The data about the performance of the audience and the "experts" in *Who Wants to Be a Millionaire?* comes from an interview with a spokeswoman for the show.

Pages 4–5: There are innumerable studies of "group intelligence," loosely defined. Among some of the most important and interesting are Kate H. Gordon, "Group Judgments in the Field of Lifted Weights," *Journal of Experimental Psychology* 7 (1924): 398–400; Hazel Knight, "A Comparison of the Reliability of Group and Individual Judgments," unpublished master's thesis, Columbia University (1921); Herbert Gurnee, "Maze Learning in the Collective Situation," *Journal of Psychology* 3 (1937): 437–43; R. S. Bruce, "Group Judgments in the Fields of Lifted Weights and Visual Discrimination," *Journal of Psychology* 1 (1935): 117–21; and Marjorie Shaw, "A Comparison of Individuals and Small Groups in the Rational Solution of Complex Problems," *American Journal of Psychology* 44 (1932): 491–504.

A good overview of these studies—albeit one that is more skeptical about their import than I am—is Irving Lorge, David Fox, Joel Davitz, and Marlin Brenner, "A Survey of Studies Contrasting the Quality of Group Performance and Individual Performance, 1920–1957," *Psychological Bulletin* 55 (1958): 337–72.

Jack Treynor describes his jelly-bean experiment in Treynor, "Market Efficiency and the Bean Jar Experiment," *Financial Analysts Journal* 43 (1987): 50–53.

One historical example of an attempt to employ group intelligence that I do not discuss elsewhere is the Delphi method, which was devised at the Rand Institute in the early 1950s. Delphi was an attempt to tap into the collective wisdom of a group of experts while avoiding the small-group dynamics that often skew group judgments. There's a good discussion of its history in Harold Linstone and Murray Turoff, *The Delphi Method: Techniques and Applications* (Reading, MA: Addison-Wesley, 1975). The original Rand Institute papers on collective decision making—including a number of studies before the Delphi method was formulated—are fascinating. See, for instance, A. Kaplan, A. L. Skogstad, and M. A. Girshick, "The Prediction of Social and Technological Events," Rand Institute paper P-93 (April 1949). All of these papers are still available from Rand. Also published in *Public Opinion Quarterly* 14 (Spring 1950): 93–110.

Pages 6–7: Norman L. Johnson, "Collective Problem Solving: Functionality Beyond the Individual," Los Alamos working paper LA-UR-98-2227 (1998); and Johnson, "Diversity in Decentralized Systems: Enabling Self-Organizing Solutions," Los Alamos working paper LA-UR-99-6281 (1999), available at http://ishi.lanl.gov/diversity/documents_div.html.

Pages 7–11: Michael T. Maloney and J. Harold Mulherin, "The Stock Price Reaction to the Challenger Crash: Information Disclosure in an Efficient Market" (December 7, 1998), http://ssrn.com/abstract=141971. A revised version of the paper, entitled "The Complexity of Price Discovery in an Efficient Market: The Stock Market Reaction to the *Challenger* Crash," is forthcoming in *Journal of Corporate Finance*. As many have already noted, the stock market seems not to have done a good job in assigning responsibility for the *Columbia* disaster. On the day the *Columbia* disintegrated during reentry, the stock of Alliant Techsystems, the current owner of Thiokol (which still makes booster rockets for the shuttle), plummeted, although it now seems clear that the disaster was caused by foam insulation hitting the *Columbia*'s wing when it launched. In effect, traders assumed that what had been true in 1986 was also true in 2003. This points to one of the many problems with the stock market as a collective decision-making mechanism (which we'll look at in later chapters), namely that investors are prone to herd and to imitate each other. The reaction to the *Challenger* disaster took place in a relatively pristine environment, in the sense that there were no precedents to look to and no preconceived wisdom shaping the crowd's opinions.

Pages 13–15: An excellent overview can be found in Raymond D. Sauer, "The Economics of Wagering Markets," *Journal of Economic Literature* 36 (1998): 2021–64. Sauer's paper includes a discussion of most of the important attempts to disprove the efficiency of the sports-betting market.

The data on horse-racing odds predicting race outcomes is in Sauer (2033–34). It comes from perhaps the most remarkable single piece of evidence on the predictive abilities of betting markets, which is Arthur Hoerl and Herbert Fallin's study of all 1,825 races that were run at the Aqueduct and Belmont Park racetracks in 1970. Hoerl and Fallin compared the objective winning frequency of every horse in every race with the odds that the market had given them. They wanted to know two things: Were the odds (which are subjective probabilities) good predictors of the frequency with which horses won, and was the market's ranking of the horses' chances a good predictor of the order in which horses finished?

Here's what they found: with only a few exceptions, the market's ranking of the horses predicted exactly the order in which horses finished. This was true no matter how many horses were in the race (the sizes of the fields varied that year from five horses to twelve): the favorite finished first most often, the second-favored horse finished second most often, and so on. They also calculated the average finishing position of the horses, and that number declined monotonically with the rank of the horse, without a single mistake.

Even more impressive, at least to my statistically naïve eyes, is how well the odds predicted the frequency of victory. Take, for instance, the 312 races run that year in which seven horses ran. In those races, the favorite was predicted to win 33 percent of the time. It won 34 percent of the time. Second-place horse: 22 percent predicted, 21 percent real; third-place: 16 percent/16 percent; fourth-place: 12 percent/12 percent; fifth-place: 9 percent/8 percent; sixth-place, 6 percent/8 percent; and seventh-place 3 percent/2 percent. The results were similar, though not quite as dazzling, in the other races. In other words, the subjective forecasts of Aqueduct and Belmont Park bettors almost perfectly predicted objective probabilities. See Arthur E. Hoerl and Herbert K. Fallin, "Reliability of Subjective Evaluations in a High Incentive Situation," *Journal of the Royal Statistical Society* 137 (1974): 227–30.

See also William O. Brown and Raymond D. Sauer, "Fundamentals or Noise? Evidence from the Professional Basketball Betting Market," *Journal of Finance* 48 (1993): 1193–209.

Evidence for the NFL market's late-season inefficiency can be found in Richard Borghesi, "Price Predictability: Insight from the NFL Point-Spread Market" (2003), www.cba.ufl.edu/fire/phdstudents/papers/borghesipercent20pricepercent20predictability.pdf.

The long-shot bias is documented in Richard H. Thaler and William T. Ziemba, "Parimutuel Betting Markets: Racetracks and Lotteries," *Journal of Economic Perspectives* 2 (1988): 161–74.

Pages 16–17: Lawrence Page, Sergey Brin, Rajeev Motwani, and Terry Winograd, "The PageRank Citation Ranking: Bringing Order to the Web" (1998), http://dbpubs.stanford.edu/pub/1999-66. See also Brin and Page, "The Anatomy of a Large-Scale Hypertextual Web Search Engine" (1998), http://www-db.stanford.edu/~backrub/google.html.

Pages 17–19: The data on the Iowa Electronic Markets' performance comes from Joyce Berg, Robert Forsythe, Forrest Nelson, and Thomas Rietz, "Results from a Dozen Years of Election Futures Market Research," University of Iowa working paper (2000), http://www.biz.uiowa.edu/iem/archive/BFNR_2000.pdf.

See also Robert Forsythe, Forrest Nelson, George R. Neumann, and Jack Wright, "Anatomy of an Experimental Political Stock Market," *American Economic Review* 82 (1992): 1142–61; and Joyce Berg, Forrest Nelson, and Thomas Rietz, "Accuracy and Forecast Standard Error of Prediction Markets," Tippie College of Business mimeo (2001), http://www.biz.uiowa.edu/iem/archive/forecasting.pdf.

The IEM Web site has a page with links to research into the potential efficacy of prediction markets: http://www.biz.uiowa.edu/iem/archive/references.html.

One important thing to note is that most of these papers, while they document the relative accuracy of the IEM's forecasts, offer a different explanation for that accuracy than the one I offer here. These authors attribute the success of the IEM not to the collective wisdom of the crowd of all IEM traders but rather to a small minority of rational and foresighted investors—the "marginal investors" or "marginal traders"—who keep the market smart by buying or selling whenever IEM prices start to get out of whack (that is, whenever they deviate from what their true value should be). Most IEM traders, the argument goes, are biased and not especially well-informed, and if they were really shaping the prices in the market, those prices would often be wildly inaccurate. But in fact it's the marginal investors who dictate what the IEM does.

The idea of the "marginal investor" is also invoked by many economists to explain why financial markets are relatively efficient. It is an intuitively appealing concept, because it allows us to retain our faith that a few smart people have the right answers while still allowing the market to work. But it's a myth. There is no marginal investor in the sense of a single investor (or small group of investors) who determines the prices that all investors buy and sell at. No trader—even in the stock market, where some investors control enormous amounts of money—has enough capital to outweigh the aggregated buying and selling power of all the other investors. (It is, of course, possible for a single investor to overpay for an asset and thereby acquire it, but in that case there is only one buyer in the market, so of course one buyer sets the price.) That means that the decisions taken by any one investor or small group of investors will be overridden immediately if the "crowd" disagrees with them.

This is obviously true of the IEM, where the stakes people can use to buy and sell contracts are limited to $500. As a result, if the aggregate judgment of most IEM traders was really irrational and inaccurate, the effect of their inaccurate trading would overwhelm the attempts of smart investors to resist it. To take a concrete example from the 1988 IEM presidential market, the accuracy of which was explicitly attributed to marginal traders: according to Forsythe, et al., there were 22 marginal traders and 170 nonmarginal traders in the 1988 market. The average marginal trader did invest twice as much money as the average nonmarginal trader. But this means that the "smart" traders controlled only about a quarter as much money as the "dumb" ones did. If the supposedly dumb traders' judgment was collectively bad, there would have been no way for the smart traders to counterbalance it.

In their 1992 paper, Forsythe et al. provide convincing documentation that those they identified as marginal traders were keener judges of news events and more objective in their judgments than most of the IEM traders (who tended to let their political feelings get in the way). Nonetheless, the marginal traders, on their own, simply did not have the means to set prices, so they could not have been solely responsible for the accuracy of the group's judgment.

More important, in a market like the IEM or in the stock market, it doesn't make sense for some investors to be "marginal" and others "nonmarginal." All investors can move in and out of the market with equal ease. And in any case, two investors with the same amount of capital have the same influence on market prices, even if one of those investors is actively buying and selling and the other is sitting on his hands. Buying or selling a security does not affect a security's price more than not buying it (if you don't own it) or not selling it (if you do own it) does. And a decision to hold on to a stock is just as consequential as the decision to sell it. In that sense, even though some investors are more influential than others (because they control more capital), all investors are marginal. And the price of a stock or of a security always incorporates the judgment of every investor in a market, even if that judgment manifests itself in inaction, which amounts to an effective statement that the current price is right.

This doesn't mean that some investors aren't smarter than others, nor does it mean that having smart traders in a market doesn't matter. The more informed investors are, the better their collective judgment is likely to be (as long as they are also diverse and their judgments are independent). And, as we've seen, whenever a group is asked to solve a cognition problem, chances are that a small minority will do better than the group as a whole and much better than most of the individual members of the group. The data from 1988 convincingly shows that the "marginal traders" were strong supporters of Bush, which was, of course, the accurate judgment to make. But the fact that some traders were strong supporters of Bush is, of course, hardly surprising: if they hadn't been there's no way the market could have reached a collectively intelligent judgment. The market would have been less intelligent had these traders not been part of it, but, to make an obvious point, it would also have been less intelligent had there been no Dukakis supporters in it (then Bush's chances of winning would have been overrated). Retrospectively identifying those participants in a market who were right is not useful (because in any group, some people are going to be more right than others), unless you believe that the same people are always going to be right.

The judgment of all the traders in a market, however they're identified, is part of the market's judgment and helps make it either more or less accurate. In 1988, these "marginal" traders moved it in the right direction. But they did not, on their own, make the market smart, because it is, in the end, impossible for the collective judgment of a large group to be intelligent if the aggregated (not individual) judgment of a large chunk of its members (unless they control only a small amount of capital) is stupid. It also seems telling that in pari-mutuel-betting markets there is no "marginal bettor."

All bettors who bet on a particular horse receive the same odds, and the final odds are determined by the bets of everyone in the pool, so it's a pure weighted-average judgment. These markets are, as we've seen, the most accurate betting markets in existence.

Pages 19–20: Information about the Hollywood Stock Exchange can be found in David Pennock, Steve Lawrence, C. Lee Giles, and Finn Arup Nielsen, "The Power of Play: Efficiency and Forecast Accuracy in Web Market Games," NEC Research Institute technical report 2000-168 (2000), http://artificialmarkets.com/am/pennock-neci-tr-2000-168.pdf. The data on the Oscar predictions seems more impressive than the data on box-office forecasts.

See also David Pennock and Michael P. Wellman, "A Market Framework for Pooling Opinions," unpublished paper (2001); and Pennock and Wellman, "Representing Aggregate Belief Through the Competitive Equilibrium of a Securities Market," Thirteenth Conference on Uncertainty in Artificial Intelligence (July 1997): 392–400, http://dpennock.com/publications.html. These papers are interesting because they demonstrate that the price of a state-contingent security—which just means a security that pays out or doesn't depending on whether a future state of affairs comes to pass or doesn't—represents the collective, weighted-average judgment of all investors in the market for that security.

A useful paper on using securities markets as a form of testing out new products is Nicholas Chan, Ely Dahan, Adlar Kim, Andrew Lo, and Tomaso Poggio, "Securities Trading of Concepts," MIT eBusiness working paper no. 172 (2002), http://ebusiness.mit.edu/research/papers/172_Chan_STOC.pdf.

See also Charles Plott, J. Wit, and W. C. Yang, "Parimutuel Betting Markets as Information Aggregation Devices: Experimental Results," Caltech Social Science working paper 986 (April 1997).

Robin Hanson of George Mason University has written extensively on extending decision markets into other realms, including science and government. His papers on the subject are collected at http://hanson.gmu.edu/ifpubs.html#Hanson. See especially Hanson, "Could Gambling Save Science? Encouraging an Honest Consensus," Social Epistemology 9 (1995): 3–33.

The Innovation Futures Web site is open to all comers and costs nothing to play. It's at http://www.technologyreview.com/trif/trif.asp.

It's also worth looking at the NewsFutures and TradeSports Web sites to get a sense of the range of contracts now being offered, although there has been no serious study of the efficiency or accuracy of these markets.

Page 20: One issue that needs to be considered is how to judge the accuracy of probabilistic forecasts. For instance, in March of 2003 a TradeSports futures contract on the removal of Saddam Hussein by the end of April cost about 80 cents (with a payoff of $1). So the market believed there was an 80 percent chance that Saddam would be gone before May arrived. (Some people question whether in fact this is what an "80¢" price means, but it seems like a reasonable extrapolation.) And so, in fact, he was. Was the market's prediction right? Was there an 80 percent chance that he would be gone? After all, it's a single event. We can't replay history ten times and see if, in fact, eight of the ten times he fell by the end of April while two of the ten times he somehow stayed in power. The right answer, probably, is that we can only test predictive accuracy over time, by judging how often events predicted to happen 80 percent of the time actually did happen. If the market is smart, then over time, eight of ten events that were given 80 percent probabilities should occur.

Page 21: One logical approach would seem to be use a weighted average, with the weights roughly proportional to people's level of confidence in their guesses. Theoretically, at least, that's how stock markets and betting markets work. It's likely that weighting does not make as much of a difference in improving the group's accuracy as we think it does, because there is no evidence that people with good information are more confident about their forecasts than people with bad information. But weighting at the least does no harm—since even if accuracy makes no difference to confidence, the weighted wrong guesses will still be canceled out by the weighted right ones. And if there is a correlation between good information and confidence, then weighting the votes will help. The easiest way to see this is mathematically. If a person's information is good, his guess will be better than the group's collective guess. Any guess that's more accurate than the group's moves the group's judgment closer to the truth, so we want good guesses to be as influential as possible.

One other note: Arrow's impossibility theorem—which shows how, once a group has to decide among more than two choices, there is no voting system that will meet a set of seemingly easy conditions and ensure that the vote's outcome will reflect the group's real preferences—should not apply to groups solving cognition problems, because, at least in theory, solving these problems is not a matter of aggregating *preferences.*

2. The Difference Difference Makes: Waggle Dances, the Bay of Pigs, and the Value of Diversity

Pages 23–26: There has never been, as far as I can tell, a scholarly biography of Ransom Olds, but lively accounts of his career can be found in Duane Yarnell, *Auto Pioneering* (Lansing: privately printed, 1949); and Glenn Niemeyer, *Automotive Career of Ransom E. Olds* (East Lansing: Bureau of Business and Economic Research, 1963).

Pages 26–27: An excellent account of the waggle dance, and much else besides, can be found in Thomas Seeley, *The Wisdom of the Hive* (Harvard: Harvard University Press, 1996). A book worth reading.

Page 28: Rajiv Kumar Sah and Joseph E. Stiglitz, "Human Fallibility and Economic Organization," *American Economic Review* 75 (1985): 292–97.
Sah and Stiglitz, "The Architecture of Economic Systems: Hierarchies and Polyarchies," *American Economic Review* 76 (1986): 716–27.

Pages 28–29: Jeff Bezos drew the analogy between the Cambrian explosion and the Internet in a number of places, including an interview in *Business Week* (September 16, 1999), http://www.businessweek.com/ebiz/9909/916bezos.htm.

Page 30: Scott Page describes this experiment in "Return to the Toolbox," unpublished paper (2002). Also see Scott Page and Lu Hong, "Problem Solving by Heterogeneous Agents," *Journal of Economic Theory* 97 (2001): 123–63.

Pages 30–31: The seminal paper is James G. March, "Exploration and Exploitation in Organizational Learning," *Organization Science* 2 (1991): 71–87. The quotes are from pages 86 and 79.

Pages 32–34: The study of chess players can be found in Herbert A. Simon and W. G. Chase, "Skill in Chess," *American Scientist* 61 (1973): 394–403. The Chase quote is from James Shanteau, "Expert Judgment and Financial Decision Making," paper prepared for *Risky Business: Risk Behavior and Risk Management,* edited by Bo Green (Stockholm: Stockholm University, 1995). This paper includes an excellent survey of expert studies. Also see Shanteau, "Domain Differences in Expertise," Kansas State University unpublished paper (2002), http://www.ksu.edu/psych/cws/downloads.htm.

Pages 33–34: The numbers on mutual-fund performance are from John Bogle, *John Bogle on Investing* (New York: McGraw-Hill, 2001): 20.

J. Scott Armstrong, "The Seer-Sucker Theory: The Value of Experts in Forecasting," *Technology Review* 83 (June–July 1980): 16–24.

Shanteau, "Expert Judgment and Financial Decision Making": 2. See also Shanteau, "Why Do Experts Disagree," in *Risk Behaviour and Risk Management in Business Life*, edited by B. Green et al. (Dordrecht: Kluwer Academic Press, 2000): 186–96.

Terrance Odean, "Volume, Volatility, Price, and Profit When All Traders Are Above Average," *Journal of Finance* 53 (1998): 1887–934.

Pages 35–36: Richard Larrick and Jack B. Soll, "Intuitions About Combining Opinions: Misappreciation of the Averaging Principle," INSEAD working paper 2003/09/TM (2003), http://ged.insead.edu/fichiersti/inseadwp2003/2003–09.pdf.

Pages 36–38: The definitive account of groupthink can be found, of course, in Irving Janis, *Groupthink: Psychological Studies of Policy Decisions and Fiascoes* (Boston: Houghton Mifflin, 1982). See also Irving Janis and Leon Mann, *Decision Making: A Psychological Analysis of Conflict, Choice, and Commitment* (New York: The Free Press, 1977).

Pages 38–39: Solomon Asch, *Social Psychology* (Englewood Cliffs, NJ: Prentice-Hall, Inc., 1952). See also Asch, "Effects of Group Pressure upon the Modification and Distortion of Judgments," *Groups, Leadership and Men*, edited by Harold Guetzkow (New York: Russell & Russell, 1963 [1951]): 177–90.

3. Monkey See, Monkey Do: Imitation, Information Cascades, and Independence

Page 40: The account of the circular mill can be found in William Beebe, *Edge of the Jungle* (New York: Holt, 1921).

A compelling account of self-organization in nature and in human society is Steven Johnson, *Emergence* (New York: Scribner, 2001). There are obvious resonances between Johnson's book and my own, although in his model local influence is important and generally beneficial, while I see independence as essential and see influence as, on the whole, inimical to good cognitive judgments. On the other hand, local influence is clearly a good thing when it comes to coordination problems. More to the point, *Emergence* is only tangentially concerned with decision making, and is more interested in, as the title suggests, self-organization and the emergence of order.

Page 42: There's an excellent discussion of the conceptual foundations of methodological individualism and of its limits in Kenneth J. Arrow, "Methodological Individualism and Social Knowledge," *American Economic Review* 84.2 (1994): 1–9.

The Simon quote is from Herbert J. Simon, *Administrative Behavior*, 3rd edition (New York: Free Press, 1976): xvi.

The essential article on the idea of embeddedness and its relationship to economic thinking is Mark Granovetter, "Economic Action and Social Structure: The Problem of Embeddedness," *American Journal of Sociology* 91 (1985): 481–510. See also Ronald S. Burt, *Structural Holes: The Social Structure of Competition* (Cambridge: Harvard University Press, 1992).

Pages 43–44: The street-corner experiment is described in Stanley Milgram, Leonard Bickman, and Lawrence Berkowitz, "Note on the Drawing Power of Crowds of Different Size," *Journal of Personality and Social Psychology* 13 (1969): 79–82.

Pages 44–47: David Romer's brilliant analysis can be found in David Romer, "It's Fourth

JAMES SUROWIECKI

Down and What Does the Bellman Equation Say? A Dynamic-Programming Analysis of Football Strategy," working paper, University of California, Berkeley (2003). Also published as NBER working paper w9024 (2002), http://papers.nber.org/papers/w9024.

Page 48: Michael Lewis, *Moneyball* (New York: Norton, 2003).

Pages 49–50: David S. Scharfstein and Jeremy C. Stein, "Herd Behavior and Investment," *American Economic Review* 80 (June 1990): 465–79.

Page 51: John Maynard Keynes, *The General Theory of Employment, Interest, and Money* (New York: Harbinger, 1964): 158. *The General Theory* was originally published in 1936.

Pages 51–53: The account of plank-road fever is taken from Daniel B. Klein and John Majewski, "Plank Road Fever in Antebellum America: New York State Origins," *New York History* (January 1994): 39–65.

Pages 53–54: The literature on informational cascades is voluminous and ever-growing, and an excellent guide to it is a Web page that Ivo Welch maintains at http://welch.som.yale.edu/cascades/. Two important articles are Sushil Bikhchandani, David Hirshleifer, and Ivo Welch, "A Theory of Fads, Fashion, Custom, and Cultural Change as Informational Cascades," *Journal of Political Economy* 100 (1992): 992–1026; and Bikhchandani, Hirshleifer, and Welch, "Learning from the Behavior of Others: Conformity, Fads, and Informational Cascades," *Journal of Economic Perspectives* 12 (1998): 151–70.

See also Abhijit V. Banerjee, "A Simple Model of Herd Behavior," *Quarterly Journal of Economics* 107 (1992): 797–817; H. Henry Cao and David Hirshleifer, "Conversation, Observational Learning, and Informational Cascades," Dice Center working paper no. 2001–5 (2001), http://papers.ssrn.com/sol3/papers.cfm?abstract_id=267770; and Suzanne Lohmann, "The Dynamics of Informational Cascades: The Monday Demonstrations in Leipzig, East Germany, 1989–91," *World Politics* 47 (1994): 42–101.

Pages 53–55: A rigorous model of cascades and the way networks function is in Duncan Watts, *Six Degrees* (New York: Norton, 2002).

Page 55: A remarkably rich and human picture of how cascades work in the real world can be found in Malcolm Gladwell, *The Tipping Point* (New York: Little, Brown, 2000).

Robert Shiller, "Conversation, Information, and Herd Behavior," *American Economic Review* 85 (1995): 181–85. While Shiller is skeptical of the ubiquity of cascades, in this paper he nonetheless emphasizes the importance of social influence, as a way of explaining herding behavior.

Pages 55–56: A longer account of William Sellers's campaign to standardize the screw can be found in James Surowiecki, "Turn of the Century," *Wired* 10.01 (January 2002), http://www.wired.com/wired/archive/10.01/standards_pr.html.

Page 57: A definitive account of the "1,000 percent myth" can be found in Andrew Odlyzko, "Internet Traffic Growth: Sources and Implications," *Optical Transmission Systems and Equipment for WDM Networking II,* edited by B. B. Dingel, W. Weiershausen, A. K. Dutta, and K.-I. Sate, proceedings of the International Society for Optical Engineering (SPIE) 5247 (2003): 1–15.

Page 59: Herbert Simon, "A Mechanism for Social Selection and Successful Altruism," *Science* 250 (1990): 1665–68. Simon used the curious word "docility" to describe our willingness to mimic our elders and those who have influence in society. My account of imitation here differs substantially from Simon's insofar as he seemed to argue that most people were unable to distinguish or were uninterested in distinguishing between imitations that made sense and those that didn't.

Page 59: The story of Imo can be found in Lee Dugatkin, *The Imitation Factor* (New York: The Free Press, 2001): 170–72.

Page 60: Robert Boyd and Peter J. Richerson, "Norms and Bounded Rationality," in *Bounded Rationality: The Adaptive Toolbox*, edited by Gerd Gigerenzer and Reinhard Selten (Cambridge: MIT Press, 2001): 281–96. Boyd and Richerson have also written a number of important papers on the possibility of the evolutionary transmission of culture, which is relevant to this book's chapter on cooperation and trust.

Page 61: Ivo Welch, one of the original informational-cascade theorists, has been making this argument, while also writing about the relationship between overconfidence and entrepreneurship, for years. See Antonio Bernardo and Ivo Welch, "On the Evolution of Overconfidence and Entrepreneurs," Cowles Foundation discussion paper no. 1307 (2001).

Pages 61–62: The original paper is Bryce Ryan and Neal Gross, "The Diffusion of Hybrid Seed Corn in Two Iowa Communities," *Rural Sociology* 8 (1943): 15–24. See also Everett Rogers, *The Diffusion of Innovations* (New York: The Free Press, 1983); and J. S. Coleman, H. Menzel, and E. Katz, "The Diffusion of an Innovation Among Physicians," *Sociometry* 20 (1957): 253–70. These are the texts that established the idea of the S-curve of technological adoption and the importance of networks of influence.

Page 62: An excellent study of India during the Green Revolution is Kaivan Munshi, "Social Learning in a Heterogeneous Population: Technology Diffusion in the Indian Green Revolution," Brown University working paper (2003), http://www.econ.brown.edu/fac/Kaivan_Munshi/ag6.pdf. The paper was published in the *Journal of Development Economics*, 73 (2004): 185–213.

Pages 63–65: Angela Hung and Charles Plott, "Information Cascades: Replication and an Extension to Majority Rule and Conformity-Rewarding Institutions," *American Economic Review* 91 (2001): 1508–20.

4. Putting the Pieces Together: The CIA, Linux, and the Art of Decentralization

Pages 66–67: This account of Bill Donovan's campaign for a national intelligence agency is drawn from Larry Valero, " 'We Need Our New OSS, Our New General Donovan, Now . . .': The Public Discourse Over American Intelligence, 1944–1953," *Intelligence and National Security* 18 (2003): 91–118.

Page 67: See *Central Intelligence: Origin and Evolution*, edited by Michael Warner (Washington, DC: Center for the Study of Intelligence, 2001): 1, www.cia.gov/csi/books/cia_origin/PDFS/19.pdf. This is a remarkable collection of documents relating to the evolution of American intelligence in the postwar years.

Page 68: Roberta Wohlstetter, *Warning and Decision* (Palo Alto: Stanford University, 1962).

Page 69: Richard Shelby issued his own supplement to the Senate Intelligence Committee report. See Shelby, "September 11 and the Imperative of Reform in the U.S. Intelligence Community" (2002): 65, 21, http://intelligence.senate.gov/shelby.pdf. The core of Shelby's critique of the failure of the intelligence community is on pages 21–45 of his report.

Page 71: Friedrich Hayek's most famous essay on the subject of local knowledge is F. A. Hayek, "The Use of Knowledge in Society," *American Economic Review* 35 (1945): 519–30. See also Hayek, *Individualism and Economic Order* (Chicago: University of Chicago Press, 1948). Although the idea of the wisdom of crowds has affinities with

Hayek's work, and in particular with his conviction that social mechanisms could produce intelligent outcomes without top-down guidance, Hayek would have been, I
think, hostile to the emphasis I place on the virtues of aggregation. Hayek did not like
the idea of the market as a kind of giant calculating machine, and he was skeptical of
the quest for *a* right answer. In particular, he did not like any attempt at centralizing
intelligence, believing that it was both futile (because the multiplicity of local knowl-
edges could not be meaningfully condensed into a single judgment) and probably dangerous. The virtue of the market for him was the way it achieved its ends in a truly
decentralized fashion, with people talking to each other and transmitting information
to each other only through the vehicle of price.

While the Hayekian virtues of markets are undeniable, particularly when it comes to solving the problem of coordination, I also think Hayek's fear of socialism and of any form of
centralized authority led him to overestimate the difficulties in aggregating information
and local knowledge and to underestimate the potential benefits of such aggregation. A
pari-mutuel-betting market, for instance, is thoroughly un-Hayekian: a central authority
takes one side of all bets, and aggregates the results to produce one set of odds that applies to all bettors. But it produces an eerily accurate picture of the future.

The story of the *demes* can be found in Brook Manville and Josiah Ober, *A Company
of Citizens* (Boston: Harvard Business School Press, 2003): 144. The relevant passages
from the Bible are Exodus 18:17–26.

Pages 72–74: Ko Kowabura, "Linux: A Bazaar at the Edge of Chaos," *First Monday* 5
(2000), http://firstmonday.org/issues/issue5_3/kuwabara/index.html. See also Linus
Torvalds, *Just for Fun* (New York: HarperBusiness, 2001).

Page 76: The description of the Iraqi resistance as a self-organizing, decentralized phenomenon comes from Kevin Maney, "Military Strategists Could Learn a Thing or Two
from the Sims," *USA Today* (April 1, 2003). The line about tactics and strategy comes
from Mark Steyn, "The War? That Was All Over Two Weeks Ago," *Daily Telegraph*
(May 4, 2003).

Pages 76–77: Interesting discussions of the decentralized nature of the U.S. military can
be found in Richard Pascale, Mark Millemann, and Linda Gioja, *Surfing the Edge of
Chaos* (New York: Crown, 2000): 135–41; and Christopher Meyer and Stan Davis, *It's
Alive* (New York: Crown Business, 2000): 156–64.

Page 79: PAM is at http://www.policyanalysismarket.org.

5. Shall We Dance?: Coordination in a Complex World

Pages 84–85: William H. Whyte, *City: Rediscovering the Center* (New York: Doubleday,
1988): 56–63. See also Whyte, "The Gifted Pedestrian," *Ekistics* (May–June 1984).

Pages 87–89: Brian Arthur laid out the El Farol problem in W. Brian Arthur, "Inductive
Reasoning and Bounded Rationality," *American Economic Review* 84 (1994): 406–11.

Pages 89–90: Ann M. Bell and William A. Sethares, "Avoiding Global Congestion Using
Decentralized Adaptive Agents," *IEEE Transactions on Signal Processing* 49 (2001):
2873–79.

Pages 90–92: The Grand Central experiment is in Thomas C. Schelling, *The Strategy of
Conflict* (Cambridge: Harvard University Press, 1960): 54–67.

Page 92: Howard Rheingold, *Smart Mobs* (Boston: Perseus Books, 2002). As the similar-
ity in the titles suggests, there are obvious resonances between Rheingold's book and
this one—particularly in the possibilities for groups to cooperate and coordinate without top-down leadership. But the central concerns of the books are quite different.

Smart Mobs illuminates the way technology may make it easier for people to organize collectively to good (or, conceivably, bad) ends. (The "smart" in Rheingold's title means, for the most part, something more like "self-aware" than "wise.") What's distinctive about smart mobs is that they are aware of themselves and can, or at least someday will be able to, act collectively in a self-directed manner. That's true of some of the crowds in this book, but all other things being equal, the more self-aware a crowd becomes, the less wise (in my sense of the word) it will become, because the less independent each of its members will be.

Pages 92–93: Jonathan Rauch, "Seeing Around Corners," *The Atlantic Monthly* 289 (April 2002): 35–48.

Pages 94–96: The subway and line-jumping studies, along with many of Milgram's most interesting papers, is included in *The Individual in a Social World*, edited by Stanley Milgram (New York: McGraw-Hill, 1992). Milgram's description of how the subway study came about is from the Introduction to that book (xix–xxxiii).

Pages 97–98: An excellent discussion of the relationship between convention and economic behavior is H. Peyton Young, "The Economics of Convention," *Journal of Economic Perspectives* 10 (1996): 105–22. Also see Truman F. Bewley, *Why Wages Don't Fall During a Recession* (Cambridge: Harvard University Press, 1999); and George Akerlof, "A Theory of Social Custom, of Which Unemployment May Be One Consequence," *Quarterly Journal of Economics* 94 (1980): 749–75.

Page 98: The study is Robert E. Hall, "The Response of Prices to Shifts in Demand," Stanford working paper (2002).

Pages 98–101: A good discussion of movie theaters' fixed-price strategy can be found in Liran Einav and Barak Orbach, "Uniform Prices for Differentiated Goods: The Case of the Movie-Theater Industry," Harvard Olin discussion paper no. 337 (2001).

Pages 103–7: The original account of an experimental market is Edward Chamberlin, "An Experimental Imperfect Market," *Journal of Political Economy* 56 (1948): 95–108. Vernon L. Smith's paper on his first classroom experiment is Vernon L. Smith, "An Experimental Study of Competitive Market Behavior," *Journal of Political Economy* 70 (1962): 111–37. Many of the papers he has published over the years have been collected in two volumes: Smith, *Papers in Experimental Economics* (Cambridge: Cambridge University Press, 1991); and Smith, *Bargaining and Market Behavior* (Cambridge: Cambridge University Press, 2000).

Pages 105–6: The key paper is Kenneth J. Arrow and Gerard Debreu, "Existence of an Equilibrium for a Competitive Economy," *Econometrica* 22 (1954): 265–90. See also Arrow, "The Role of Securities in the Optimal Allocation of Risk-Bearing," *Review of Economic Studies* 31 (1964): 91–96. (Oddly, this essay was first published in French in 1953, and was only published in English eleven years later, even though it was written in English to begin with.) See also Debreu, *Theory of Value* (New York: Wiley, 1959).

Pages 106–7: Vernon L. Smith's Nobel lecture offers an excellent survey of not just experimental economics but also of current thinking about what efficient market exchange requires. See Smith, "Constructivist and Ecological Rationality in Economics," *American Economic Review* 93 (2003): 465–508.

6. Society Does Exist: Taxes, Tipping, Television, and Trust

Pages 112–14: On ultimatum games, see Vernon L. Smith, "Constructivist and Ecological Rationality in Economics," *American Economic Review* 93 (2003): 465–508. An excellent study of the way people play the ultimatum game in different countries is Alvin E.

Roth, Vesna Prasnikar, Masahiro Okuno-Fujiwara, and Shmuel Zamir, "Bargaining and Market Behavior in Jerusalem, Ljubljana, Pittsburgh, and Tokyo: An Experimental Study," *American Economic Review* 81 (1991): 1068–95.

On the capuchins, see Sarah F. Brosnan and Frans B. M. de Waal, "Monkeys Reject Unequal Pay," *Nature* 425 (2003): 297–99.

Page 115: See Alberto Alesina, Rafael di Tella, and Robert MacCulloch, "Inequality and Happiness: Are Europeans and Americans Different?," National Bureau of Economic Research working paper no. 8198 (2001). A later version of this paper is available at http://www.people.hbs.edu/rditella. See also Jennifer L. Hochschild, *What's Fair? American Beliefs About Distributive Justice* (Cambridge: Harvard University Press, 1981); and Hochschild, *Facing Up to the American Dream: Race, Class, and the Soul of the Nation* (Princeton: Princeton University Press, 1996).

Page 116: Samuel Bowles and Herbert Gintis, "Prosocial Emotions," Santa Fe Institute working paper no. 02–07–028 (2003); and Bowles and Gintis, "Origins of Human Co-operation," in *Genetic and Cultural Evolution of Cooperation,* edited by Peter Hammerstein (Cambridge: MIT Press, 2003). See also Ernst Fehr and Simon Gachter, "Fairness and Retaliation: The Economics of Reciprocity," *Journal of Economic Perspectives* 14 (2000): 159–81; and Ernst Fehr, Urs Fischbacher, and Simon Gachter, "Strong Reciprocity, Human Cooperation and the Enforcement of Social Norms," *Human Nature* 13 (2002): 1–25.

A genuinely fascinating paper on the subject of fairness is Robert J. Shiller, Maxim Boycko, and Vladimir Korobov, "Popular Attitudes Toward Free Markets: The Soviet Union and the United States Compared," *American Economic Review* 81 (1991): 385–400.

Page 117: The classic text in the field remains Robert Axelrod, *The Evolution of Cooperation* (New York: Basic Books, 1984). Axelrod's more recent work, though, has moved beyond a single-minded focus on reciprocal altruism to investigate other explanations for the rise of cooperation. See, among other papers, Rick L. Riolo, Michael D. Cohen, and Robert Axelrod, "Evolution of Cooperation Without Reciprocity," *Nature* 414 (2001): 441–43; Cohen, Riolo, and Axelrod, "The Role of Social Structure in the Maintenance of Cooperative Regimes," *Rationality and Society* 13 (2001): 5–32; and Axelrod, "On Six Advances in Cooperation Theory," *Analyse und Kritik* 22 (2000): 130–51. All of these papers are available at http://wwwpersonal.umich.edu/~axe/research_papers.html.

Page 118: Robert Wright's argument is, needless to say, much more sophisticated and nuanced than my short appropriation of it. See Robert Wright, *Nonzero: The Logic of Human Destiny* (New York: Pantheon, 2000).

Page 119: On the Quakers, see Jacob M. Price, "The Great Quaker Business Families of 18th Century London," *Overseas Trade and Traders: Essays on Some Commercial, Financial, and Political Challenges Facing British Atlantic Merchants, 1600–1775* (Brookfield, VT: Ashgate, 1996); James Walvin, *The Quakers: Money and Morals* (London: Trafalgar Square, 1998); and Peter Mathias, "Risk, Credit, and Kinship in Early Modern Enterprise," in *The Early Modern Atlantic Economy,* edited by John J. McCusker and Kenneth Morgan (Cambridge: Cambridge University Press, 2000): 15–35.

Pages 120–21: Thomas Schelling, *Choice and Consequence* (Cambridge: Harvard University Press, 1985): 210. See also Kenneth J. Arrow, "Observations on Social Capital," in *Social Capital: A Multifaceted Perspective,* edited by Partha Dasgupta and Ismail Seregeldin (Washington, DC: The World Bank, 1999); and Arrow, "The Economics of Moral Hazard—Further Comment," *American Economic Review* 58 (1968): 537–38.

The thinker who's done the most to make it clear how important healthy institutions are to economic growth is the economist Douglass North. See, among many others, Douglass C. North, "Economic Performance Through Time," *American Economic Review* 84 (1994): 359–68; and North, "Institutions," *Journal of Economic Perspectives* 5 (1991): 97–112.

Avner Greif, "Contract Enforceability and Economic Institutions in Early Trade: The Maghribi Traders' Coalition," *American Economic Review* 83 (1993): 525–48; and Greif, "Self-Enforcing Political Systems and Economic Growth: Late-Medieval Genoa," in *Analytic Narratives,* edited by Robert H. Bates et al. (Princeton: Princeton University Press, 1998): 23–63.

There is an especially rich discussion of the Enlightenment faith that commerce was "sweet" in Albert O. Hirschman, *The Passions and the Interests* (Princeton: Princeton University Press, 1977).

Richard Tilly, "Moral Standards and Business Behavior in Nineteenth-Century Germany and Britain," in *Bourgeois Society in Nineteenth-Century Europe,* edited by Jurgen Kocka and Allen Mitchell (Oxford: Berg, 1993): 182–86.

Page 122: John Mueller, *Capitalism, Democracy, and Ralph's Pretty Good Grocery* (Princeton: Princeton University Press, 1998).

Page 123: See Clifford Geertz, "The Bazaar Economy: Information and Search in Peasant Marketing," *American Economic Review* 68.2 (1978): 28–32.

Pages 124: The Knack quote is from Stephen Knack, "Trust, Associational Life and Economic Performance," in *The Contribution of Human and Social Capital to Sustained Economic Growth and Well-Being,* edited by John F. Helliwell (Hull, CAN: Human Resources Development Canada and Organisation for Economic Co-operation and Development, 2001): 181.

The paper is Stephen Knack and Philip Keefer, "Does Social Capital Have an Economic Payoff? A Cross-Country Investigation," *Quarterly Journal of Economics* 112 (1997): 1251–88.

Pages 125–26: See Joseph Henrich et al., " 'Economic Man' in Cross-Cultural Perspective: Behavioral Experiments in 15 Small-Scale Societies," Santa Fe Institute working paper (2001), available at http://www.santafe.edu/sfi/publications/WorkingPapers/01-11-063.pdf; and Henrich et al., "In Search of *Homo Economicus:* Experiments in 15 Small-Scale Societies," *American Economic Review* 91 (2001): 73–78.

Pages 133–34: Mancur Olson, *The Logic of Collective Action* (New Haven: Yale University Press, 1965).

Page 138: See Joel Slemrod, "On Voluntary Compliance, Voluntary Taxes, and Social Capital," *National Tax Journal* 51 (1998): 485–91.

See also Margaret Levi, "A State of Trust," in *Trust and Governance,* edited by Valerie Braithwaite and Margaret Levi (New York: Russell Sage Foundation, 1999).

Pages 139–40: Ernst Fehr and Simon Gächter, "Cooperation and Punishment in Public Goods Experiments," *American Economic Review* 90 (2000): 980–94. See also the previously cited papers by Fehr et al. on fairness and reciprocity.

Page 140: John T. Scholz and Mark Lubell, "Adaptive Political Attitudes: Duty, Trust, and Fear as Monitors of Tax Policy," *American Journal of Political Science* 42 (1998): 903–20; and Scholz and Lubell, "Trust and Taxpaying: Testing the Heuristic Approach to Collective Action," *American Journal of Political Science* 42 (1998): 398–417.

PART II
7. Traffic: What We Have Here Is a Failure to Coordinate

Pages 146–47: An excellent survey of congestion pricing is C. Robin Lindsey and Erik T. Verhoef, "Traffic Congestion and Congestion Pricing," Tinbergen Institute discussion paper TI2000–101/3 (2000). See also Katushiko Nakamura and Kara Maria Kockelman, "Congestion Pricing and Roadspace Rationing: An Application to the San Francisco Bay Bridge Corridor," *Transportation Research Part A: Policy and Practice* 36 (2002): 403–17.

Pages 147–48: There is a good discussion of Singapore's traffic system in Dan Baum, "The Ultimate Jam Session," *Wired* 9.11 (November 2001), http://www.wired.com/wired/archive/9.11/singapore_pr.html. Baum's piece is very good on traffic problems generally. See also Rex Toh and Sock-Yong Phang, "Curbing Urban Traffic Congestion in Singapore," *Logistics Transportation Journal* (1997); and Teo Poh Keng, "Singapore to Adopt Toll System," *The Nikkei Weekly* (March 16, 1998): 18.

Pages 150–51: For a remarkably clear and concise explanation of the science behind jams, see Philip Ball, "Further On Down the Road," *Nature* (November 26, 1998); and Ball, "Jams Tomorrow," *The New Scientist* (January 15, 2000).

Page 151: Kai Nagel, Peter Wagner, and Richard Woesler, "Still Flowing: Approaches to Traffic Flow and Traffic Jam Modeling" (2003), forthcoming in *Operations Research*.

Pages 152–53: K. Smilowitz, C. F. Daganzo, M. J. Cassidy, and R. L. Bertini, "Some Observations of Highway Traffic in Long Queues," *Transportation Research Record* 1678 (1999): 225–33; and Daganzo, Cassidy, and Bertini, "Possible Explanations of Phase Transitions in Highway Traffic," *Transportation Research* 33A (1999): 365–79.

See also M. J. Cassidy and B. Coifman, "The Relation Between Average Speed, Flow and Occupancy and the Analogous Relation Between Density and Occupancy," *Transportation Research Record* 1591 (1997): 1–6; and M. J. Cassidy and R. L. Bertini, "Observations at a Freeway Bottleneck," in *International Symposium of Traffic and Transportation Theory,* edited by A. Cedar (Amsterdam: Elsevier, 1999): 107–24.

Pages 155–57: Dirk Helbing and Bernardo Huberman, "Coherent Moving States in Highway Traffic," *Nature* 396 (1998): 738–40; and Huberman and Helbing, "Economics-Based Optimization of Unstable Flows," *Europhysics Letters* 47 (1999): 196–202.

Pages 156–57: Dirk Helbing and Martin Treiber, "Jams, Waves, and Clusters," *Science* 282 (1998): 2001–3.

8. Science: Collaboration, Competition, and Reputation

Pages 158–60: The SARS story can be found in WHO, "A Multicentre Collaboration to Investigate the Cause of Severe Acute Respiratory Syndrome," *The Lancet* 361 (2003): 1730–33.

Page 162: Paula Stephan, "The Economics of Science," *Journal of Economic Literature* 34 (1996): 1220–21.

Page 162: Etienne Wenger, Richard McDermott, and William M. Snyder, *Cultivating Communities of Practice* (Boston: Harvard Business School Press, 2002): 10.

Page 162: D. J. de Solla Price and Donald B. Beaver, "Collaboration in an Invisible College," *American Psychologist* 21 (1966): 1101–17.

Harriet Zuckerman, "Nobel Laureates in Science: Patterns of Productivity, Collaboration and Authorship," *American Sociological Review* 32 (1967): 391–403.

Page 163: Barry Bozeman and Sooho Lee, "The Impact of Research Collaboration on Scientific Productivity," paper prepared for presentation at the annual meeting of the American Association for the Advancement of Science (February 2003): 24–25.

Pages 164–67: Robert K. Merton, "The Matthew Effect," *Science* 159 (1968): 56–63.

Pages 166–67: There is an excellent discussion of Henry Oldenburg and the creation of the Royal Society in Lisa Jardine, *Ingenious Pursuits* (New York: Doubleday, 1999). See also Joel Mokyr, *The Gifts of Athena: Historical Origins of the Knowledge Economy* (Princeton: Princeton University Press, 2002): 36, 54. Mokyr's book is a wondrous history of the rise in the West of what he calls "open science," which required a historically unprecedented free access to knowledge.

Pages 170–72: Robert K. Merton, "The Matthew Effect II: Cumulative Advantage and the Symbolism of Intellectual Property," *Isis* 79 (1988): 606–23.

Page 171: Richard Lewontin's paper is cited in Merton, "The Matthew Effect II": 608.

9. Committees, Juries, and Teams: The Columbia Disaster and How Small Groups Can Be Made to Work

Pages 173–82: All the data and information on the *Columbia* disaster comes from the remarkable *Columbia Accident Investigation Board Report Volume 1: August 2002*; and from James Glanz and John Schwartz, "Engineers: NASA Leaders Ignored Safety Pleas," *The New York Times* (September 26, 2003). The *Columbia* report is available at http://www.nasa.gov.

Page 177: The Ralph Cordiner quote can be found in Leonard Sayles and George Strauss, *Human Behavior in Organizations* (New York: Prentice-Hall, 1966): 219.

Page 183: One classic study of the importance of leaders in structuring discussion is N. R. F. Maier and A. R. Solem, "The Contribution of a Discussion Leader to the Quality of Group Thinking: The Effective Use of Minority Opinions," *Human Relations* 5 (1952): 277–88.

Pages 183–84: Garold Stasser, "The Uncertain Role of Unshared Information in Collective Choice," in *Shared Knowledge in Organizations*, edited by Leigh L. Thompson, John Levine, and David Messick (New York: Lawrence Erlbaum, 1999).

Pages 184–86: On group polarization, see: J. A. F. Stoner, *A Comparison of Individual and Group Decisions Involving Risk*, unpublished master's thesis, MIT School of Industrial Management (1961); D. G. Myers and M. F. Kaplan, "Group-Induced Polarization in Simulated Juries," *Personality and Social Psychology Bulletin* 2 (1976): 63–66; and A. Vinokur and E. Burnstein, "Novel Argumentation and Attitude Change: The Case of Polarization Following Group Discussion," *European Journal of Social Psychology* 8 (1978): 335–48.

Pages 185–88: An excellent look at the evidence for small-group decision making, group polarization, and the value of differing opinions is Cass Sunstein, *Why Societies Need Dissent* (Cambridge: Harvard University Press, 2003).

Page 187: The experiments with the military fliers were done by E. P. Torrance. See E. P. Torrance, "Some Consequences of Power Differences on Decisions in B-26 Crews," United States Air Force Personnel and Training Research Center research bulletin 54–128 (1954); and Torrance, "Some Consequences of Power Differences in Permanent and Temporary Three-Man Groups," in *Small Groups*, edited by A. P. Hare et al. (New York: Knopf, 1955).

Page 188: Brock Blomberg and Joseph Harrington, "A Theory of Flexible Moderates and Rigid Extremists with an Application to the U.S. Congress," *American Economic Review* 90 (2000): 605–20.

Pages 189–90: Alan S. Blinder and John Morgan, "Are Two Heads Better Than One? Monetary Policy by Committee," National Bureau of Economic Review working paper 7909 (2000). See also Clare Lombardelli, James Proudman, and James Talbot, "Committees versus Individuals: An Experimental Analysis of Monetary Policy Decision-Making," Bank of England working paper 165 (2002), available at http://www.bankofengland.co.uk/wp/index.

10. The Company: Meet the New Boss, Same as the Old Boss?

Pages 192–95: There's a good discussion of Zara's logistical wizardry in David Bovet and Joseph Martha, Value Nets (New York: John Wiley & Sons, 2000).

Pages 196–97: See Ronald Coase, The Firm, the Market, and the Law (Chicago: University of Chicago Press, 1988); the D. H. Robertson quote is on page 35. See also Oliver Williamson, Markets and Hierarchies: Analysis and Antitrust Implications (New York: The Free Press, 1975); Williamson, "Calculativeness, Trust, and Economic Organization," Journal of Law and Economics 36 (1993): 453–86; and The Nature of the Firm, edited by Oliver Williamson and Sidney Winter (New York: Oxford University Press, 1991), which includes the original Coase essay.

Pages 201–2: Alfred Chandler Jr.'s histories of the rise of corporate capitalism are essential. See Chandler, The Visible Hand (Cambridge: Belknap/Harvard University Press, 1977); and Chandler, Scale and Scope (Cambridge: Belknap/Harvard University Press, 1990). His earlier books, Strategy and Structure (Cambridge: MIT Press, 1969 [1962]) and Pierre S. DuPont and the Making of the Modern Corporation (New York: Harper, 1971) are also valuable.

Page 202: See Elton Mayo, The Human Problems of an Industrial Civilization (London: Routledge, 2003 [1938]); and Mayo, Social Problems of an Industrial Civilization (Work, Its Rewards, and Its Discontents) (Manchester, New Hampshire: Ayer Books, 1977 [1945]). William H. Whyte writes explicitly about Mayo's impact on the corporation in Whyte, The Organization Man (New York: Simon and Schuster, 1956): 32–46.

Page 203: For the anecdote about the headlight meetings and for a discussion of bureaucratic sclerosis at General Motors, see Nitin Nohria, Davis Dyer and Frederick Dalzell, Changing Fortunes: Remaking the Industrial Corporation (New York: Wiley, 2002): 119–20.

Page 204: In 1980, there were five levels separating the head of Toyota from a factory-floor supervisor. At Ford, there were fifteen. See Thomas J. Peters and Robert H. Waterman, In Search of Excellence (New York: Harper & Row, 1982): 313.

Page 204–5: Maryann Keller, Rude Awakening (New York: Morrow, 1989): 127.

Page 205: Peters and Waterman, In Search of Excellence: 18.

Page 206: A very different analysis of hierarchy, emphasizing its virtue as an efficient information-processing mechanism, is in Roy Radner, "Hierarchy: The Economics of Managing," Journal of Economic Literature 30 (1992): 1382–415.

Pages 207–8: Chris Argyris is cited in Stephan H. Haeckel, Adaptive Enterprise (Boston: Harvard Business School Press, 1999): 151.

Page 208: Donald Roy, "Goldbricking in a Machine Shop," American Journal of Sociology 7 (1952): 427–42.

Pages 208–9: A shorter version of Jensen's argument can be found in Michael C. Jensen, "Corporate Budgeting Is Broke—Let's Fix It," Harvard Business Review (November 2001). The longer paper is Jensen, "Paying People to Lie: The Truth About the Budgeting Process," Harvard Business School working paper 01–072 (2001), http://papers.ssrn.com/papers=267651.

Pages 210–11: For a defense of the bottom-up model see Joseph Blasi and Eric Kruse, *In the Company of Owners* (New York: Basic Books, 2003); and for a critique of it see James Hoopes, *False Prophets* (Cambridge: Perseus Publishing, 2003). See also William Joyce, Nitin Nohria, and Bruce Roberson, *What Really Works: The 4 + 2 Formula for Sustained Business Success* (New York: HarperCollins, 2003).

Pages 210–11: Alfred P. Sloan, *My Years with General Motors* (New York: Doubleday, 1964).

Page 213: The definitive Western account of the Toyota Production System can be found in James P. Womack, Daniel T. Jones, and Daniel Roos, *The Machine That Changed the World: The Story of Lean Production* (New York: HarperCollins, 1991).

Page 215: Keller, *Rude Awakening*: 101.

Page 216: Frederick Winslow Taylor is cited in Stephan H. Haeckel, *Adaptive Enterprise* (Boston: Harvard Business School Press, 1999): 30.

Page 217: Rakesh Khurana, *Searching for a Corporate Savior* (Princeton: Princeton University Press, 2002).

Page 217: As an example, this article claims that Chambers has "created more shareholder value" than virtually any other high-tech CEO; see http://www.edgewater.com/site/news_events/in_the_news_articles/042501_VARBusiness.html.

Results from the Burson Marsteller 2001 survey "Building CEO Capital" available at: http://www.bm.com/insights/ceo_rep.html.

Page 218: See, among others, Mark Sirower, *The Synergy Trap* (New York: The Free Press, 1997). The value of the average firm that is acquired in a merger does not shrink, so perhaps you could say that CEOs of acquired firms are doing a good job. But it's the CEOs of acquiring firms who do the initiating and bear most of the responsibility for the decision, since once a concrete takeover offer is made the responses of the target company's CEO are limited.

Page 219: Sydney Finkelstein, *Why Smart Executives Fail* (New York: Portfolio, 2003): 49.

Pages 219–20: Armen Alchian, "Uncertainty, Evolution, and Economic Theory," *Journal of Political Economy* 58 (1950): 213, 214. Alchian is sometimes read as arguing that the market's winnowing effect guarantees that the winner will be the best company imaginable, and will be maximizing profits. He is explicitly not saying this, arguing instead that the ability to realize profits is always relative, because it always depends on how capable one's competitors are. So the fact that a company is profitable may just be the result of the fact that its competitors are not very good.

Page 220: Finkelstein, *Why Smart Executives Fail*: 47–48.

Page 221: Charles R. Plott and Kay-Yut Chen, "Information Aggregation Mechanisms: Concept, Design and Implementation for a Sales Forecasting Problem," Caltech working paper 1131 (March 2002).

Pages 221–23: This discussion of Innocentive's experiment is based on a conversation with Alph Bingham of Innocentive.

11. Markets: Beauty Contests, Bowling Alleys, and the Stock Prices

Page 225: In response to all the hysteria, the New York Stock Exchange economist Edward Meeker wrote a book defending short sellers in 1932. See Edward J. Meeker, *Short Selling* (New York: Harper & Brothers, 1932). See also Charles M. Jones and Owen A. Lamont, "Short-Sale Constraints and Stock Returns," *Journal of Financial Economics* 66 (2002): 207–39.

Pages 229–30: See Brad M. Barber and Terrance Odean, "Trading Is Hazardous to Your Wealth: The Common Stock Performance of Individual Investors," *Journal of Finance* 55 (2000): 773–806.

Pages 229–34: An especially good account of the relationship between behavioral finance and traditional finance theory is Robert Shiller, "From Efficient Markets Theory to Behavioral Finance," *Journal of Economic Perspectives* 17 (2003): 83–104. There's also lots of good material on irrationality in Shiller's *Irrational Exuberance* (Princeton: Princeton University Press, 2000). The limits of arbitrage are well explained in Andrei Shleifer, *Inefficient Markets: An Introduction to Behavioral Finance* (New York: Oxford University Press, 2000). And a mountain of evidence and intelligent analysis is marshaled in support of the proposition that investor psychology matters in Kent Daniel, David Hirshleifer, and Siew Hong Teoh, "Investor Psychology in Capital Markets: Evidence and Policy Implications," *Journal of Monetary Economics* 49 (2002): 139–209. Karim Jamal and Shyam Sunder, "Bayesian Equilibrium in Double Auctions Populated by Biased Heuristic Traders," *Journal of Economic Behavior and Organization* 31 (1996): 273–91.

See also Richard H. Thaler, "The End of Behavioral Finance," *Financial Analysts' Journal* (November–December 1999): 12–17; and Daniel Kahneman, Paul Slovic, and Amos Tversky, *Judgement Under Uncertainty: Heuristics and Biases* (New York: Cambridge University Press, 1982), which is the jumping off point for much of the work in behavioral finance.

Page 233: See George Akerlof's Nobel lecture, "Behavioral Macroeconomics and Macroeconomic Behavior" (December 8, 2001) for a discussion of people's problems saving.

Page 235: Fischer Black, "Noise," *Journal of Finance* 41 (1986): 533.

Page 236: Robert Shiller, *Market Volatility* (Cambridge: MIT Press, 1993). The best definition of "market efficiency," I think, is that the market is efficient if it consistently provides a better forecast of the future discounted free cash flow of companies than any other individual or system provides.

Pages 237–41: Just how small the world of arbitrageurs was in the summer of 1998 is shown in Roger Lowenstein, *When Genius Failed: The Rise and Fall of Long-Term Capital Management* (New York: Random House, 2000). Donald MacKenzie focuses on the role of imitation in the crisis. Because other arbitrageurs tried to emulate LTCM, funds were caught holding the same positions, leaving them concerned with only one thing: getting out before everyone else did. See Donald MacKenzie, "Mathematizing Risk: Markets, Arbitrage and Crises," paper presented at the Organizational Encounters with Risk workshop, London School of Economics Centre for the Analysis of Risk and Regulation (May 2002), http://www.sociology.ed.ac.uk/Research/Staff/LSE.pdf.

The LTCM debacle also points up problems with the familiar theory that arbitrageurs keep financial markets efficient. According to this theory—which is similar, if not identical, to the idea of the "marginal trader" mentioned in a footnote to the discussion of the IEM—most investors are foolish, perhaps irrational sheep, who make regular mistakes in pricing financial assets. The arbitrageurs are the clever and ruthless wolves (or sharks), who recognize every mistake, and in doing so drive the price of assets back to their true value. So it's the wolves who really set the market price, while the sheep are just there to make mistakes that give the wolves a financial incentive to participate.

Although this theory is a popular, if undertheorized, one, it's built on a number of flawed assumptions. If most investors are, in fact, "irrational" in the sense that they are making, in aggregate, systematic mistakes in pricing financial assets, then even if the intelligent arbitrageur comes along to push the market back toward rationality, there is no reason to believe the sheep won't go back to being irrational once the wolf has finished pouncing. If investors are irrational, they do not know they're irrational. They think they're as right as the wolf does. Smart investors don't have enough capital to outweigh the buying or selling power of all the other investors in an asset, so it's unclear how their rationality can offset the irrationality of the foolish investors (assuming for argument's sake that they are irrational).

The implicit assumption behind the idea that arbitrageurs are what keep market prices rational seems to be that once the smart investors act, all the other previously irrational investors will snap to and realize that they've been foolish. But there is no reason, theoretical or empirical or experimental, to believe that this is the case. If a large group of investors is irrational, having someone come along and make a trade that implies they're wrong is not suddenly going to make them change their mind. They'll just go back to being irrational once his capital is exhausted.

One response to this argument is that, if that happens, the arbitrageur will make money from his trade, while the irrational people will lose from theirs, and over time that will make prices rational. But this misses the important point: a rational arbitrageur can only make money if prices eventually become rational. James Chanos, the short seller, has said: "We can only hope that eventually the market will realize 2+2=4." But it can't be the arbitrageur alone who makes prices rational, because then he won't make any money. (If the arbitrageur's buying and selling makes the price rational, then his profits will be minuscule.) The only way for arbitrageurs to truly prosper is if the market, on its own, moves toward rationality. But if most investors are sheep, why would the market do that?

LTCM is a perfect case study of this. In many of the markets it was participating in, LTCM was the biggest player. It should have been, in the theory, the "marginal investor"—the one who sets the price of the asset. But when things started going south, the fact that LTCM was such a huge player did not protect it. Even though LTCM controlled so much capital, the absence of buyers meant that the value of its assets plummeted. LTCM's positions were rational ones, and it was the wolf in the market. But when the sheep started running, LTCM got trampled.

Although this was an extreme case, the principle is always true: whatever the price of an asset (rational or irrational), it is that price because that's what the weighted-average judgment of all the investors in the market says it should be. So if financial markets are efficient at all, that means that the judgment of most investors, when aggregated, must not be irrational. (It will not be as accurate as it would be if you included the judgment of the "marginal traders," but it cannot be irrationally off base if the market price is to be accurate.) Or, to put it differently, it means that collectively, the "sheep" are wolves.

Pages 241–44: A fascinating account of the cultural mainstreaming of bowling is in Andrew Hurley, *Diners, Bowling Alleys, and Trailer Parks: Chasing the American Dream in Postwar Consumer Culture* (New York: Basic Books, 2002). Charles Schwab talked about the bowling bubble in an interview in Charles Fishman, "Face Time with Charles Schwab," *Fast Company* (July 2001): 66.

Page 247: John Maynard Keynes, *The General Theory of Interest, Employment, and Money* (London: Macmillan, 1936): 156.

Page 249: Per Bak, *How Nature Works* (New York: Springer-Verlag, 1996).

Pages 249–50: Colin F. Camerer, "Taxi Drivers and Beauty Contests," *Engineering & Science* 1 (1997): 17–19.

Page 251: An interesting look at what we know about the causes of bubbles is Kevin Hassett, *Bubbleology* (New York: Crown Business, 2001).

Page 252: Andy Serwer, "I Want My CNBC," *Fortune* (May 24, 1999).

Page 253: Jeffrey Busse and T. Clifton Green, "Market Efficiency in Real Time," *Journal of Financial Economics* 65 (2002): 415–37.

See also Marcia Vickers and Gary Weiss, "Wall Street's Hype Machine," *Business Week* (April 3, 2000), http://www.businessweek.com:/2000/00_14/b3675001.htm; and James J. Cramer, "The Box Moves Stocks," *TheStreet.com* (December 6, 1999), http://www.thestreet.com/comment/wrong/834200.html.

Page 254: Paul Andreassen, "On the Social Psychology of the Stock Market: Aggregate Attributional Effects and the Regressiveness of Predictions," *Journal of Personality and Social Psychology* 53 (1987): 490–98. This is really one of the more interesting papers in the experimental economics literature, and yet it's rarely mentioned.

Page 255: Jack Treynor, "Market Efficiency and the Bean Jar Experiment," *Financial Analysts Journal* 43 (1987): 50–53.

Pages 256–57: Leon Mann, "The Baiting Crowd in Episodes of Threatened Suicide," *Journal of Personality and Social Psychology* 41 (1981): 703–9.

Pages 257–58: Mark Granovetter, "Threshold Models of Collective Behavior," *American Journal of Sociology* 83 (1978): 1420–43.

12. Democracy: Dreams of the Common Good

Pages 259–61: An idea similar to Deliberation Day is proposed in James Fishkin, *Democracy and Deliberation* (New Haven: Yale University Press, 1992). Fishkin followed that with *The Voice of the People: Public Opinion and Democracy* (New Haven: Yale University Press, 1996). The National Issues Convention got considerable national attention, and five hours of it were broadcast live on PBS and C-SPAN. Bruce Ackerman and Fishkin described their idea of a Deliberation Day in Bruce Ackerman and James Fishkin, "Deliberation Day," a paper they delivered at the Deliberating About Deliberative Democracy conference, University of Texas (February 2000); Ackerman and Fishkin, *Deliberation Day* (New Haven: Yale University Press, 2004) is forthcoming. In the latest version of the idea, Deliberation Day is spread out over two days, with employers required to give their workers one of the two days off.

Pages 261–62: Richard Posner, *Law, Pragmatism, and Democracy* (Cambridge: Harvard University Press, 2003): 164, 131–32.

Page 263: James Buchanan's 1986 Nobel lecture offers an interesting look at the philosophical and conceptual foundations of public-choice theory, which he has described elsewhere as being about "politics without romance": http://www.nobel.se/economics/laureates/1986/buchanan-lecture.html.

The James Buchanan and Gordon Tullock quote is cited in Mark Kelman, "On Democracy-Bashing: A Skeptical Look at the Theoretical and 'Empirical' Practice of the Public Choice Movement," *Virginia Law Review* 74 (1988): 235, 252.

Page 264: The William Riker quotes are cited in Brian Barry, *Sociologists, Economists, and Democracy* (Chicago: University of Chicago Press, 1978): 15, 17, 32.

Page 265: Kinder and Kiewiet argued that voters were "sociotropic" rather than "egotropic" in Donald R. Kinder and D. Roderick Kiewiet, "Economic Discontent and Political Behavior: The Role of Personal Grievances and Collective Economic Judgments in Congressional Voting," *American Journal of Political Science* 79 (1979): 10–27; and Kinder and Kiewiet, "Sociotropic Politics: The America Case," *British Journal of Politics* 11 (1981): 129–61.

David Sears and Carolyn Funk, "Self-Interest in Americans' Political Opinions," in *Beyond Self-Interest,* edited by Jane Mansbridge (Chicago: University of Chicago Press, 1990): 147–70. See also David Sears, Richard Lau, Tom Tyler, and Harris Allen, "Self-Interest vs. Symbolic Politics in Policy Attitudes and Presidential Voting," *American Political Science Review* 74 (1980): 670–84.

Pages 265–66: Laments about the ignorance of the American voter have been a perennial in American politics for more than a century. Good discussions of the informed voter can be found in Michael Delli Carpini, "In Search of the Informed Voter: What Americans Know About Politics and Why It Matters," http://www.mtsu.edu/~seig/paper_m_carpini.html; and Michael Schudson, "America's Ignorant Voters," *Wilson Quarterly* 24 (2000): 16.

More detailed looks can be found in Michael Delli Carpini and Scott Keeter, *What Americans Know About Politics and Why It Matters* (New Haven: Yale University Press, 1997); and Michael Schudson, *The Good Citizen: A History of American Civic Life* (Cambridge: Harvard University Press, 1999).

Page 268: Posner, *Law, Pragmatism, and Democracy:* 206.

NOTE: A full bibliography will be available at www.wisdomofcrowds.com and also at www.surowiecki.com beginning in May of 2004.